ZERO DAY THREAT

ZERO DAY THREAT

The Shocking Truth of How Banks and Credit Bureaus
Help Cyber Crooks Steal Your Money and Identity

*zero day threat (n.): a hazard so new that
no viable protection against it yet exists*

BYRON ACOHIDO AND JON SWARTZ

UNION SQUARE PRESS
An imprint of Sterling Publishing Co., Inc.

New York / London
www.sterlingpublishing.com

Library of Congress Cataloging-in-Publication Data Available

10   9   8   7   6   5   4   3   2   1

Published by Sterling Publishing Co., Inc.
387 Park Avenue South, New York, NY 10016
© 2008 by Byron Acohido and Jon Swartz
Distributed in Canada by Sterling Publishing
c/o Canadian Manda Group, 165 Dufferin Street
Toronto, Ontario, Canada M6K 3H6
Distributed in the United Kingdom by GMC Distribution Services
Castle Place, 166 High Street, Lewes, East Sussex, England BN7 1XU
Distributed in Australia by Capricorn Link (Australia) Pty. Ltd.
P.O. Box 704, Windsor, NSW 2756, Australia

Sterling ISBN-13: 978-1-4027-5695-5
          ISBN-10: 1-4027-5695-X

CONTENTS

	Prologue	1
	Introduction	4
Chapter 1	Built for Speed	7
Chapter 2	System Stimulation	22
Chapter 3	System Fissures	32
Chapter 4	Self-Anointed Avenger	46
Chapter 5	The Convenience Quotient	60
Chapter 6	Predators and Opportunists	71
Chapter 7	Perpetuating Errors	86
Chapter 8	Cost of Doing Business	95
Chapter 9	Vulgar Cheats and Swindles	110
Chapter 10	Hungry Sharks	123
Chapter 11	Perception Challenge	135
Chapter 12	Larger Rings	145
Chapter 13	Public Acceptance	158
Chapter 14	Gaps in the System	171
Chapter 15	Keys to the Puzzle	182
Chapter 16	Self-Contained Units	197
Chapter 17	Under Siege	214
Chapter 18	What Must Be Done	231
	Epilogue	243
Appendix A	Personal Security and Advocacy	248
Appendix B	Survey of Security Experts	256
	Glossary	265
	A Note on Sourcing	274
	Acknowledgments	282
	Index	285
	About the Authors	298

Prologue

March 29, 2005, Edmonton

Guns drawn, Detectives Bob Gauthier and Dave Shenning of the Edmonton Police Service stood outside the door of the third-floor walk-up apartment and listened. Gauthier turned the doorknob and pushed. The door was unlocked. Dead silence. The detectives entered, followed by several uniformed constables, and fanned out.

"Police! Search warrant. Anybody in here?" Gauthier bellowed. He and Shenning scanned the flat. Gauthier noted a compact kitchen to his left and, beyond that, an adjacent living area; to the right, the door to the bathroom; across the foyer, two doors leading to the bedrooms. A sliding glass door on the far side of the living room led to a balcony.

Bereft of any furniture to speak of, the apartment was thoroughly trashed. It looked to Gauthier, a lifelong hockey player who, at age forty-eight, still played goalie on the police league team, as if a rampaging winger had gone berserk in the place. Shattered glass from unknown knickknacks and dinnerware littered the floor. Elongated gashes marred the walls, as if someone had been doing drills with his hockey stick and the walls got in the way. The glass oven door was obliterated.

Something stirred behind the bedroom door to the left. Gauthier stepped quickly inside the room, .40-caliber Glock handgun ready to shoot, followed by Shenning. A scrawny young male, clad in a rumpled T-shirt, cotton sweatpants, and dirty socks, lay on a mattress on the floor. He was groggily stirring into consciousness.

Gauthier recognized him as Socrates, a twenty-one-year-old meth addict and tech whiz kid he'd arrested four months earlier in a seedy downtown establishment called the Beverly Motel. Socrates's laptop PC had been sitting on the motel bed that December day, hooked up to a dial-up Internet access account linked to an e-mail folder containing a cache of stolen PayPal account log-ons and passwords. Socrates had spent several days in jail and faced charges of possession of stolen identity data, but subsequently skipped out on a scheduled court appearance. A warrant had been issued for his arrest.

Not long thereafter, reports got back to Gauthier, a veteran drug detective, and his partner, economic crimes detective Al Vonkeman, that Socrates had resurfaced with a cell of drug-addicted collaborators holed up somewhere in the south end. Word was that Socrates had built a Golden Goose PC with a Plexiglas front panel, flashing blue lights, and multiple hard drives that could make nuggets of cash magically appear in bank accounts.

Police heard about the Golden Goose computer largely because it had become a topic of marvel among the city's meth addicts, known as speeders, and crack cocaine addicts, called crackheads. The south-end cell had taken to recruiting street addicts, rewarding them handsomely to set up local bank accounts in their own names, or with fake IDs if they preferred. The accounts functioned as safe havens, referred to as "drops," into which Socrates could direct online deposits of ill-gotten funds. Edmonton's circle of drug dealers and drug traffickers took notice of a spike in demand touched off by an influx of disposable income into the hands of some of their regular customers. Lots of folks, on both sides of the law, relished getting ahold of the Golden Goose computer.

Now, in late March, the creator and tender of the Golden Goose PC looked as if Gauthier could knock him out by blowing on him. "I know you," the detective deadpanned, as he began to pat down the suspect. "We've been looking for you."

Socrates turned pallid and began hyperventilating. In a rising panic, he begged Gauthier to hand him a large-mouth juice container sitting on the floor across the room. It was half full of murky fluid with bits of foreign matter floating in it. Gauthier obliged, and Socrates gulped the filthy fluid.

Shenning by now had scoped out the rest of the apartment and came back to report that there was nothing of consequence—no computer or electronic equipment of any sort. Continuing the pat down, Gauthier grabbed one of Socrates's ankles and then the other. But instead of a weapon or dope stashed in the suspect's sock, the detective found a neatly folded sheet of printer paper.

"What's this!" said Gauthier, unfolding the printout. "Ooh, look at this."

Socrates wheezed, "Omigod. Omigod. Omigod." His thoughts began racing. Oh, shit. Oh, shit. I'm fuckin' screwed. Just screwed right over. I'm going to jail. On the printout were full profiles—names, account numbers, online account log-ins and passwords—for a dozen Royal Bank of Canada customers. These were the choicest nuggets from the richest vein stored on the hard drive of the Golden Goose, now gone missing. The holder of this data would have had quick and easy Internet access to accounts holding a cumulative $2 million Canadian, then worth about US$1.6 million.

Wheezing and rattling, Socrates asked Gauthier if it would be OK for him to smoke a cigarette. He knew it would be his last stimulant for a long stretch. He knew he faced kicking meth and cigarettes cold turkey in a jail cell. What he didn't know at the time was that his cohorts weren't about to let him stay on the sidelines for very long.

Introduction

Convenience, as much as anything, defines Western culture. For many of us it has become unthinkable to go anywhere without a cell phone and unnerving to be more than a few minutes removed from access to our e-mail. In this digital age, the notions of getting caught short of cash or forgetting to replenish your checkbook before leaving home have become quaint anachronisms. We live in a time where you can complete a credit or debit card transaction in a retail establishment, on the phone, or on the World Wide Web, in less time than it would take to break a $100 bill or show identification for a personal check.

Yet with greater convenience comes rising risk. It turns out that the amazingly swift credit-issuing and payments system we've come to rely on is rife with paper-thin membranes. The financial industry—banks, credit card companies, credit bureaus and data aggregators—designed it that way. A pliable system, after all, is endlessly extendable. With such a system, convenience often trumps security, and that was fine as long as criminal exploitation could be managed at an acceptable level, which has been the case for most of the past five decades since the time financial convenience began.

But a number of variables changed drastically as the last millennium drew to a close. Consumers saved less, borrowed more, and used magnetic-striped payment cards more pervasively. Digital technology flourished and the Internet age took off. Eager to exploit the Internet's convenience, merchants, media companies, tech companies, and the financial industry stampeded into electronic commerce.

What few saw coming was the extent to which enterprising hackers, con artists, and thieves, ranging from video-game-addled adolescents to well-funded Russian crime gangs, would follow suit and swarm e-commerce as well. Since 2000, the systematic harvesting of personal and financial data has accelerated to an astounding level. Meanwhile, financial fraud scams that make clever use of stolen identity data have mushroomed in scope and variety, playing off the many and varied commercial transactions that can be executed anonymously from any Internet-connected PC anywhere in the world, simply by typing in the correct user name and password. More recently, cyberspies have joined the party, probing the same soft membranes, hacking into government and corporate databases. These elite database hackers stealthily roam even private intranets, scooping up large caches of personal and financial data and hunting down military and trade secrets.

In tech security circles, one of the most feared phenomena is something called a zero day threat. It refers to a virus designed to take advantage of a security hole for which no patch exists. No patch exists because the bad guys discover the hole—and deploy a malicious program to take advantage of it—before the good guys are even aware of the vulnerability. "Zero day" is a reference to the period of time during which there is nothing stopping an intruder from taking full advantage of a freshly discovered flaw.

In much the same sense, our entire convenience-crazed society is facing a zero day threat posed by data harvesters and financial scammers as they accelerate their Internet-enabled criminal activities with near impunity. No true protection exists, because banks and credit bureaus publicly deny their true scope of losses; because technology companies have only just begun discussing a sweeping security overhaul of the Internet that is clearly needed; and because consumers remain blissfully ignorant. Most of us, for instance, fail to realize that by simply possessing a Social Security number, we face a rising risk of becoming the victim of credit fraud. Few of us appreciate how each time we use online banking and shopping services, we put our personal and financial data into active play for data thieves.

The authors had little inkling of this pervasive threat in the summer of 2003 when each was filing separate news reports for USA Today on spam and PC viruses, respectively. The mainstream press at the time certainly reported on spam and viruses as though they were mutually exclusive topics. The genesis of this book began when the reporters teamed up that summer to look into what commonalities there might be, if any, between spam and virus attacks. A working premise soon began to gel around examining the notion that the cybercrime underground, in fact, operates according to the same business principals as any other capitalist market. But as research progressed, myriad complexities surfaced. We confirmed that spammers, virus writers, data harvesters, and financial scammers indeed acted according to the principals of supply, demand, and profits. But we also came to see how cybercrooks actually play a somewhat limited role in that they are merely opportunists slipping into doors, windows, closets, and vaults left ajar in the rush to commercialize the Internet. We discovered that there were much more complex contagions eroding the security and privacy of sensitive data, and those corrupters had more to do with the business practices and marketing strategies of the financial services and technology industries.

The stories herein contain many astounding revelations. They have been assembled with the intent of helping to foster an improved understanding among the public at large about the intricacies of keeping personal data secure and private in the Internet age. Each chapter is written in three recurring sections—"Exploiters," "Enablers," and "Expediters"—that progress in parallel through the book. The "Exploiters" sections take the reader deep into the world of drug addicts, scam artists, and crime lords who carry out the gritty aspects of data theft and financial fraud. The "Enablers" sections guide readers through the history and current practices of credit card companies, banks, credit bureaus, and data brokers. And the "Expediters" sections recount the role of the technologists—the good guys and the bad guys—from Microsoft Chairman Bill Gates to a rogues' gallery of virus writers and database hackers continually probing tech systems for fresh flaws. Additionally, the stories of ordinary citizens who have experienced data theft and financial fraud are interspersed throughout.

The authors' intent is not so much to alarm as it is to illuminate the underlying drivers that are working in concert to expose all of us to a perpetual zero day threat, in terms of the imminent risks of becoming a victim of data theft and identity fraud. In doing so, it is our sincere hope that readers come away better equipped to deal with security and privacy issues likely to confront all of us to one degree or another.

This is a work of journalism. All characters and events are real, though some pseudonyms have been used for the personal safety of our sources.

CHAPTER 1
Built for Speed

Exploiters
Summer 2003, Edmonton

Marilyn had to think quickly. The security guard appeared out of nowhere. She was sitting behind the wheel of her black Chevy Cavalier, parked in an alley alongside a sprawling building, newly built beside the highway leading out to Sherwood Park, an upper-middle-class suburb northeast of Edmonton.

Inside the building a few hundred workers manned phone lines, taking service calls from customers of Neiman Marcus, the upscale U.S. department store chain. Many of the phone calls were to process credit card applications. The detritus of this process—discarded notepads, customer account records, and the like—were flushed out of the brick building in plastic garbage bags hurled into a burly recycling bin in the alley. Marilyn's accomplice, Frankie, was rooting in the recycling bin as the guard approached.

"What are you doing here?" said the guard.

"Oh, hi," Marilyn said sweetly. A soft-spoken, attractive blonde, then thirty-five, with a friendly demeanor, Marilyn passed herself off as an absent-minded employee hunting for a lost daily planner. "It's my first week here," she said. "I think I might have knocked it in with the recyclables. My kid brother is trying to see if he can find it."

Frankie stepped away from the Dumpster clutching a large plastic bag.

"We were just going to take this stuff home to see if we can fish it out," said Marilyn.

"Oh. I'll help you," the guard volunteered. He handed Frankie another bag. "Maybe it's in one of these."

Driving away, the Cavalier's trunk stuffed with plastic bags, Marilyn and Frankie shared a laugh. Later, at Marilyn's condo, they would smoke a bowl of crystal meth and reminisce about other close calls—and big scores— while making their regular rounds of the recycling bins and garbage Dumpsters around greater metropolitan Edmonton. Their rounds included binning, or Dumpster diving, in trash receptacles behind banks, trust companies, telecom companies, hotels, car rental agencies, restaurants, video rental stores—anywhere a business might throw out paperwork.

Frankie often would carry a plastic bag half full of empty soft-drink cans as a ready-made alibi; if challenged he could say he was collecting soft-drink cans for the return deposits. Once, Frankie had rooted through a Dumpster shared by several businesses of a retail strip mall, including a neighborhood branch of the Bank of Nova Scotia. He fished out the branch manager's daily planner, which contained override access codes for all of the branch's account holders, as well as the manager's e-mail password and voice-mail PIN.

"Nothing was ever shredded," says Frankie. "All the information you ever wanted was in there."

Marilyn had met Frankie in the spring of 2003 through a mutual acquaintance, her boyfriend, who happened to be Frankie's drug connection. Up until her divorce in 2001, Marilyn describes herself as a "model citizen," college educated, two children, management career, everything going well. But then her marriage hit the rocks, and she picked the wrong boyfriend, a meth dealer. She became a meth addict. "He was domineering, and I was vulnerable from the divorce," she says.

By the time Marilyn and Frankie teamed up, Frankie was something of a legend in local drug-trafficking circles. Living with his divorced father, he ran with the wrong crowd and became a meth addict at sixteen. Passionate, creative, but easily manipulated, he quickly demonstrated a high aptitude for committing fraud. One day an acquaintance who happened to work at the Canadian cellular phone company Rogers Communications showed him how to fish discarded phone contracts out of Rogers's Dumpsters, then call in to reopen the accounts with new working numbers.

Frankie soon began Dumpster diving at the offices of other businesses around Edmonton and harvested a bounty of documents: customer profiles, employee manuals, passwords, internal phone directories. He focused on securing stolen credit card numbers, which he used to buy electronic gear, pay for hotel rooms, and set up cell phone accounts. Around his high school campus, Frankie was known as the guy who always had cells phones to sell. The phone account would always be under someone else's name, prepaid with a stolen credit card number, and guaranteed to work for six months. The price: $250. The typical purchaser: drug dealers.

By early 2003, Frankie, at age nineteen, was running a cottage industry business from his bedroom in his dad's apartment in Mill Woods, a middle-class, racially mixed suburb in south Edmonton. It became widely known in the speeder community that Frankie would pay in cash or drugs for certain kinds of records. Thieves began lurking near certain bank branches after hours, when the janitorial crews were on duty. Often the janitor would stock-pile plastic bags of trash in the public-access foyer, where the ATMs were located. When the janitor returned inside to finish up, the trash bags had disappeared from the foyer. At other bank branches, locks on garbage Dumpsters kept needing to be replaced.

Word got back to Edmonton Police Service Detectives Allan Vonkeman and Bob Gauthier about a kid and his girlfriend amassing bank records and running a counterfeit ring out of a suburban Mill Woods apartment. Vonkeman, then forty-four, an erudite tactician, and the slightly older Gauthier, a street-smart drug investigator, given to cynical wisecracks, had first met as young constables working the north-end neighborhoods of this prosperous oil city on the Canadian plains. Edmonton is home of the world's largest shopping mall, complete with an indoor water park the size of a domed football stadium. Vonkeman, an Edmonton native son, and Gauthier, who migrated inland from British Columbia, each took different paths to becoming detectives.

Going with the flow, in a very Canadian way, they took it upon them-selves to turn their friendship into a professional partnership when Vonkeman walked in the door for his first day on the job as an economic crime specialist. No supervisor asked them to team up. Someone threw a left-over identity theft case on Vonkeman's desk. Meth was involved. He phoned his old pal Gauthier, and the two worked together almost exclusively on drug–identity theft cases ever since.

On March 19, 2003, Vonkeman and Gauthier, backed by uniformed constables, battered in the dead bolt of the spacious three-bedroom apart-ment in Mill Woods where Frankie and his dad lived. Dad, a printing supplies salesman, was on the living room couch watching ESPN SportsCenter. Frankie's bedroom door, as usual, was closed. As Gauthier entered the bedroom, .40-caliber Glock pistol drawn, he saw Frankie and his girlfriend both sitting cross-legged on the floor. They had just finished smoking a bowl of crystal meth. Frankie grabbed a hatchet and brandished it at Gauthier. The detective coaxed him into putting it down.

The bedroom floor was littered with paperwork from all five major Canadian banks: deposit and withdrawal slips, loan documents, registered savings plans (the Canadian equivalent of IRAs), account summaries. Similar records overflowed from three cardboard filing boxes. There was a desktop computer in the room, and a scanner and printer, which Frankie had been using, not very successfully, to produce counterfeit Canadian $5 bills. The backsides of some samples were upside down. "You could tell he was still playing with them, trying to get them right," says Vonkeman. "You could tell he was working on the quality and the quality was improving."

The next day Vonkeman got quick approval from his division sergeant to invite local TV news crews to a press conference at which he neatly displayed an array of the confiscated bank records on a large conference table. Such a thing would never have happened in the United States without protracted wrangling. Public disclosure of sensitive investigations rarely originates from beat cops in the United States, where media exposure of police work almost always is a carefully orchestrated, top-down affair. That evening the top local news story in Edmonton was about how a nineteen-year-old kid had amassed a cache of bank records, examples of which showed up on the TV screen with the bank names clearly visible. It wasn't long before each of the five banks contacted Edmonton police and Vonkeman was dispensing advice on how they should secure their outflow of trash. The banks took his advice.

"Our thing wasn't to give the banks a black eye, but you know what, we've had next to nothing for a problem with bank records since that point in time," says Vonkeman. "Our banks have gone through great lengths to make sure they train their people, and the trash is in a vault or being shredded."

Later, Vonkeman arranged for Marilyn to meet in person on several occasions with different bank security officials to debrief them on how easy it was to breach their systems. He also arranged for CTV reporter Lloyd Robertson to interview Frankie on camera (keeping the young man's visage in shadows) for a nationally broadcast news story on identity theft. Gauthier, meanwhile, gave a long interview to *Edmonton Journal* cops reporter, Florence Loyie, in which he attributed a spike in property crimes to a spiraling increase in meth use.

"I think it's because of the effects of meth," Gauthier told Loyie. "When you have a guy staying up three or four days, they have nothing better to do than think up new crimes, new scams."

Enablers
6,803 Transactions per Second

Somewhere in the western United States, at the edge of an upscale suburban community, a cluster of attractive commercial buildings covering approximately the same footprint as three soccer fields blends imperceptibly into a pristine high-tech business park. With smoke-tinted windows and aluminum trim, the five-story main building appears to house the headquarters of a prosperous company. It is flanked on either side by a matched set of brick warehouses, each about three-stories high, with minimal windows. There is nothing indicating what activity is taking place behind the brick walls—no corporate logo, no signage of any kind, save a street number, posted near the security gate.

The last thing a passerby might guess is that the brick facade actually camouflages impregnable concrete bunkers inside which massive amounts of financial data are being crunched, second to second, nonstop, 24 by 7 by 365. In the basement, multiple backup systems stand at the ready to ensure that not a single second is ever lost to downtime.

The average citizen would be hard-pressed to guess that the nondescript brick buildings contain a staggeringly complex and astoundingly capable credit-issuing and payments system. The technology within the buildings is built for one thing: speed. Omnipotent computers continually process vast quantities of credit and debit card transactions, enabling our retail purchases to unfold quickly and conveniently. The technology within has helped accelerate our use of revolving debt and has brought us to the brink of becoming a cashless society. And yet, despite sophisticated safeguards, the technology within has also proved to be all too susceptible to fraud.

The compound is home to Operations Center Central, or OCC, the newest, most advanced of four processing centers that make up VisaNet, the digital brain that handles a large percentage of the world's Visa payment card transactions. (The others are located in the eastern United States, Europe, and Asia.) Fresh data arrives at VisaNet in 1,500-byte chunks every time someone swipes a Visa payment card through a card reader or types a Visa account number into an online shopping cart.

VisaNet each year authorizes some 45 billion transactions, worth $2.4 trillion, or about 60 percent of the world's card-based transactions. Similar payment systems, operated by MasterCard, American Express, and Discover Card, handle most of the rest. Together, such processing centers make up a linchpin to the global economy, the essence of what makes it ultraquick and convenient for consumers to almost instantly acquire everything from a high-definition TV to a double cheeseburger by presenting a credit or debit payment card.

Though the financial industry is notoriously secretive about its inner workings, Visa granted one of the authors a rare guided tour of OCC, including a walk-through of its primary "server farm"—a highly secured, climate-controlled hall the length and width of a football field containing row upon row of powerful computers. The first thing one notices upon entering the server farm is the steady thrum of air conditioners hugging the outer walls. The air units continually draw out computer-generated heat, maintaining a constant room temperature of precisely 70.5 degrees Fahrenheit. At either end of the hall, machines set to keep the relative humidity at 45 percent spit measured blasts of moisture into the air—the only movement noticeable in the otherwise completely static space.

Frenetic electronic energy, nonetheless, continually courses through the hall. Strolling across the server farm is like penetrating deep inside the brain and nervous system of a simpleminded beast capable of incredible feats of narrowly focused intellect. Computer servers housed in seven-foot-high metallic cabinets stand, sentinel-like, in neat rows, resembling stylish refrigerators. Brightly colored strands of cables sprout from the top of each cabinet—orange for fiber optics, blue for Ethernet—forming tributaries that feed into color-coded streams crisscrossing the ceiling in meticulously arranged traffic patterns.

This arrangement allows synapses to fire, unseen and unheard, on a Herculean scale. On a typical day, the beast's brain approves 100 million payment card transactions from around the world; during the height of the 2006 Christmas shopping season it green-lighted a record 6,803 transactions per second, sustained over a one-hour period on December 22, 2006.

This represented a 7 percent increase over the 6,363 transactions per second executed on December 23, 2005. This ability to process a massive volume of electronic transactions with aplomb makes it possible for 1.6 billion Visa cardholders to enter 20 million merchant locations around the world and complete financial transactions in 174 different currencies.

Even more astounding than the sheer volume of transactions VisaNet is capable of processing is that it handles each request in well under two seconds, or what Jean Bruesewitz, Visa USA's senior vice president of processing and emerging products, refers to as "in flight." VisaNet verifies the name and address of the cardholder and confirms that sufficient cash or credit is available to complete the transaction. What's more, a sophisticated fraud-detection program, called Advanced Authorization, cross-checks each transaction for a variety of fraud indicators. If something suspicious turns up—say a cardholder suddenly begins buying ostentatious items in a distant country—an alert gets fired off to the card-issuing bank, which can then make a decision about whether to stop the transaction and contact the cardholder.

"We've brought everything together to a centralized point where we can get a view of everything that account is doing," says Bruesewitz. "From a fraud-mitigation standpoint, it comes to one place and you have a real view of how that card is being used. It gets real exciting when you talk about doing this while the authorization request is in flight and you've got six thousand swipes going on every second. It's pretty amazing."

As digital technology advances apace, Visa expects to add suspicious patterns to the security review, which should, Visa executives assert, make VisaNet more effective at deterring fraud. Visa is also continually upgrading VisaNet. In particular, it has begun calling for wider use of a "contact-less" payment system built around debit cards, credit cards, and portable devices embedded with a computer chip that is read when the user holds the payment instrument near a special terminal.

Exemplifying just how effectively the financial industry has brought the exponential rise in computing power to bear on the singular task of making it faster and ever-more convenient to buy and borrow, Visa expects to add more payment flexibility and intensified security reviews while driving down the time it handles each card swipe to less than one second, from the current average of 1.4 seconds.

"We're not sacrificing security for speed," says Brian Triplett, Visa's senior vice president of emerging product development. "We're doing more and more security faster."

Yet, the approach of supplying more safeguards faster has an intrinsic limitation. Banks can, and often do, calibrate their automated systems to err on the side of approvals, thereby enabling fraudulent transactions to sail through just as fast as legitimate ones. Visa's brain can raise all the red flags in the world. But it's what the credit-issuing banks decide to do with security warnings in the second or two that elapses while approving a transaction that matters. Since banks began embracing automated systems in the 1960s, fraudsters have proven to be endlessly enterprising in finding ways to test and exploit such systems. One rule has stood the test of time: the faster and more convenient banks and credit card companies make the payment system, the more opportunities they open for crooks.

Expediters

White Hats, Black Hats, Gray Hats

The year is 1999—the close of the twentieth century. "Livin' la Vida Loca," Harry Potter, and *The Blair Witch Project* dominate pop culture. John F. Kennedy, Jr., piloting a small plane to a Martha's Vineyard wedding, crashes; his wife, her sister, and he die in the tragic accident. Major news organizations hype what turns out to be an inert Y2K threat. Antitrust regulators bear down on Microsoft for using illegal monopolistic practices, while tech darlings Amazon.com and Netscape help inflate the dot-com bubble. Internet stocks launch into the stratosphere.

As dynamic as 1999 was, it was a comparative age of innocence when it comes to Internet security. Online shopping and online banking were in a nascent stage. Hacking was the dominion of computer geeks, invariably young males, seeking bragging rights. In the anonymity of cyberspace, the frail nerd pushed around by jocks in the schoolyard could log on to the Internet and emerge as a giant among peers by contriving the cleverest ways to exchange copyrighted music or to cheat at video games. In cyberspace, ethics became pliable, and reality altered, especially for impressionable teenage boys, says Ohio University telecommunications professor Mia Consalvo, author of *Cheating: Gaining an Advantage in Video Games.*

The introverted lad who would never dare to shoplift a CD from a music store or cheat playing a board game with flesh-and-blood acquaintances might think nothing of pirating a first-run movie or finding a shortcut to beat a popular online game.

"We now have kids who grew up as digital natives," says Consalvo. "This is the first generation to grow up with computers in the home since the time they were born. They've grown up knowing that it's easier to get away with things online, and there can be a little bit of confusion about what's right and what's wrong, especially during the teen years when you're sorting out your identity anyway."

As the new millennium dawned, the splashiest way to achieve geekdom immortality was to advance beyond piracy and cheating and create a headline-grabbing piece of malicious software, or malware, as antivirus companies called it.

In May 1999, the Melissa e-mail virus would establish a new malware high-water mark. Melissa lured naive victims into opening viral e-mail attachments with messages like

"Check this!! This is some wicked stuff," or "Question for you. It's fairly complicated so I've attached it."

Clicking on the attachment activated a brilliantly invasive packet of coding. Melissa made copies of itself, which it then e-mailed to the first fifty names in the infected computer's e-mail address book. Thus the next fifty potential victims would receive copies of the tainted attachment thinking it sent by a trusted source. If just a handful of the fifty fell for it, followed by a handful after that, and a handful after that, and so on, the e-mail virus would spread exponentially.

Indeed, Melissa propagated so rapidly that the e-mail systems at Microsoft, Intel, Lockheed Martin, and other big corporations crashed under the sheer volume of e-mail generated by the virus. Melissa's author, David L. Smith, thirty, of Aberdeen Township, New Jersey, would ultimately spend twenty months in jail for infecting hundreds of thousands of computers with Melissa, which he reportedly named after a favorite stripper.

A bit old to be a hobbyist hacker, Smith, who worked as a troubleshooter at AT&T Labs, bragged in hacker chat rooms about spreading viruses under the bad-guy nickname Kwyjibo. But he also maintained a good-guy persona, using the name Doug Winterspoon to help people clean up infections caused by the evil Kwyjibo. "He had a bit of a Peter Pan complex," says Roger Thompson, cofounder and CTO of Exploit Prevention Labs, one of a cadre of virus hunters who helped track down Smith.

Some hackers would consider a couple of years in lockup a small price to pay for securing a place in hacking lore. And if imitation is the highest form of flattery, then Smith secured the preeminent accolade: many of Melissa's techniques were to become commonplace in e-mail worms to follow.

The Love Bug, also known as the ILOVEYOU virus, for instance, copied Melissa's propagation engine. The author was Onel de Guzman, twenty-four, a lovesick student at the Amaconda programming institute in Manila's upscale Makati district. De Guzman's claim to fame was concocting the compelling e-mail subject line "ILOVEYOU" and the irresistible attachment "LOVE-LETTER-FOR-YOU.TXT.vbs," partly to impress an instructor whom he had a crush on.

De Guzman took psychological manipulation, or "social engineering," as psychologists and law enforcement officials call it, to another level. ILOVEYOU sped westward from the Philippines, tricking workers into clicking on the attachment as they arrived at the office to start their workday. Following the arc of the rising sun, the Love Bug triggered an avalanche of e-mails around the globe, crippling systems and causing $5 billion in damages.

De Guzman's masterstroke carried some nasty twists. It corrupted picture and music files and installed a password-stealing program. Why? De Guzman, who escaped punishment because his home nation lacked computer-hacking laws, would later reveal in a CNN interview that he launched the virus partly as a joke, but mostly to test his programming skills. De Guzman insisted that he was a creative programmer, not a malicious hacker, who aspired to a career in the tech field.

"If I may have done something wrong, if I stirred up a controversy, then I would like to apologize for it," de Guzman told CNN. But he also blamed Microsoft for releasing sloppily built copies of its ubiquitous PC operating system, Windows. "The liability should lie in the hands of the software developers that come out with programs that are defective," he told CNN.

De Guzman's indignation—and his eagerness to expose security flaws in Windows—reflected a deep antipathy toward Microsoft that was widely held in the hacker community. This sentiment had been festering since the mid-1980s. Back then, an upstart Harvard dropout named Bill Gates turned the chummy techie community upside down by lambasting the common belief that software should be cheap or free. Gates coined the phrase "software pirates" to describe anybody who didn't pay Microsoft for its "intellectual property." Gates went on to become the richest man in the world, in large part by using illegal tactics to crush the competition and monopolize the market for Windows, the operating system running 90 percent of the world's personal computers, and for the Office suite of clerical programs, and Internet Explorer Web browser, which command similar market shares. Microsoft would prosper, despite being heavily sanctioned by antitrust regulators in the United States and Europe for resorting to illegal anticompetitive practices.

One ramification of Microsoft's prosperity was that by the start of the twenty-first century, Windows would become the favorite target of hackers and malware writers. Three categories of Windows hackers, each with distinctive motives, emerged: white hats, black hats, and gray hats.

White hats were good-guy hackers who took to incessantly exposing new Windows vulnerabilities. White hats argued that the intense scrutiny would compel Microsoft to take security more seriously and patch security flaws with more alacrity. Black hats were the bad guys. Black hats searched for vulnerabilities, too, but were just as apt to wait for the white hats to discover them, then take advantage. Gray hats were somewhere in between, sometimes contributing to the cause of good, other times behaving more like black hats.

In this frenzied world of conflicting motivations, a kind of arms race took shape among white hats, black hats, and gray hats. Each group hustled to be the first to find the next gaping Windows security hole, referred to as a "vulnerability." The number of known Windows vulnerabilities—flaws that could be exploited over the Internet—would balloon tenfold in four years, from 417 in 1999 to 4,129 in 2002, according to the CERT Coordination Center. (CERT is the U.S. Computer Emergency Readiness Team, a quasi-governmental organization established in 2003 at Pittsburgh's Carnegie Mellon University to help protect the nation's

Internet infrastructure.) Hackers were forced to pick sides in a polarized debate over when to disclose a newly discovered security hole. Proponents of "full disclosure" championed the practice of broadly announcing new vulnerabilities immediately upon discovery, the better to compel Microsoft (or other software vendors whose products were found lacking) to expedite a security patch. Opponents of full disclosure advocated notifying the software vendor first and giving the vendor a grace period of several weeks to prepare a patch before publicly announcing the new flaw.

Whether for or against full disclosure, white hats and gray hats—who referred to themselves as "researchers"—soaked up the stature gained from being the first to announce a new security hole. As with the virus-writing community, vulnerability researchers coveted bragging rights. Black hats, of course, were all for full disclosure since it broadened their opportunities to wreak havoc.

Each new Windows vulnerability made public was like opening a previously unnoticed trapdoor to hundreds of millions of Internet-connected PCs. As Microsoft scrambled to keep up with patches, black hats gravitated to the easiest holes to exploit. A flurry of attacks made the headlines in 2000 and 2001. The Anna Kournikova virus masqueraded as a photo of the celebrity tennis star. Bubble Boy infected PCs as soon as the user opened the e-mail; no need to click on the attachment. Nimda used five different methods to infect PCs and to self-propagate. SirCam bored into corporate servers.

It became trivial for hackers of modest technical savvy to infect Internet-connected Windows PCs in the home and in corporate settings. Yet the implications were profound. An intruder essentially usurped full control of the infected PC. It became the common practice of black hats to leave a back door open on an infected PC through which any intruder could install and run any program.

It almost seemed as if the youths who dabbled in copyright piracy and video game cheating had progressed to more serious forms of politically motivated hacking, sort of like advancing to hard narcotics after becoming inured to a gateway drug. Sarah Gordon, a senior researcher at Symantec Security Response, and an expert on the psychology of virus writers and hackers, doubts that a strong correlation can be drawn between simple cheating and more malicious forms of hacking. But she concedes it's plausible.

"In some cases, yes, they will trip down that path," says Gordon. "On the Internet, there are no other people involved, and no one you can see. There's just enough depersonalization and desensitization to come up with an excuse [to cheat or hack] with very little inner conflict."

Hacking began to cause increasingly heavy collateral damage. Hackers began routinely installing a small program, called a bot, short for robot. A bot sits on the hard drive and receives instructions from a controller over an IRC (Internet relay chat) channel. An IRC channel is nothing more than a private instant messaging line—the same technology used for popular public instant messaging services such as AOL's AIM, Microsoft's Windows Live Messenger, and Yahoo! Chat.

A hacker in command of an IRC channel through which dozens, hundreds, or even thousands of bots report for duty, is called a bot herder. Among black hats, one measure of skill became how good you were at assembling large bot herds and using them to launch so-called DDoS (distributed-denial-of-service) attacks.

In a DDoS attack, the controller instructs all of the bots in a bot herd to simultaneously flood a targeted Web address with repeated nuisance messages, thus crippling the Web site. In February 2000, a black hat calling himself Mafiaboy installed bots on computers at Yale and Harvard universities and used them to crash CNN's Web site for four hours and create chaos at the Web sites of Yahoo, eBay, Amazon, Dell, Excite, and E-Trade. He bragged in chat rooms that the FBI would never catch him.

With help from the Royal Canadian Mounted Police (RCMP), the FBI traced Mafiaboy to a large Montreal home in an upscale subdivision astride the Club De Golf St. Raphael. A dozen RCMP agents raided the residence at 3 a.m. and arrested a fifteen-year-old boy, who instantly became a cause célèbre, the subject of editorial cartoons and a Free Mafiaboy campaign. Mafiaboy pleaded guilty to fifty-six criminal counts related to the attacks and was sentenced to eight months in a detention home.

Mafiaboy's father told reporters the youth played sports and had other interests. "He's not fixated on computers to the point where it would damage his health," the father said. "I think he learned a big lesson and he'll put it to good use."

As the Mafiaboy furor subsided, Code Red slithered into the headlines. Code Red was created to take advantage of a security hole in Microsoft's IIS software, used to serve up Web pages. The IIS vulnerability had been discovered by a black hat–turned–white hat, Marc Maiffret, cofounder and chief hacking officer of eEye Digital Security.

This is how Maiffret describes how he became a vulnerability researcher: "The short version is: Bad home life, computers were an escape, learned about phone phreaking, eventually led to hacking, eventually led to doing illegal things, which caused me to be raided by the FBI when I was seventeen, which caused me to have a wake-up call to do something with my life, in which I cofounded eEye, became the chief hacking officer, and have been one of the people shaping the security landscape ever since."

Maiffret had advised Microsoft about the flaw in IIS in early 2001. He waited patiently to take credit for it on June 18, once Microsoft had a patch ready. At the time, simply issuing a patch didn't mean the patch would get installed on all vulnerable machines in a timely manner. Patches can crash programs and foul corporate systems, and in 2001 they weren't a high priority for many companies.

In mid-July—Friday the thirteenth, to be exact—twenty-five days after Microsoft released the IIS patch, Maiffret and some colleagues, energized by swigs of a megacaffeinated soft drink, worked through the night to reverse engineer Internet traffic logs from an IIS Web server that had bogged down. They uncovered an automated program that was snaking around the Internet in search of unpatched IIS Web servers. Each time the program found one, it posted "HELLO! Hacked By Chinese!" on the Web page.

Maiffret christened the program Code Red, a reference to the Asian defacement "and because Code Red Mountain Dew was the only thing that kept us awake while we disassembled the exploit."

Unlike an e-mail virus, Code Red spread on its own with no action required by the PC user. Maiffret and his cohorts had uncovered the first major self-propagating worm.

Code Red did double duty. It also organized infected machines into bot herds standing at the ready to launch DDoS attacks against designated Web addresses. Its first target: www.whitehouse.gov, the White House's Web site.

Code Red compromised 225,000 IIS Web servers in half a day, and set up a DDoS attack to shut down www.whitehouse.gov. The White House dodged the attack. Yet, Code Red would linger on the Internet for years, breaking into millions of PCs. And it established a model for what would become a familiar cycle. Vulnerability researchers would find a fresh security hole; Microsoft would issue a patch; black hats would race to exploit as many PCs as possible before the patch got widely distributed.

"No one was really patching their systems, or aware of the threat that their businesses were exposed to by running Microsoft software," says Maiffret. "Code Red was the wake-up call not only to an industry but truly to the entire world, which had grown dependent on computers and Microsoft."

CHAPTER 2
System Stimulation

Exploiters
Summer 2003, Edmonton

Frankie quickly posted bail after his March 2003 arrest, and not long afterward slipped back into meth use. He picked up where he had left off doing financial fraud. "I needed to feed my drug habit and make a living," he says. Meeting Marilyn seemed a godsend. Marilyn's managerial experience and math skills meshed perfectly with Frankie's moxie. Marilyn scanned the classified ads and took note when hiring notices were publicized for two major call centers moving to the city. One was for Neiman Marcus; the other was Convergys, which handled customer service calls from Sprint cell phone subscribers in the United States.

The Dumpster behind the Convergys call center in suburban Mill Woods proved to be a convenient and reliable jackpot. It happened to be located in a nondescript strip mall just two blocks from Frankie's dad's apartment, and it brimmed with valuable data. "We'd get credit check information from Equifax, credit card numbers to make payments, Social Security numbers, date of birth, addresses," says Marilyn. "They would make a printout, then just throw it out."

Soon Marilyn and Frankie were able to delegate Dumpster diving to others and concentrate on fine-tuning schemes to make the most of pilfered data. They became adept at developing what they referred to as "full profiles." Given just a name and home address culled from the trash, Marilyn would dispatch a street addict to the residence with instructions to scour the occupant's garbage for bank statements (a big score) or even a debit card receipt (still valuable). Depending on whether the victim was a woman or man, she or Frankie would phone the victim's bank and pose as the customer.

If the bank rep asked for a recent transaction as proof of identity, citing information from a receipt plucked from the garbage, along with a bit of improvised playacting, often was sufficient to win the rep's full help. Marilyn or Frankie would then get the rep on the phone to change the billing address, request a replacement debit card and PIN number, apply for credit cards and credit line increases, and add other account users.

Once in control of a bank account, they would send runners, usually addicts working for $200 cash or the equivalent in dope, to make a $1,000 or $2,000 ATM withdrawal, depending on the particular bank's limits, from the breached account. The runners were instructed to hit the ATM machines just before and after a unit was serviced late at night, thus getting two days of maximum withdrawals within a few hours. Enter Biggie, a longtime video gaming buddy of Frankie, and a fixture in the Edmonton speeder scene. The middle of three boys from a protective middle-class family, Biggie was garrulous and outgoing, a born networker, with a short attention span. Biggie recruited and handled the runners, and often controlled splitting up the loot.

Marilyn, Frankie, and Biggie began to aggressively probe and test financial systems designed to enable convenient commerce. Staying awake for days, sometimes weeks, at a time in hotel rooms or dingy residences, called sketch pads, where speeders and crackheads congregated, Marilyn, Frankie, and Biggie would plot intricate variations of proved scams or concoct wild, blockbuster capers.

Marilyn at one point concocted a surefire scheme to extract $10,000 in forty-eight hours. It involved making a series of deposits from breached accounts with overdraft protection into certain ATM machines, with runners making withdrawals within a certain window of time. But she could never get all the moving parts to mesh. Someone would be too high, or get arrested, or back out. "And that kind of like destroys the whole operation, right. So it never got very far," says Marilyn.

In western Canada, the crystalline form of methamphetamine, often referred to as ice, or glass, is preferred over the powered form. Speeders typically buy an eight ball—an eighth of an ounce of crystals—for $100 to $250, depending on supply and demand. Speeders heat the crystals in a small glass pipe, called a bowl, and inhale the fumes. Depending on the quality of the crystals, a pungent ammonia smell can be stifling; the odor stems from the incomplete cleansing of solvents used as part of the manufacturing process. An eight ball can keep a moderate user buzzed for two or three days.

Methamphetamine is a cheap, highly addictive street derivative of the amphetamine family of stimulants first used by the Nazis during World War

II to keep elite tank crews and combat pilots sharp. Amphetamine was widely distributed as small white diet pills in the 1950s and 1960s and it became popular among college students pulling all-night studies and long-haul truck drivers. A "St. Louie halfway" meant a dose of "crosstops" or "bennies" that would get you halfway across the country, while a "West Coast turnaround" meant enough for a cross-continent trip. Amphetamines virtually disappeared by the mid-1970s. But a new, hypercharged formulation—distilled from the cold medication ephedrine—turned up in Hawaii and California in the late 1980s. Available in forms that can be smoked, snorted, eaten, or injected, methamphetamine migrated to the Pacific Northwest in the early 1990s and has since spread across North America.

Methamphetamine artificially stimulates the sympathetic nervous system. It triggers a cascading release of norepinephrine, dopamine, and serotonin in the brain. These are the naturally produced chemicals that arouse excitement, fear, and pleasure. It elevates heart rate, blood pressure, and body temperature. It dilates pupils, inhibits stomach activity, and quickens the release of adrenaline. Ingested in low doses, it can make users feel more confident, lose weight, stay alert, and enjoy sex more. Repetitive tasks, such as hand washing, house cleaning, or working puzzles can become hypnotic. Prolonged use of high dosages can lead to acute sleep deprivation, which in turn can lead to paranoid delusions, hallucinations, violence, and self-destructive behavior. Chronic elevated blood pressure can cause brain vessels to burst or the heart to fail.

Going days, sometimes more than a week, without sleeping, Frankie's and Marilyn's cell members were continually fearful of two things: the police, and an even more clear-and-present threat—their larcenous fellow addicts. Biggie once passed out, certain he had $2,000 in his wallet, and woke up alone, with no wallet. Marilyn often fantasized about a big score that would give her the impetus to return to a normal life.

"But nothing ever got really big. We probably used a quarter of the stuff we had," she says. "Somebody rips you off, or you never collect what you're owed. You feel like you can do anything. But you can't stay focused. You lose your train of thought. You have to move fast when you're doing fraud, and speeders don't move fast."

Enablers

A Cashless Society

Largely invisible to the general public, our built-for-speed credit-issuing and payments system has been half a century in the making. Its roots can be traced to 1949, when a Manhattanite named Frank McNamara got ready to pay for his meal at a ritzy New York eatery called Major's Cabin Grill only to discover he had forgotten his wallet in another jacket. That embarrassment sparked inspiration. McNamara persuaded a group of restaurateurs to allow a select group of patrons to "charge" for their meals upon presenting a wallet-sized piece of cardboard. In 1952 he set up a company to settle what was owed and the Diners Club charge card was born.

Accepted by select restaurants, hotels, and merchants, a Diners Club card became a status symbol wielded by business expense account holders and the well-heeled, who invariably paid off the entire balance each month. American Express and Carte Blanche soon followed. Then, in 1958, Bank of America successfully introduced the BankAmericard throughout California. Other banks had dabbled in charge cards on a local scale. But the BankAmericard was the first charge card made widely available for the average citizen. The BankAmericard had one small, but profound, distinction from Diners Club–type charge cards: it allowed users to pay off just part of what they owed, carrying the balance as an unsecured loan. Thus was born revolving consumer credit.

To expand its fledgling credit card business into other states, Bank of America in 1966 struck upon the idea of licensing the BankAmericard to other financial institutions. At about the same time, several competing credit card cooperatives were taking shape across the country that would subsequently merge to become MasterCard. Soon Bank of America could no longer run its credit card business efficiently enough to keep its widely scattered stable of licensees happy.

Enter a brash thirty-eight-year-old credit card program director named Dee Hock, from the tiny National Bank of Commerce in Seattle. Hock in 1970 led a licensees' rebellion and rose from obscurity to help form, then head up a corporation called National BankAmericard Inc., or NBI, assigned to independently run BankAmericard operations on behalf of its member financial institutions. Through the 1970s, the charismatic Hock built a legacy as a visionary architect and champion of an ultrafast and convenient global payments system. Under Hock's leadership, NBI hustled to recruit bank members across Europe and Asia, and overtook MasterCard as the most widely used payment card on the planet. Part of that had to do with Hock leading a drive to rechristen the BankAmericard with a name more befitting a global payment tool. In 1977 BankAmericard became Visa.

Hock was also driven to take advantage of the best available technology. In the early 1970s he persuaded NBI's directors to gamble $3 million on building an electronics payment system dubbed the Bank Authorization System Experiment I (BASE I). Prior to the popularization of plastic payment cards, there had been only three major advancements in how Westerners settled financial transactions. The ancient Lydians began using coins in place of bartering around 700 B.C.E., the Italians introduced an early form of checks in the twelfth century, and colonists living in the Commonwealth of Massachusetts are credited with inventing paper money in the seventeenth century.

BASE I was a catalyst for the fourth major advancement: the wide use of a card-based payment system. BASE I, and systems like it, became the cornerstone on which the financial industry would begin to infuse mind-boggling speed and flexibility into electronic payments. Prior to BASE I, processing a credit card transaction had been a cumbersome hands-on affair. Merchants were required to place the credit card on top of a paper sales slip fitted onto a "zip-zap" machine. Cranking the handle back and forth imprinted the card's embossed name and account number onto the triplicate sales slip.

One copy of the sales slip went to the card-issuing bank, one went to the customer, and one stayed with the merchant. Settlement relied on manual handling of the paper trail. Cardholders could generally charge small purchases with little hassle, but transactions above a "floor limit" (usually $50) had to be authorized by the bank. That necessitated a phone call to a bank employee, who manually verified the card user's available credit. Such phone calls typically took several minutes, limiting credit card use for major purchases.

BASE I came along in 1973 and incorporated mainframe DEC computers into the payment process. No longer did a store clerk have to get verbal approval from a bank employee for charges above the $50 floor limit. Instead, BASE I processed the authorization and transmitted an approval code via a phone line to a payment terminal sitting near the cash register. Processing time dropped to less than a minute.

Building on the success of BASE I, Hock a year later rolled out BASE II, which computerized the settlement process, paving the way for zip-zap machines and the paper trail to be phased out. By the mid-1980s most merchants helped speed the transactions process up even more by switching to electronic point-of-sale card readers. The card readers transferred data from a magnetic stripe on the back of the payment cards directly to the processing computers. Transactions now could be done in five to twenty seconds.

Exponential expansion of the card-based payment system followed. Refined and security hardened at the end of the twentieth century, the electronic payment system became an essential cog of the twenty-first century. A simple physical device—the magnetic striped plastic card—emerged as the linchpin enabling the financial services industry to connect each individual consumer to the payment system, and, ultimately, integrate the payment system into the Internet.

Befitting the role he played in ushering in the age of electronic payments, Hock is widely quoted in books about banking and finance. In Martin Mayer's *The Bankers: The Next Generation*, Hock has this to say about BASE I and BASE II, the progenitors of VisaNet: "It was necessary to reconceive, in the most fundamental sense, the nature of bank, money, and credit card; even beyond that to the essential elements of each and how they might change in a microelectronics environment. Several conclusions emerged: First: Money had become nothing but guaranteed, alphanumeric data recorded in valueless paper and metal. It would eventually become guaranteed data in the form of arranged electronics and photons which would move around the world at the speed of light."

Hock's commentary typifies the financial industry's long-held holy grail: the attainment of a cashless, checkless society. Indeed, our built-for-speed electronic payments systems, of which VisaNet is at the vanguard, take us as close as we've ever been. They allow us to whip out a plastic card and acquire just about any good or service, pretty much anywhere in the civilized world, and be surprised, even annoyed, if the entire transaction doesn't clear, lickety-split.

Expediters

Spam Plague

The nuisance factor was getting out of hand.

As e-mail viruses and self-propagating worms multiplied in the wake of Code Red, cleanup expenses and lost productivity spun out of control. In late 2001, consulting firm Computer Economics pegged the projected damage caused by Code Red at a record $2 billion, with plenty more to come. A refined variant, Code Red II, lingered on through the fall, knocking out Microsoft Network's free Hotmail service, Qwest's Internet access service, and the Associated Press's Web site.

And Code Red was just one of dozens of actively spreading pieces of malware. E-mail viruses replicating thousands of messages each second, and self-spreading worms aggressively scanning the Internet acted like bad cholesterol: the surfeit of traffic clogged the Internet's bandwidth and slowed everything down.

To make matters worse, another fast-rising, seemingly indomitable force had begun to clog the Internet: spam. Tech companies such as Yahoo and AOL pioneered sending e-mail ads to consumers, and banks and merchants soon joined them. But spam really took off when a battalion of entrepreneurs with murky ethics, attracted by the compelling economics of junk e-mail, jumped in to become bulk e-mailers catering to advertisers of dubious wares.

For a comparatively tiny expense, a bulk e-mailer could fire off tens of millions of junk e-mail ads for an advertiser selling offshore prescription drugs, get-rich-quick schemes, or pornography. The advertiser gladly paid a fraction of a penny for each spam sent, knowing he or she stood to make a tidy profit if just 1,000 out of 1 million pieces of spam resulted in a sale.

Almost overnight, a community of several hundred bulk e-mailers sprang up and began by sending spam from their own home computers. Meanwhile, an extensive and determined antispamming community quickly took shape, led by the volunteer antispam groups SpamHaus and Spamcops. These antispam crusaders took it upon themselves to monitor e-mail traffic and alert Internet service providers to blacklist egregious spammers. And thus began a series of parries and thrusts between bulk e-mailers and the antispam groups that would ultimately drive spammers to form an alliance with elite virus writers.

But first the bulk e-mailers would exhaust the easy pickings. "A spammer would sign up for an account with an ISP on Friday and let loose a torrent of spam over the weekend," says Joe Stewart, senior security researcher at SecureWorks, who has made a study of the evolution of spam. By the time complaints reached the Internet service provider on Monday morning, "the spammer would have already abandoned the account." But with help from the antispam crusaders, ISPs began keeping an eye out for weekend spammers and cutting them off.

So now the bulk e-mailers had to get a bit more geeky. They began to search out e-mail systems with "open relays." Such systems were plentiful on college campuses. The spammers found they could route spam through the open relays, and make it look like the junk mail came from the colleges. Ever vigilant, SpamHaus and Spamcops began swiftly notifying ISPs and convinced them to blacklist messages from e-mail systems with open relays. This caused the colleges to tighten their e-mail systems by shutting the relays.

As the inventory of open e-mail relays dwindled, bulk e-mailers got even geekier. "At this point, they took a cue from something hackers had long done to hide their identities while attacking systems," says Stewart. "They began to utilize proxy servers."

A proxy server intercepts incoming data-exchange requests to see whether it can fulfill the requests. If it cannot, it relays the request to another server. In the early days of the Internet, it was easy to locate "open proxies" sitting on computer servers because they used a standard protocol and communicated over assigned ports. (Ports are communications channels designated to handle certain types of traffic; for instance, port 80 carries Web-page traffic; port 25 carries e-mail.)

Borrowing from virus writers, who had mastered the art of relaying viruses through open proxies, spammers devised a way to route spam through open proxies, thus obscuring where the spam came from. SpamHaus and Spamcops reacted quickly, organizing a campaign to blacklist traffic coming from open proxies and thus choking off spam once more. Next move: spammers.

As the year 2001 drew to a close, spam and viruses swarmed into home computers like never before, and bogged down more and more corporate systems. Consumers and corporate users were getting more than annoyed—they began to lose confidence in Windows. Linux, the free open-source-code operating system built and continually improved by volunteer programmers, began to get more attention. IBM jumped in as a big Linux backer, offering to help government agencies and corporate clients replace their Windows-based systems with corporate-grade Linux systems.

None of this was lost on Microsoft founder and CEO Bill Gates. On January 15, 2002, Gates moved boldly to rectify the situation with a memo sent to each one of his 47,000 employees. Gates took the unprecedented step of halting all development work on Windows to launch an initiative he called "Trustworthy Computing." He dispatched 7,000 Windows software programmers to boot camp on how to write secure code, and set in motion a complete overhaul of how Microsoft designed, tested, and released new software programs. Gates would no longer tolerate rushing to market with buggy software, bloated with superfluous, lightly tested features. Instead Microsoft software developers—many hired directly out of top-ranked programs at Stanford and MIT, and groomed for speedy production of cool new features—would have to be retrained. An ambitious if obtusely named initiative called SDL (Security Development Lifecycle) embodied the paradigm shift Gates sought. With SDL, Gates commanded his software developers to embrace new and unfamiliar habits designed to root out coding errors and eradicate security holes in Windows from day one.

"In the past, we've made our software and services more compelling for users by adding new features and functionality, and by making our platform richly extensible," Gates wrote. "We've done a terrific job at that, but all those great features won't matter unless customers trust our software."

To Gates's credit, Microsoft would pour vast resources into making the Windows XP operating system, and its successor, Windows Vista, more hack proof. Indeed, Microsoft would set an example for rivals such as Apple, Google, and Adobe on the wisdom of being forthcoming about security weaknesses and diligent about mitigating them. Yet, at the same time, Microsoft could not escape its DNA as a tech company enamored of new bells and whistles. It would continue to push aggressively into emerging new markets for Internet-enabled software services, such as online search, instant messaging, and digital entertainment, without fully accounting for the new opportunities it was creating for cyberintruders. For every security hole Microsoft patched or avoided in Windows, white hat, black hat, and gray hat hackers would uncover scores of fresh vulnerabilities in Internet Explorer, Instant Messenger, Word, Excel, and PowerPoint.

Michael Cherry, a longtime tech-security analyst for Seattle-based research firm Directions on Microsoft (which is completely independent of the software giant) uses an analogy from the physical world to describe Microsoft's security challenges. Cherry likened Gates's epiphany about security, and Microsoft's launch of the SDL initiative, to a homebuilder who decides to follow a methodology drafted in broad outline.

"Having a process is better than no process, and a good process keeps evolving and growing," says Cherry. "But you have to be careful. The methodology is just a set of guidelines and principals that is supposed to get designers, developers, and testers thinking about security issues. But it doesn't guarantee security."

A contractor's methodology might require solid core construction and dead bolts for all exterior doors, notes Cherry. But a designer can still position a window close enough to an exterior door so that a burglar can break the glass, reach in, and release the dead bolt.

"Sometimes all the methodology does is give you a false sense that you have addressed the problem, and people are more interested in checking off that they completed the step than in what they actually did as part of the step," says Cherry.

CHAPTER 3
System Fissures

Exploiters
2004 Global

On the morning of the 9/11 terrorist attacks, a few blocks from the World Trade Center, Terrance DeFranco was at his desk at Baird, Patrick & Co., where he was chief of investment banking. DeFranco had been mulling a career change. He had an inkling to run a start-up tech company. The 9/11 tragedy spurred him to leave behind fourteen years in investment banking and pursue his dream.

DeFranco knew about a company that had developed technology to decipher patterns in large databases. He saw the technology as ripe for wider commercial deployment in what in 2001 looked to be a promising field: identity-theft deterrence. DeFranco secured investors to help him buy the company, recruited some hotshot computer programmers, and by 2004 was ready to take the revamped company public, renaming it Edentify. He left New York City behind with no regrets and set up headquarters near his boyhood home in Bethlehem, Pennsylvania. And just like that, he was in the vanguard defending against an onslaught of data harvesters and scam artists probing for fissures in a financial transactions system designed for convenience and speed.

Edentify set out to help financial institutions spot suspicious patterns in use of Social Security numbers (SSNs). SSNs with tweaked names, changed addresses, and a slew of new accounts opened in a short time indicated identity thieves at work. Using stolen data, crooks would open credit lines and take out loans piggybacked on the good credit standing of the victim. A tier of accomplices usually helped. Some supplied the stolen data necessary to get started. Others helped extract cash from the faked accounts.

"New-account fraud," as security experts call it, is really an old scam. It first turned up when credit card usage began to rise in the 1970s. But back then, crooks had to be bold enough to show up in person and fill out a paper application. Everything was much more traceable. The risk was greater, and the scalability—the potential for opening a large number of accounts—was minimal.

Automated transactions and the Internet changed all of that. "Now you can open 10,000 of these accounts in the time it used to take to open one," says Avivah Litan, vice president and research director at Gartner Research, a prominent technology-industry consulting firm. "And it can all be done on a faceless Internet. You never have to show up in person."

DeFranco often uses the following representative example to illustrate the wide latitude identity thieves enjoy while using stolen SSNs to commit new-account fraud: First, the fraudster obtains Tina Ahern's SSN. Next, the crook applies online for a pay-as-you-go cell phone account under the name Tina A. Hern, using Tina Ahern's SSN but a different billing address. A few months later—after paying the cell phone bill and thus establishing a payment history and new billing address for Tina A. Hern—the thief successfully applies for a credit card using the name Christina Hern, instead of Tina A. Hern, or Tina Hern, with two digits of the SSN inverted.

After making a few payments, Christina Hern requests a credit limit increase to $3,000, then to $5,000, and finally to $10,000. Along the way, the crook applies for another credit card, this time under the name Herman Christianson, using Christina Ahern's SSN and billing address. Tuned for speed, and readily accepting of close-enough data, the credit bureau's automated system sees only the combined payment behaviors of the various accounts the crook has opened using Tina Ahern's credit history. So the credit bureau issues the credit-issuing bank a valid credit report and credit score for Herman Christianson.

The bank's computer system, in turn, sees only an acceptable credit history and credit score; the bank approves a new credit card for Herman Christianson and mails it to him at the address listed on the loan application. The crook keeps adding new accounts, upping the credit limit on each account, until he or she decides it's time to "bust out," says DeFranco. On the appointed day, the scammer makes large cash withdrawals out of each account, transferring the funds over the Internet to a "drop" account controlled by a trusted accomplice, known as a "drop specialist." Knowing law enforcement rarely bothers with thefts under $5,000, the scammer makes sure no transfer exceeds that amount.

As Edentify won more clients and checked more financial records, it found evidence of crooks manipulating SSNs in systematic fashion and on a wide scale. From 2004 to early 2007, Edentify would analyze more than 500 million names paired with Social Security numbers. It would discover some 5 million SSNs being used fraudulently, including one number that was being used by thirty-five different individuals.

"Criminals are finding gaps in the system and exploiting them by intentionally manipulating identities," says DeFranco. "This is something that is done through trial and error. Fraudsters can afford to do trial and error because they are operating from the anonymity of the Internet."

As Terrance DeFranco ramped up his dream company in the eastern United States, Marilyn, Frankie, and Biggie began collaborating in Edmonton with an introverted young man named Socrates. A digital native, Socrates was never far from his laptop PC. When he wasn't losing himself for hours on end playing Counter-Strike, a shoot-'em-up online video game, Socrates enjoyed downloading and watching pirated first-run movies. He liked to smoke a little pot but had never tried meth until he ran into Marilyn in late 2003.

Socrates had little inkling of it at the time, but he was destined to become a renowned figure in the Edmonton underworld. He would become a revered hacker enabling the Edmonton cell to rise from petty local scams to raking in thousands of dollars a day partnering with cybercrooks from Oklahoma, Quebec, Bulgaria, and Romania. He would apply his computing skills toward setting up the Edmonton cell to provide a much-in-demand service: drop specialists for hire.

Enablers
Easy-Credit Quicksand

A cute, seemingly innocuous, animated banking commercial appeared on black-and-white television sets throughout California in 1959. It featured a sprightly, baton-wielding orchestra conductor pitching use of a wallet-sized plastic card: the BankAmericard, the first widely promoted, all-purpose charge card. Dressed in coattails, the conductor directed a lively choir of singers harmonizing the refrain "yeeess" to "convenient shopping" for "shoes, gasoline, housewares."

No one, not even the bank executives who approved the ad campaign, had any inkling how massively consumer credit would mushroom. In lifting his baton, Bank of America's cartoon conductor marked the start of a stunning transformation. Over the next few decades, America would discard its long-held pay-as-you-go ethos and morph into a society whose citizens habitually and increasingly live beyond their means.

The winsome tone of the cartoon commercial belied Bank of America's bold gamble. Up until that time, individual banks had dabbled in issuing charge cards for local use. But no bank had been able to persuade a wide spectrum of merchants to accept a bank-specific payment card. And none dared delve into the uncharted waters of liberally offering revolving credit to the masses. The BankAmericard, in effect, made unsecured loans of $300 to $500 available to all Bank of America customers.

This opened the door to a profound departure from the traditional use of credit. Farmers historically relied on bank loans to carry them through the cycle of planting, harvesting, and selling crops. And as America entered the twentieth century—and steadily became more urbanized—the issuance of informal lines of credits from relatives, local merchants, and the family doctor or dentist played a crucial role.

Millions of working-class families took to carefully managing various loans and IOUs while regularly socking a little something away toward a major purchase or for rainy-day emergencies. Thus the U.S household savings rate rarely dipped below 8 percent throughout the 1900s. Through the first three-quarters of the millennium, in particular, families were able to steadily improve their standard of living by emphasizing frugality and patience. Getting a washing machine or new family car was achievable, though it often required sacrifice and delayed gratification.

The easy credit made so readily available by obtaining a BankAmericard blew that kind of thinking out of the water. Bank of America struck upon a business model that, in theory, would spark a continually escalating cycle of borrowing. To begin the sequence, consumers had to embrace the habit of satiating their material desires straightaway.

A credit card was a tool that supplied unprecedented buying power and financial flexibility to make that possible. Suddenly a new wardrobe, a Christmas shopping spree, or even an exotic vacation was within Joe Average's immediate reach. Merchants could easily see the potential for a boost in sales, not to mention efficiency gains in cash flow and inventory management. And the bank stood to pocket 18 percent in consumer interest and 6 percent in merchant handling fees. The BankAmericard, in short, proffered a "win-win-win" decades before that catchphrase would enter the business lexicon. Its success galvanized the banking industry.

Bank of America sold BankAmericard franchises to major banks in Illinois, Michigan, and elsewhere. Soon a rival group, led by Chemical Bank and Manufacturers Hanover, formed the Interbank Card Association, which later became MasterCard.

"Bank of America started its own credit card, which gave the impetus for all these banks in the Midwest and on the East Coast to get into credit cards, as well," says banking consultant Darold D. Hoops, president of Huntersville, North Carolina–based Town & Country Consulting. "It was to stave off Bank of America."

Convenience was an elemental driver that made speed—both in mass distribution of new credit cards and in executing cardholder transactions—an imperative. The more widely credit cards were distributed and used, the more system speed was required to execute a rising volume of transactions in a timely manner. Bank of America's bold business proposition swiftly took root. In 1957 the BankAmericard was nonexistent. By 1963 consumers used it to make $111.1 million worth of purchases, and by 2006 Visa payment cards settled a phenomenal $2.4 trillion in transactions. Visa today accounts for 64 percent of payment card transactions worldwide, with MasterCard holding a 30 percent share, followed by American Express and Discover Card, each with 3 percent shares.

But it wasn't until the U.S. Supreme Court's 1978 ruling in the landmark Marquette Bank case that credit cards began to form the basis of the hyper-fast credit-issuing and electronic payments system as we know it today. At the time, Jimmy Carter was president, a global oil crisis was rapidly unfolding, and runaway inflation pushed interest rates into the 20 percent range. Credit card operations overnight had become a big money loser for banks, which were forced to borrow money at high rates, and issue credit restricted by rate caps, generally 12 percent, imposed by state usury laws.

The high court affirmed Marquette's assertion that its credit card business should be governed solely by the usury laws of the state in which the operation was physically located. The decision absolved the bank from having to heed local interest rate caps imposed by the state where the cardholder resided. South Dakota and Delaware immediately seized upon the opportunity by liberalizing their usury laws in order to lure credit card issuers to relocate on friendlier soil.

In response, Citibank in 1981 moved its credit card operations, then and now one of the world's largest, from New York to Sioux Falls. Delaware similarly lured the credit card divisions of several large East Coast banks to Wilmington. By the mid-1980s, all of the big banks, as well as the new "monoline" banks that dealt strictly in credit cards, such as MNBA and Capitol One (Capitol One now does other forms of banking), set up shop in either Sioux City or Wilmington.

The stage was set for the financial industry to take the notion first conveyed by Bank of America's cartoon conductor—say yes to a credit-fueled lifestyle—and really run with it. Conservative lending practices went by the wayside, replaced by predatory marketing tactics designed to take full advantage of the speed built into the system. Marketing campaigns began to take aim at teenagers, college students, and lower-income citizens, folks who could least afford to carry a high debt load. The heightened risk of such borrowers defaulting on loans was offset by the steep consumer interest rates permitted by South Dakota and Delaware.

U.S. consumers responded big-time to this democratization of debt. Put simply, they began to borrow profligately and forget about saving. From 1980—about the time the financial industry got serious about extending consumer credit far and wide—through December 2006, outstanding revolving consumer credit rose more than fifteenfold, from $55 billion to $880 billion. During that same two-and-half-decade span, total consumer debt—including revolving debt and nonrevolving car loans, mortgages, and home equity loans—rose sevenfold, from $352 billion to a whopping $2.4 trillion. By the end of 2006, American consumers cumulatively held outstanding debt roughly matching the gross national product of Germany, the world's third most productive nation.

Meanwhile, the median household income of young families (those whose head of household ranged in age from twenty-five to thirty-four) stood at $45,485 at the end of 2004, a meager 0.08 percent higher than the $41,986 median income earned by young families in 1980, as adjusted for inflation. The financial industry is given to arguing that many families made smart use of debt to extend their buying power and enhance their quality of life; bank officials don't care to discuss the many more families for whom servicing unprecedented levels of burdensome debt has become a way of life.

The extent to which American consumers have become bogged down in easy-credit quicksand is starkly underscored by a relatively recent shift in the century-long pattern of U.S. households saving at least 8 percent of disposable income. In an unprecedented plunge, the savings rate slipped to 7 percent in 1994 and continued plummeting—to negative 0.6 percent by mid-2005.

Instead of saving up for a major purchase or the proverbial rainy day, consumers by the start of the twenty-first century had become accustomed to spending like there was no tomorrow, flashing plastic and taking out home equity loans to buy plasma TVs, lease gas-guzzling SUVs, and book exotic vacations. Bank of America's cartoon orchestra conductor would approve.

Expediters

"billy gates . . . fix your software!!"

Precocious teenagers, disaffected computer geeks, egotistical virus researchers, determined spammers, all sharing varying degrees of disdain for Microsoft, most coveting each others' respect and admiration—these were the enemies Bill Gates rallied his troops to repel in early 2002.

Gates had no way of knowing it at the time, but a cataclysmic shift in the attacker community was under way. A dozen years had slipped by since the Berlin Wall came tumbling down. Eastern Europe was crawling with educated, tech-savvy young men who were left to scratch for menial work in a perennially depressed economy. In North America, the dot-com bubble had burst, wiping out thousands of cushy tech jobs. With all this technical skill running around, the purist hacker's mind-set was ripe for corruption. Hacking for profit was on the verge of becoming the new imperative.

The earliest manifestation of this change would surface on the Internet, in the private chat channels, where spammers began to communicate with virus writers, and on security bulletin boards, where researchers and virus hunters dissected obscure malware. This is where Joe Stewart, senior security researcher at SecureWorks, hung out.

Stewart never planned on becoming a virus hunter. Born in Athens, Ohio, he split time growing up between his mom's home in Florida and his dad's place in Arizona. An inveterate tinkerer, he and a sixth-grade buddy fiddled endlessly with a Radio Shack TRS-80 color desktop computer, staying after school every day to figure it out and teaching themselves how to program in BASIC. This was in the mid-1980s. Shortly thereafter, Stewart convinced his dad to buy a then-state-of-the-art Commodore VIC-20 desktop computer and progressed even further, sometimes running up $300 in long-distance phone charges to log on to the early techie bulletin boards.

By the time Stewart turned sixteen in the late 1980s, he considered himself fairly computer savvy. But he dropped out of computing for several years to dabble in becoming a rock musician, until one day in 1996 when his mom gave him her worn-out desktop computer. It had an outdated 386 microprocessor; Mom had purchased an upgraded 486 for herself.

"The motivation of being broke and having a wife and baby to support really kicked my learning back into high gear," says Stewart. Four years later, Stewart found himself part of a select group of perhaps 200 virus hunters, the vast majority young males. These Internet sleuths worked at tech-security companies such as Symantec, McAfee, Trend Micro, Computer Associates, Sophos, F-Secure, MessageLabs, Postini, and several dozen smaller niche players. They had in common with mainstream software programmers a high aptitude for math and problem solving, but they also brought something extra to the table—a healthy sense of injustice.

"I've always admired a good hack—but modern viruses are not displays of skill; they are simple brutes that are polluting and pillaging the Internet landscape," says Stewart. "It's the powerful taking advantage of the weak. I'm disgusted at how they [criminal hackers] are so ready and willing to destroy what I view as one of mankind's greatest developments, all for their own selfish greed."

Stewart rose rapidly in his chosen field and landed the position of lead network intrusion analyst at LURHQ, a Myrtle Beach, South Carolina, tech-security firm that would later merge with SecureWorks. In August 2002, Stewart caught wind of a mysterious new type of proxy server that could be installed on compromised PCs in stages. This allowed the virus writer to send parts of the malware from different Web sites, the better to elude the virus hunters.

"The complete installation would happen in stages, sometimes over several days," says Stewart. "The subsequent stages completely replace the first stage. Once the second stage takes over, the virus is removed and no longer spreads from that host."

Once fully installed, this new type of proxy server could be used to relay spam or participate in DDoS attacks. It was ominous for another reason: Because standard proxy servers relayed data over "well-known ports," they were easy to blacklist. But this new type could use any port.

Internet port numbers are categorized in three ranges: ports 0 through 1,023 are the so-called well-known ports, assigned to very specific purposes; ports 1,024 through 49,151 are available for general use; and ports 49,152 through 65,535 are for private communications. With this new proxy server, the entire range of ports was now in play for hackers.

On January 9, 2003, virus hunters took note of an obscure little e-mail virus, which they came to refer to as SoBig.A, launched from the spoofed e-mail address big@boss.com. SoBig.A used a variety of enticing subject descriptions to get victims to click on a tainted attachment.

Once activated, it launched into two tasks: spreading itself to every e-mail address it could find, and visiting a designated Web site, hosted at www.geocities.com, for further instructions. When Stewart visited the Geocities Web site, he found a Web-page link that led nowhere: www.blahblahblahblah.com. Stewart had a hunch. He repeatedly checked the Web site over a period of several hours, and, sure enough, caught the virus writer periodically dropping in the real link.

"He was trying to protect the progression from analysis," Stewart says.

The real link directed the infected PC to another Web page to download stage two of the malicious program, and then to yet another Web page to download stage three. "It was quite successful at this," says Stewart. "Thousands of proxy servers were surreptitiously installed on computers worldwide."

SoBig.A got choked off when Internet service providers—AOL, MSN, EarthLink, and others—began to block all e-mail from big@boss.com, and Web site host Geocities cut off the designated Web site.

But SoBig.A's author wouldn't be discouraged so easily. On May 19, SoBig.B began spreading. It purported to come from support@microsoft.com and contained several improvements. For instance, it ran every time the user turned on his or her computer, and it sought to spread itself to any corporate servers that happened to be sharing a data-exchange link with the infected PC. By far, SoBig.B's most distinctive new feature was this: the virus turned itself off after two weeks.

The day SoBig.B expired, SoBig.C appeared with more improvements. It, too, turned off after two weeks. SoBig.D followed, then SoBig.E. Like infectious bacteria mutating in response to antibiotics, each variant tried different ways to counter Geocities, which moved quickly to shut down the Web sites the infected PCs were instructed to report to.

"All the versions were very similar; they just kept improving, version after version, like a software development project," says Mikko Hyppönen, chief research officer at F-Secure. "It was done professionally. Someone was investing money."

After SoBig.E went mute in mid-July, no more variants followed, leaving Stewart, Hyppönen, and their fellow virus detectives to believe the SoBig virus family had run its course. They were wrong. But before anyone could contemplate the deeper significance of a virus strain that steadily improved with each iteration, MSBlast stormed the Internet.

MSBlast took absolutely no one in the close-knit community of vulnerability researchers and virus sleuths by surprise—quite the opposite. Something like MSBlast had been widely predicted early in the summer of 2003 after a Polish group of white hats, calling themselves the Last Stage of Delirium, notified Microsoft about a gaping hole in a Windows component called remote procedure call, or RPC, which allowed PCs to share files and use the same printer.

The Polish researchers had discovered that it was possible to overwhelm RPC by sending it too much data. Once overwhelmed, RPC would let the attacker have full access to the computer. This flaw existed on PCs running Windows XP, Windows 2000, Windows NT, and Windows Server 2003— hundreds of millions of machines worldwide. Any Windows computer connected to the Internet with RPC enabled was a ripe target.

On July 16, Microsoft issued a patch for the RPC hole and gave the Last Stage of Delirium credit for flushing it out. Nine days later, a group of Chinese researchers calling themselves Chinese X Focus posted a "proof of concept" RPC exploit on several security bulletin boards. The exploit showed how to overwhelm RPC and take control of the machine. It was only a matter of time before a black hat stepped forward to copy or improve upon the Chinese exploit—and release it on the Internet. The glory was there for the taking.

The inevitable occurred on August 11, just twenty-six days after Microsoft issued the RPC patch. Hardly anyone had installed the patch. A self-propagating worm, christened MSBlast, began searching out unpatched PCs and infecting them at an incredible rate. In contrast to the SoBig e-mail viruses, which had been handled like a series of carefully controlled pilot tests, MSBlast raced out of the starting blocks and cried out for attention.

Stewart was among the first virus hunters to reverse engineer MSBlast. He found this cryptic message buried inside the code:

```
billy gates why do you make this possible? Stop making
money and fix your software!!
```

That brash admonishment told the virus hunters that MSBlast's author almost certainly came from the subculture of braggarts who get a charge out of wreaking havoc on the Internet to make a name for themselves. By contrast, SoBig's creator was a model of discreetness, clearly cut from different cloth.

"When it came to the motive behind a particular piece of malware, we were starting to see it separate into two groups: profit versus nonprofit," says Stewart. "The nonprofit virus author wants to raise public awareness of viruses, but the for-profit virus author does not. Ideally, the for-profit author wants to use your computer for as long as possible without being discovered."

MSBlast was anything but quiet. Within twenty-four hours, MSBlast breached 120,000 computers around the world; each infected computer, in turn, scoured the Internet for more vulnerable targets to infect. At its peak, MSBlast infected 4,000 PCs an hour. Corporate systems crashed under the surge of traffic.

A number of tech-security experts remain convinced to this day that the intense spreading of MSBlast contributed to a major power blackout that darkened New York, Toronto, and Detroit on August 14; while the fast-spreading worm may not have directly caused the outage, it very well could have crippled computer systems that could have kept the outage from spreading.

MSBlast did more than spread like wildfire. To add insult to injury, it implanted a bot instructed to stand by for an August 15 DDoS attack on windowsupdate.com, the Web site where Microsoft distributed security patches. Microsoft went into crisis mode to blunt the impending assault, and managed to do so at the eleventh hour. The software giant narrowly escaped infamy. Imagine the irony of a Windows virus spread via an unpatched security hole knocking out the Web site that distributed Windows patches.

The full scope of how invasive MSBlast turned out to be wouldn't be known until Microsoft assigned an anti-malware program manager named Matthew Braverman to analyze the effectiveness of the MSBlast cleanup tool. Braverman found that within six months of making the removal tool publicly available, "Microsoft recorded approximately 25 million downloads and 12 million executions. In other words, over 25 million unique computers were identified as being infected by MSBlast," Braverman wrote in his report.

MSBlast also left behind an easy-to-find back door. During the time those 25 million PCs were infected with MSBlast, any novice hacker could have skipped along and slipped in bots of his or her own—or any spamming group could have implanted proxy servers.

MSBlast's creator was never caught. However, on August 29 FBI and Secret Service agents stormed an apartment in Hopkins, Minnesota, and arrested Jeffrey Lee Parson, eighteen, a senior at Hopkins High School. They were led to the apartment Parson shared with his parents by a clue buried in the coding of a variant of MSBlast. The clue was the address for a Web site belonging to Parson where he stored a stash of viruses alongside lyrics to songs from Judas Priest, "Weird Al" Yankovic, and Megadeth.

It turned out that the six-foot-four, 320-pound Parson was responsible only for a copycat variant of MSBlast that infected 48,000 PCs and caused an estimated $1.2 million in damage, prosecutors said. U.S. District Court judge Marsha Pechman described Parson as a lonely teenager who created his "own reality," rarely leaving his bedroom. He served an eighteen-month jail sentence.

"Jeffrey Lee Parson foolishly considered himself an untouchable," says Ken Dunham, director of the rapid response team at iDefense, a VeriSign company. "His arrest proved how overconfident some adolescents can become in the security of their own online worlds."

The tumult over MSBlast must have struck SoBig's profit-minded author as a golden opportunity. What better time to release the ultimate SoBig e-mail virus than when MSBlast's braggart author commanded the full attention of virus hunters, law enforcement, and the media?

On August 18, an e-mail luring recipients to open an attachment containing pornographic images began circulating all across the Internet. SoBig.F was now on the loose. It fired off copies of itself to every e-mail address it could find on the hard drive, using a technique called "multi-threading" for faster spreading.

Borrowing a refinement from SoBig.E, the attachment came in the form of a zip file so as to pass through e-mail systems that had begun to deny executable (.exe) attachments. Borrowing from SoBig.D, it implanted a bot tasked to report to not one, but twenty different Web servers around the world—PCs compromised by earlier SoBig variants, now standing at the ready to release the second and third stages of the attack.

"The worm writer learned two lessons from the endless cycle of Geocities closing the sites—stealth and redundancy," says Stewart.

But the SoBig.F bots never downloaded stages two and three. The virus hunters and law enforcement agencies collaborated to get Internet service providers to take nineteen of the twenty Web servers off-line. Seeing the good guys closing in, SoBig's backers held off sending further commands through the one Web server left standing on August 22.

Chalk one up for the good guys. Yet an ominous unease lingered in the aftermath of MSBlast and SoBig. Defending the Internet had become magnitudes of order more complex. It was one thing to repel immature braggarts out to bedevil giant corporations and make political state-ments; it was quite another to also have to deter well-funded criminal elements methodically refining tried-and-true hacking techniques to make a profit.

The MSBlast worm appeared to be the work of a vigilante looking to chastise Microsoft, much like Onel de Guzman, the author of the ILOVEYOU virus, had done. By contrast, whoever was behind the SoBig family of viruses did not want attention of any kind. The incremental improvements in each version—from SoBig.A in January to SoBig.F in August—progressed exactly like a professional software development project. SoBig's creators appeared to be dead serious about perfecting a virus that could infect a large number of computers for the express purpose of turning them into spamming machines and making a ton of money.

"The proof point is simply in the design of the virus," says Stewart. "The typical moneymaking virus installs spam proxies or tries to steal passwords. We saw these activities with SoBig, but not with MSBlast."

Hacking's age of innocence was fast coming to a close.

CHAPTER 4

Self-Anointed Avenger

Exploiters

Fall 2003, Edmonton

The oldest of three children in a stable, churchgoing family, Socrates recalls getting hooked on computers as a young kid. Introverted, soft-spoken, and respectful of his parents, Socrates taught himself about all things digital. He became savvy enough around computers to land a job as a technical engineering draftsman not long after graduating from high school. He earned enough to get himself an apartment and buy a state-of-the-art desktop PC. By all outward appearances, by age twenty, he seemed well positioned to make his way in the world.

In his leisure time, Socrates spent endless hours at his keyboard smoking a little pot and playing Counter-Strike, a popular online video game in which participants role-play either as a terrorist out to plant bombs, take hostages, and assassinate enemies, or as a counterterrorist determined to neutralize the terrorists. Comrades communicate by text messaging one another, using Internet slang, on an IRC (Internet relay chat) channel. Chat channels are virtual meeting rooms where people from all over the world convene to exchange text messages in real time about topics of common interests. As with most online, multiplayer video games, cheating on Counter-Strike is not uncommon. For instance, some players will use "wallhacks"—cheat code that renders solid objects semi-transparent. This allows the cheater to spot and take aim at rivals hiding behind solid objects.

When he wasn't playing Counter-Strike, Socrates would navigate to mIRC.com, a popular public Web site that serves as a gateway to thousands of chat channels. He gravitated to certain chat rooms where cinema buffs bragged about being the first to post digital copies of the latest Hollywood blockbusters on the Internet for free downloading. He became an avid collector of pirated first-run Hollywood blockbusters. Increasingly, Socrates lost track of time. His punctuality—and ultimately attendance—at work suffered. He was fired in the summer of 2003.

"I was always at home, stuck on my computer," he says. "I was too obsessed with doing what I was doing online, rather than going to work. I lost my apartment. Lost everything I owned. Then I started using heavier drugs. I started smoking meth."

In the fall of 2003, Marilyn was trying to work out a new fraud scheme and had heard about a kid named Socrates who knew his way around computers and chat rooms. She had actually been acquainted briefly with Socrates years before. "I ran into him through a mutual friend when he lost his job," she says. "I was, like, 'Hey maybe you can help me out with something?'"

Marilyn introduced Socrates to Biggie and Frankie. By then Frankie was trying to lie low. Several weeks after almost getting shot by Detective Gauthier, he had been arrested a second time and was out on bail, awaiting disposition of a slew of criminal charges. A third bust would guarantee serious jail time.

Frankie, too, had been haunting IRC chat channels. He had found his way to chat rooms where participants from such countries as Romania, Austria, and Egypt expressed keen interest in the data Frankie was collecting from bank records in Dumpsters and mailboxes. The cash-extraction capabilities Frankie boasted about also caught their attention. But Frankie never pursued the chat channel connections very far. He got his charge out of conning customer reps into doing his bidding. And he loved graphic design, using Adobe Photoshop to produce counterfeit checks, Canadian currency, and drivers' licenses.

Socrates, who felt most comfortable immersed in the virtual world, stepped in and picked up where Frankie left off. He handled the techie end of a scheme to exploit security holes in an online banking service unique to Canadian banks, called e-mail transfers. Canadian banks allowed their online banking customers to transfer up to $1,000 via e-mail to anyone with a valid e-mail address. In a few clicks, the recipient of an e-mail transfer could download the funds into his or her online account and have instant access to the cash at an ATM machine.

Marilyn and Frankie would get on the phone to cajole bank reps into changing the passwords and PIN numbers on accounts for which they had basic information, culled from records plucked from the trash or stolen from mailboxes. Biggie opened bank "drop" accounts all around town, using his true identity, into which he could download e-mail transfers, then withdraw the cash from an ATM machine shortly thereafter. He took charge of the recruitment and handling of runners who likewise opened drop accounts for the cell's use.

The cell discovered that the banks generally would take no action to sanction drop-account holders for making withdrawals soon after large deposits were made into their accounts. After all, there was nothing illegal in withdrawing cash that was sitting in your own account. Once the bank suspected illicit funds had been transferred into an account, the most it would do was close the drop account and decline to open another one for the runner. The cell also learned that bank branches don't necessarily communicate with one another. A runner whose account got shut down at one branch could scoot across town and open a drop account in a different branch of the same bank.

With Marilyn and Frankie assembling the pieces of data needed to breach accounts, and Biggie controlling the flow of extracted cash, Socrates's job fell right in his comfort zone. Using a laptop computer, Socrates took command of the virtual components; he went online to access the breached accounts and trigger e-mail transfers into the drop accounts controlled by the cell.

The cell also had hundreds of stolen credit card numbers to work with. Marilyn, always good at math, mastered the art of "tumbling." She could take a pair of sixteen-digit credit card numbers and decode the algorithm that would produce other working numbers in the same range. Socrates and Frankie went online and, using stolen credit card numbers, ordered the tools of their trade: computers, graphics software to manufacture fake IDs, and online services, such as Vonage Internet phone accounts.

The Vonage phone numbers came in handy if the cell needed to transfer cash from a breached bank account located in a different Canadian city. One way to defeat the bank's security measures involved making a cash transfer to a $500 money order made out to Biggie and designated for pickup at an Edmonton Western Union office. If the bank's fraud-detection system flagged the transfer as suspicious, triggering a phone call to verify the account holder, the bank employee would call the phone number listed with the account. Of course, Marilyn, beforehand, would change the number to a Vonage phone account, picking a number using the area code from the city where the account originated. There was no way for the bank rep to detect that it was a Vonage number, one of many issued to a meth addict in Edmonton. Upon answering, Marilyn, in a sweet voice, would confirm the authenticity of the money order.

Enablers
Analogue Defenses

Just as payroll-packing trains drew the attention of Jesse James in the nineteenth century, the electronic payments system of the twentieth century beckoned to those with larcenous intent. Not long after banks in the 1960s began to mail credit cards unsolicited to bank patrons, theft from mailboxes and bribery of postal workers became a problem. The card-based payment and settlement system presented fresh opportunities to enterprising scam artists. In the late 1960s a ring of thieves in Chicago, with ties to organized crime, obtained copies of valid credit card sales slips—the triplicate rectangular sheets onto which merchants imprinted transactions. Coconspiring merchants supplied the slips.

The thieves then took a hospital-issue embossing tool and stamped out newly embossed cards on rectangles of white plastic. The coconspiring merchants then used the white plastic cards to imprint batches of charges just below the $50 authorization floor limit. Hemmed in by a manual settlement process that considered imprinted sales slips as good as gold, the banks had no choice but to credit the merchant's account. The merchant then split the proceeds with the card counterfeiters.

Bank card consultant Darold Hoops, of Town & Country Consulting, at the time was cutting his teeth as a banking industry payment cards security expert. Hoops helped Continental Bank of Chicago and Chemical Bank get their credit card businesses up and running before leading the fraud and security team at MasterCard, where he went toe to toe with payment card thieves and scammers.

"With the white plastic cards they made sales drafts that looked exactly like drafts made by our embossed credit cards," recalls Hoops. "The rule was if it was $50 or more you had to call the bank to authorize. So they made up a bunch of sales slips for $49.95, and after the deposits were credited to the merchant's account they would split it with the crooks."

Continental Bank came up with the idea of adding an oversized embossed symbol that would be difficult to mimic on all of its credit cards, says Hoops. The credit card associations later added embossed symbols—a flying V for Visa and a scripted MC for MasterCard—for which no standard embossing tool existed. The white plastic caper epitomized the never-ending cat-and-mouse chase the financial services industry had to engage in as it moved to extend the global payments system through the 1970s and 1980s. Like water seeping into unsealed cracks and crevices, thieves found hole after hole in the card-based payments system.

Some of the speed that came with automation was put to work shoring up security leaks. Visa estimates that in its first year of operation, the BASE I processing system spotted enough suspicious patterns to save its member banks $30 million. For the most part, banks did a commendable job staying step for step with criminals. Physical security features added to the standard credit card made a big difference.

For instance, counterfeiters made millions reselling goods purchased with bogus cards created by ironing the embossed card numbers flat and re-embossing new numerals. So card issuers began always printing the first four-digits of the account number in tiny printed numerals near the corresponding embossed digits. If the two didn't match, merchants were advised to seize the card and call police. Another deterrent to counterfeiters: the nifty 3D hologram that covers the last four embossed digits. The shimmering holograms—a dove on Visa; twin globes on MasterCard—helped merchants spot ironed-down cards and also made it more difficult for a scammer to look over an unsuspecting consumer's shoulder and memorize his or her account number during a public transaction.

By the mid-1990s, the card-based payment system was perceived to be running reliably. Widespread use of dedicated terminals placed near cash registers made bank authorizations routinely as quick as thirty seconds. The risk of fraud was low enough to pave the way for wide use of debit cards and so-called affinity credit cards tied to loyalty programs run by airlines, car rental agencies, and hotels. At the same time, corporate America hustled to apply the galloping advances in digital technology to everything from genetic research to video games, and the financial industry directed technology at issuing credit ever faster, making dispersal of consumer goods and services ever more convenient.

Fraud, an inescapable corollary, was viewed as being comfortably under control and considered a manageable cost of doing business. The benefits of a payment system built for speed far outweighed the risk and monetary consequences of fraud. After all, a payments system that rapidly issued revolving credit and executed sales transactions allowed consumers to enjoy unprecedented power to acquire material goods. Merchants gained efficiencies in managing cash flow and financial planning. And banks found a fresh wellspring of profits: interest rates, processing fees, and penalty fees.

Banking consultant Hoops, who played an insider's role in helping to engineer this transformation, credits banking leaders of his generation for striking a "delicate balance" between convenience and security, while shaping and refining a trustworthy credit-issuing and payments system, without which our fast-paced consumer-driven economy would never have materialized.

"You can find the risk-reward scenario all over in the free-enterprise system," says Hoops. "The U.S. market really wanted and was willing to pay for convenience, and all of the organizations involved developed their products primarily with this in mind."

Yet history tells us that speed also translates into opportunities for crooks. Not long after the eighth-century Lydians invented solid-gold coins, fraudsters began manufacturing coins made of base metal plated with a thin layer of gold. Fast-forward to the twentieth century: soon after early credit card issuers set a $50 floor limit, thus speeding up small charges, scam artists began fabricating white plastic cards and imprinting an avalanche of $49.95 sales drafts.

For all their speed and sophistication, best-of-breed security systems—like VisaNet's Advanced Authorization fraud-detection program—have their limitations. First, they are programmed with algorithms based on fraud reports submitted by the banks, so cutting-edge schemes by definition aren't accounted for. Second, their use is voluntary; banks have complete leeway to decide when a transaction is suspicious enough—and poses a large enough loss—to warrant contacting the cardholder.

Between Thanksgiving and New Year's Day banks routinely "throttle down" and make fewer calls to consumers about suspicious activity, says John Pironti, chief information risk strategist at Getronics. "Banks have a library of security tools they can use, all kinds of different questions they could ask about a transaction. But the more investigation and analysis they do, the higher the probability of finding fraudulent activity, which slows down the system. So during high-volume times, like Christmas, they remove deep inspection controls so they can process transactions faster.

"The dirty little secret of the processing world is that banks don't always accept all of the security data sent to them," says Pironti. "Or if they do, they don't necessarily use it or interpret it."

Expediters
Virus Wars

```
Subject: Hi
```

So began the Virus Wars of 2004. It would pit the new breed of for-profit virus writers against an idealistic German teenager. Collateral damage would reverberate around the globe: tens of millions of PCs compromised; hospitals, banks, and transportation systems briefly knocked out. The world would never be the same. After 2004, hacking would become almost exclusively a for-profit criminal exercise, and the Internet—the emergent information superhighway—would become a thoroughfare of thieves.

It would start with an innocuous-looking sliver of e-mail moving across the Internet in Australia and New Zealand on January 19, 2004, a Monday morning. It was the beginning of a new workweek. Windows PC users in the Southern Hemisphere logged on to company computers and began absent-mindedly cleaning out e-mail in-boxes left dormant over the weekend. Thousands hastily clicked open the e-mail marked "Hi" and read this message:

```
Test =)

dhygvlueqqh

Test, yep.
```

Lulled into thinking this was some sort of techie-looking test required for one vague reason or another, many took the next step and clicked on the attached icon, a Windows calculator, with the file name:

```
otnvvjevrg.exe
```

A functioning calculator, indeed, popped up on the screen. Unseen, a virus, dubbed Bagle.A, went to work. Bagle.A efficiently replicated itself to every e-mail address it could find on the infected PC and quietly opened a back door through which the intruder could return later and install a proxy server. After spreading for two weeks, Bagle.A—like the early variants of SoBig—went dormant.

On January 26, a much more aggressive e-mail virus grabbed the spotlight in America. Craig Schmugar was one of the first to see it spreading. A virus research manager at McAfee's Anti-Virus Emergency Response Team Labs near San Francisco, Schmugar christened the virus Mydoom, after spotting the word "mydom," short for "my domain," in the virus code. "It was evident early on that this would be very big," Schmugar told Newsweek.com editor Jennifer Barrett. "I thought having 'doom' in the name would be appropriate."

Mydoom's author created many flavors; the virus poured into e-mail inboxes using one of a variety of subject headers:

```
error

status

test

hello

server report

mail delivery system

mail transaction failed
```

And the pretense to get a PC user to click on the viral attachment was much more refined than Bagle.A's silliness:

```
The message cannot be represented in 7-bit ASCII
encoding and has been sent as a binary attachment
```

or

> The message contains Unicode characters and has been
> sent as a binary attachment.

or

> Mail transaction failed. Partial message is available.

Clicking on Mydoom's attachment did more than let loose the standard address finder and e-mailing engine; it also implanted a copy of the virus on any shared Kazaa directories. Kazaa is a music-sharing service popular with teenagers and young adults. Anyone downloading music from the infected directory would also get the virus.

The virus also mixed and varied the extension of its attachments. Instead of using "text.exe," for instance, it would use "test.txt.pif" or "test.htm.zip," a ploy to slip through e-mail system filters set to block potentially hostile files. And to lower the odds of early detection, it did not send itself to e-mail addresses of government agencies, the military, or anyone at Microsoft.

While Bagle.A came and went and was barely noticed, Mydoom flooded e-mail systems like no other virus, sweeping around the globe in record time. In less than twenty-four hours, e-mail management company MessageLabs blocked more than 1 million viral e-mails, one in every twelve e-mails handled.

Mydoom also propped open a back door and planted a bot; each bot carried the same instructions: launch a DDoS attack against www.sco.com on February 1. The targeted Web site belonged to the SCO Group, a supplier of Unix computer systems and scourge of the Linux community. SCO had incurred the wrath of Linux supporters by suing IBM and Novell for donating code to Linux—code SCO claimed it partially owned.

SCO drew more ill will from the Linux crowd by posting a $250,000 reward for information leading to the arrest of Mydoom's creator. No one ever collected the reward, and on February 1, right on schedule, legions of Mydoom bots assaulted www.sco.com, forcing it to shut down for two weeks.

While Mydoom grabbed headlines, Bagle's author quietly prepared for a long-run assault. On February 17, the Bagle camp upped the ante. Bagle.B appeared on the Internet in Poland and spread to sixty-six countries in less than twenty-four hours. Taking a page from SoBig, it included instructions to self-expire in two weeks, foreshadowing improved variants to come.

As antivirus companies scrambled to thwart the twin attacks of Mydoom and Bagle, a third potent e-mail virus debuted on February 17. It was quickly named Netsky, a twist on a reference in the virus code to "Skynet," the villainous computer network in the Terminator movies starring Arnold Schwarzenegger.

Netsky incorporated just about every trick in the book. It arrived with a variety of subject lines and message texts; it replicated to all addresses found on the hard drive; it sought out shared links with corporate servers; it infected the file-sharing directories of the music download services Kazaa, BearShare, and LimeWire; and it used attachments with double extensions, such as

```
dictionary.doc.exe
```

```
basics.doc.exe
```

```
sex sex sex sex.doc.exe
```

```
hardcore porn.jpg.exe
```

Upon clicking on Netsky's viral attachment, the user would get this error message:

```
The file could not be opened!
```

Virus hunters had seen all of these techniques before. Netsky rather brilliantly combined them all. But the most distinctive thing about Netsky was its prime directive to clean out Mydoom infections. At its core, Netsky appeared to be an antivirus virus. Any doubts about this were put to rest by these cryptic messages woven into Netsky's coding:

```
<-<- we are the skynet - you can't hide yourself! - we
kill malware writers (they have no chance!) - [LaMeRz-
>] MyDoom.F is a thief of our idea! - -< SkyNet AV
vs. Malware >->->
```

```
#T#h#i#s# #i#s# #t#h#e#
#[#W#3#2#.#S#k#y#n#e#t#.#c#z#]# #A#n#T#i#V#i#R#u#S# #-#
#w#e# #w#a#n#t# #t#o# #k#i#l#l# #m#a#l#w#a#r#e#
#w#r#i#t#e#r#s#!#
```

By his own account, as told to the German news magazine *Stern*, Sven Jaschan describes himself as a shy, quiet teenager, who eschewed partying and drinking. In January 2004, while attending computer science classes at a vocational high school in Rotenburg, Germany, Jaschan says he began discussing Mydoom with his school chums. Jaschan was fascinated. Here was a program, whose name everyone knew, reproducing itself at an incredible rate. Wouldn't it be a crazy idea if someone could write something that reproduced just as quickly and deleted Mydoom? That person would become a self-anointed avenger, a hero.

Jaschan took the challenge upon himself. He spent all of his free time the next three weeks, up to ten hours a day, hunched over his computer in the basement of his parents' home in the idyllic village of Waffensen. Swigging seltzer and listening to MTV and its German equivalent, VIVA, blaring on a TV set nearby, Jaschan researched e-mail viruses and began to craft Netsky. It would take 2,000 lines of code.

Jaschan told the *Stern* reporters that his siblings and school chums knew what he was up to. "They even encouraged me to add something that would cause damage, but that was never what I wanted," claims Jaschan in the *Stern* article. Soon all the students in Jaschan's class knew what he was doing; Jaschan even claims that some of them helped him distribute Netsky. "It was just great how Netsky began to spread, and I was the hero of my class," he told *Stern*.

Graham Cluley, senior technology consultant at antivirus firm Sophos, can relate to the buzz Jaschan felt. As a college student back in 1991, Cluley won notoriety as the author of the free, text-based video games Jacaranda Jim and Humbug. He picked up spending cash soliciting donations from fans of his games, which happened to include Alan Solomon, creator of one of the early antivirus programs. Cluley took a job at Solomon's start-up company, and headed off into a career as a virus hunter.

"It's a shame that someone with obvious computer skills should turn to writing computer viruses to increase their self-esteem, rather than doing something positive like developing computer games or an innovative Web site," says Cluley.

Jaschan could not have imagined the scale of the virus war he would instigate. As Netsky drew attention, the Mydoom camp sought to regain the spotlight by issuing variants that corrupted Microsoft Office documents and launched a DDoS attack against the Recording Industry Association of America. RIAA had drawn hostility for suing people caught swapping music online.

Over in the Bagle camp, the arrival of Netsky appeared to disrupt carefully laid plans to release a barrage of Bagle variants moving at least partly in the shadow of the headline-grabbing Mydoom. With Netsky on the scene, competition for vulnerable computers to infect had suddenly intensified. Soon Bagle began attacking Netsky, forcing Netsky to retaliate. What started as a Netsky versus Mydoom war evolved into mortal combat between Netsky and Bagle, with Netsky cleaning up Bagle variants as fast as the Bagle camp could put out new ones. Buried deep inside Bagle.J, virus hunters found this cry of frustration:

```
Hey, NetSky, fuck off you bitch, don't ruine our busi-
ness, wanna start a war?
```

Through the months of March and April, Jaschan would release twenty-nine variants of Netsky, as many as five in one week, counterattacking the latest Mydoom and Bagle variants. As April drew to a close, he began looking for a way to separate himself from the pack and vanquish Mydoom and Bagle for good. He got the germ of an idea on April 13, when Microsoft issued a security patch that sent red flags fluttering throughout the tech community.

What caught Jaschan's eye was a patch to fix something called Local Security Authority Subsystem Service, or LSASS, a Windows component designed to manage security and authentication. The LSASS vulnerability looked like a repeat of the RPC security hole. It was just the previous summer, in July 2003, that Microsoft had released the RPC patch and seen its worst fears come to fruition in the form of the MSBlast worm, the infection that spread to 25 million Windows PCs worldwide.

Was history about to repeat itself? On April 25, Jaschan paid close attention when a Russian hacking group, known as House of Dabus, posted a proof of concept LSASS exploit on a French Web site. The exploit laid out programming code crafted to overwhelm the LSASS hole and take control of vulnerable Windows XP and Windows 2000 computers. "At that point, anyone with minimal programming skills could go and build a worm to hack into machines," says Johannes Ullrich, chief technology officer of the SANS Institute Internet Storm Center.

Thursday, April 29, happened to be Jaschan's eighteenth birthday. After returning home from a celebration with friends, he descended into his basement cubby and put the finishing touches on a self-propagating worm using the House of Dabus's exploit. Just sixteen days had gone by since Microsoft released the LSASS patch. Hardly anyone had applied the patch. Jaschan set his worm loose on the Internet and went to bed.

Virus hunters first spotted the worm on the move on Friday, April 30, and christened it Sasser. Crudely written, Sasser soon gathered momentum and began to spread faster—and then too fast. The worm spread so rapidly that it caused infected machines to reboot constantly. From his basement, Jaschan tried to correct the problem by releasing Sasser.B, Sasser.C, and Sasser.D, but things only got worse. Within forty-eight hours, Sasser infected at least 1.3 million PCs. In particular, it wreaked havoc with groups of PCs linked together in Windows-based local area networks commonly used in businesses around the globe. Jaschan hoped Sasser would be his coup de grâce to wipe out Mydoom and Bagle. Instead it would lead authorities to his basement lair.

Because much of Asia and Europe was heading into a three-day weekend to celebrate May Day, many companies were operating with skeleton tech-service crews.

Sasser halted rail service in Australia, paralyzed a third of Taiwan's post office, forced Finland's Sampo Bank to shut down 130 branches, and prompted Delta Air Lines to cancel several transatlantic flights. Because its effects were so blatant, it spurred other businesses and consumers to install Microsoft's LSASS patch right away. It also made Sven Jaschan a marked man.

Following the spread of MSBlast and SoBig, Microsoft had announced in the fall of 2003 that it was setting aside $5 million in reward money for the capture of notorious virus writers. A $250,000 prize awaited anyone who provided information leading to the arrest and conviction of the author of MSBlast, SoBig, or Mydoom. On May 5, two of Jaschan's school chums contacted Microsoft's German office and inquired whether a similar bounty might be available for information that led to Sasser's author. When Microsoft assented, they fingered Jaschan.

Police arrested young Sven in his home on May 7. Reporters swooped in. Sabine Jaschan, his stepmother, told a reporter for RTL News, "About four months ago he was over here for a visit and said, 'Papa, I've put out a computer worm.' And then my husband said, 'Sven, you didn't do anything stupid, did you?' He just kind of laughed nervously."

Jaschan confessed to creating Sasser and Netsky. At a hearing more than a year after his arrest, Jaschan received a sentence of twenty-one months on probation and thirty hours of community service, based largely on the fact that most of his virus writing was done before he turned eighteen. Shortly thereafter, Microsoft paid his two school chums, who for a time were investigated as suspected accomplices, $250,000.

"He said he really wanted to develop an antidote to the virus," Rainer Jaschan, Sven's father, told reporters. "He said he didn't want to cause any damage."

CHAPTER 5
The Convenience Quotient

Exploiters
Fall 2004, Edmonton

By fall 2004, the Edmonton cell controlled a matrix of local bank accounts, some breached through phone cons, some opened by Biggie and other addicts using their real names, and others opened by addicts using assumed identities and fake IDs. Enter Hula Girl, a nervy nineteen-year-old who helped out from time to time as the cell's chameleon.

Once the banks began to catch on and ban runners from opening new accounts in their own names, the cell needed another way to open drop accounts. Hula Girl got her kicks from posing in disguises and perfecting signatures for fake drivers' licenses. She then boldly opened dozens of drop accounts under assumed identities. Hula Girl took on the big risk, getting videotaped on the banks' surveillance cameras. Eventually it would catch up to her.

Socrates, by contrast, was extremely cautious. He knew investigators could monitor Internet traffic going into and out of his laptop computer. He continually moved between sketch pads and hotel rooms, changing the phone lines from which he'd sign on to the Internet. Hotel or motel rooms were ideal because anyone tracing the phone call would end at the hotel front desk. There was no easy way to pinpoint the call to a specific room.

For a two-month stretch in early 2004, Socrates, Marilyn, and a friend of Frankie found an ideal safe haven. They worked from inside a plush camper van parked in an alleyway alongside a run-down, four-story apartment building near downtown Edmonton.

Socrates extended a phone cable from the van, down a stairwell, and to the building's telephone access panel. When a tenant left for work or appeared to be sleeping, he'd patch into their phone line to get on the Internet. "We needed a safe place to use the computer, and it was so nice in the camper," says Marilyn.

Flying high on ice, Socrates immersed himself deeper in the Counter-Strike video game and the mIRC.com chat rooms. In the real world he was a jobless twenty-year-old nerd. But among the global community of Counter-Strike gamers he was a crack antiterrorist commando, and in the IRC chat rooms he was someone with a clean reputation—not tainted as a low-life "ripper" who burned people on deals. So his potential was limitless.

Soon he found his way to "carding" chat channels, where the topics under discussion all circled back, in one way or another, to identity theft. Socrates began to educate himself at freewheeling chat channels, such as ##realcashout, ##cchouse, and #carderz, about the panoply of hacking programs and cyberscams. He learned about bots and bot armies. Phishing, in particular, struck Socrates's fancy. Phishers craft and send out e-mail spam messages designed to entice the recipient to click on a link to a counterfeit banking Web site, where the victim is asked, under one ruse or another, to type in his or her log-in name and password. The sensitive data, of course, gets routed back to the phisher.

Socrates struck up a rapport with a young hacker in Oklahoma who bragged about his prowess with e-mail phishing scams.

The Oklahoman had been sending out e-mail spam purporting to be a security alert from PayPal, the online payment service owned by eBay and accepted by other online vendors, as well. Recipients were advised to confirm the validity of their PayPal user name and password by typing it into a dialogue box. Partly to prove he had, indeed, fooled a large number PayPal account holders into sending him their account access data, and partly to see if Socrates could help him extract cash from the accounts, the Oklahoman sent Socrates 500 PayPal log-in names and passwords.

Rather than store the valuable data on his laptop's hard drive, Socrates uploaded the data to an e-mail folder that came as an added feature to a Telus dial-up Internet access account he often used. He figured that would make access to the data more flexible and convenient. "If I were to lose my computer, or whatever, that way the data would still be accessible," he says.

Socrates felt safe that the Telus account couldn't be traced to him because it had been set up as a shadow account by a Telus employee, a meth addict who did it as a favor for a drug dealer. But the Telus employee got picked up on another criminal matter and ratted out the existence of the dial-up account to police. Word got back to Vonkeman and Gauthier, who soon had a printout of Socrates's PayPal log-in data in their hands. Instead of shutting down the e-mail account, Vonkeman asked Telus to leave it open and alert him anytime anyone logged on to access it.

Socrates had no immediate plans for the PayPal log-in data. He knew the data was valuable, but orchestrating schemes to extract cash from accounts just wasn't his forte. That was Marilyn's turf, and he and Marilyn had recently had a falling-out. Socrates felt certain she had cheated him out of his share of a big drop, although Marilyn denied doing so. With nothing big going down, Biggie suggested a bus trip to Calgary, 200 miles south of Edmonton, to visit an acquaintance who liked to party. It was two weeks until Christmas. Maybe a change of scenery would do them good. Maybe they'd think of a way to cash in on the PayPal log-in data cooling in the Telus e-mail folder.

Enablers

"We chase dogs."

Rationalizing that instant access to unlimited revolving debt was the heart's desire of every American, the financial industry poured billions into automating the built-for-speed payment system and extending it first to phones and then to the Internet. "In the past a loan or credit card applicant had to visit a bank branch, or at least mail in a paper application that was reviewed by a human employee. Today banks increasingly rely on auto-mated systems to process consumer loan applications and execute all types of financial transactions. The default setting: if at all possible, issue the credit; complete the transaction.

Advancing technology paved the way for U.S. consumers in 2005 to whip out an astounding 691 million credit cards and transact a record $1.8 trillion worth of purchases, according to CardWeb.com, an online publisher of information about the payment card industry. With the U.S. population topping 300 million, that means there are enough credit cards in circulation for every American man, woman, and child to wield an average of 2.3 credit cards.

Credit cards certainly are easy enough to get.

Consider what happened after Steve Borba, of Livermore, California, set up a free e-mail account to receive junk e-mail and registered it to his two-year-old pet canine, Clifford J. Dawg. Within three weeks, the pooch got a solicitation letter for a Chase Manhattan Platinum Visa, according to the *Tri-Valley Herald* of Pleasanton, California. As a joke, Borba mailed in the application listing Mr. Dawg's place of employment as the "Pupperoni Factory," noting, for security purposes, that his mother's maiden name was "Pugsy Malone."

He also scribbled on the application: "You are sending an application to a dog! Ha ha ha."

When a shiny new Chase Visa credit card embossed for Clifford J. Dawg arrived in the mail, Borba called the bank to cancel it and was told his canine's name was acquired from a marketing list. The bank rep joked that the incident should be used in a commercial with the tag line, "Dogs don't chase us—we chase them."

Rob Cockerham was in no joking mood about all the credit card offers cluttering his mailbox when he decided to conduct a similar experiment. Cockerham took a Chase MasterCard application, tore it into tiny bits, taped the application back together, changed the billing address to his father's home, and included his cell phone number. He then used the prestamped envelope to mail in the taped-together application. In short, he did everything a Dumpster-diving thief might do to get his hands on, and activate, a freshly minted credit card.

A few weeks later, the Chase MasterCard, indeed, arrived in Cockerham's father's mailbox. Cockerham posted photos and text descriptions of his test on his Web site, www.cockeyed.com, and the Torn-up Credit Card Application caper entered Internet lore. "I still can't believe it came," Cockerham told MSNBC investigative reporter Bob Sullivan. "Crazy."

Sullivan grilled Chase spokesman Paul Hartwick, who downplayed the incident as an "Internet prank." Declining to discuss Cockerham's case specifically, Hartwick acknowledged that damaged forms get transferred by machine to an electronic format, so it's plausible that a human might never handle a severely blemished application. He drew out a scenario as to how a solicitation that comes back with a changed billing address and strange phone number might, nonetheless, get approved. The bank's systems are programmed so that if the data scribbled on the application matches data from an individual of good credit standing already in its databases, then approval gets a green light.

"Chase takes these matters extremely seriously and always seeks to improve its processes to serve and protect our card members. Chase is actively involved in fraud protection. We have sophisticated systems in place to protect our customers, and to offer credit to customers who are creditworthy," Hartwick said. When Sullivan asked if Cockerham should have received the credit card, given the mangled form, the bank spokesman replied flatly, "Yes."

It is certain that the financial industry takes fraud seriously and spends billions on security systems. But it is also true that industry lobbyists spend vast resources deflecting criticism from consumer and privacy advocates, mostly by inundating federal banking regulators and members of Congress with the message that an automated transactions system built for speed provides a plethora of benefits that serve the greater public good.

The industry argument goes something like this: Credit and debit cards represent an increasingly convenient and secure form of payment, accepted at more than 23 million merchants worldwide. They can be used to make purchases and obtain cash and are virtually risk free for individual card-holders, since, for the most part, consumers aren't held responsible for unauthorized use of payment cards by fraudsters. Payment cards also happen to mesh perfectly with the rise of e-commerce; they've come to represent the predominant form of payment for Internet commerce.

What's more, the industry argues, airlines, hotels, and car rental agencies routinely issue "affinity" credit cards that offer usage rewards and perks many consumers have come to take for granted. And consider the benefits of credit card issuers taking the initiative in 2006 to make possible no-signature transactions for purchases of less than $25. By extending the convenience quotient of payment cards to incidental purchases at movie theaters, pharmacies, convenience stores, and fast-food restaurants—and popularizing the practice of paying for everyday items with plastic—banks are helping to boost the economy. After all, convenience is good for consumption, and consumption drives our economy.

But has convenience gone too far when an applicant can impersonate his dog or send in a torn-up application with a changed billing address as a joke and obtain fresh credit? And what does that say about how easy the financial industry has made it for thieves to transform convenience into criminal opportunity?

Expediters
Limitless Opportunities

With the young virus vigilante Sven Jaschan sidelined in the spring of 2004, the Mydoom and Bagle camps moved full steam ahead. The endgame for virus and worm writers became to infect millions of Windows PCs to aid in the distribution of garden-variety spam and to launch DDoS attacks.

Yet in the aftermath of the Virus Wars of 2004, compromised computers—infected Windows PCs, with back doors open to one and all, and proxy servers waiting to relay data—began to pose an expanding threat. Zombie PCs, as researchers and virus hunters called them, would become the essential tools supporting a panoply of nefarious enterprises. The multi-billion-dollar cybercrime industry was fast coming of age.

"Two thousand four ushered in a pivotal shift in computer hacker motive—from the large-scale, pandemic spread of worms and viruses aimed at achieving notoriety to the more stealthy, targeted attacks organized for financial gain," says Vincent Weafer, senior director, Symantec Security Response. "The openness and naivety of the previous generation of hackers and virus writers was increasingly being replaced by professionals who used more intense, deceptive, and sophisticated measures than had ever been seen before."

From the beginning of civilization, criminals have preyed on those susceptible to being tricked, robbed, extorted, or impersonated. At the start of the twenty-first century, the speed built into the card-based payments system, combined with the global reach and anonymity afforded by the Internet, presented criminals with limitless opportunities. Security experts and law enforcement had to derive a whole new lexicon to categorize the inventiveness of profit-minded hackers and opportunistic crime gangs.

Spyware and adware arose as extensions of the virus plague. Spyware, broadly defined, was any program installed without adequate disclosure that performed unseen functions. Purveyors of porn and gambling Web sites discovered that spyware could be used to hijack control of Web browsers and redirect PC users to visit their unseemly Web pages. Adware, a quasi-legitimate form of spyware, arrived on the scene as a sneaky way to spread pop-up advertisements for drug companies, dating services, financial services companies, and travel Web sites.

Utilizing virus-spreading methodologies, spyware and adware glommed onto PCs in a number of ways—most often without the user fully realizing what was taking place. Simply clicking on the wrong Web page or downloading a free music file could install spyware, or it could be delivered as part of a viral e-mail attachment. Spyware made it convenient for unscrupulous advertisers to spread their promotional messages Internet-wide.

The economics of spyware was every bit as compelling as that of spam. Advertisers were happy to pay a few pennies for every time one of their advertising messages popped up on the screen of a PC user. Much like in traditional advertising, only a small percentage of the audience need respond to make the exercise worthwhile. Pop-up ads quickly became like ubiquitous mini-billboards cluttering the information superhighway.

But instead of renting billboard space and hiring union laborers to paste up large signs, purveyors of porn and gambling Web sites turned to hackers-for-hire to foist pop-up ads onto unsuspecting PC users. Soon start-up online advertising distributing companies such as Gator, Claria, WhenU, and Integrated Search Technologies cropped up to sell pop-up ads a bit more out in the open; they cut deals to attach endless pop-ups to the free music and video files being swapped at Kazaa, LimeWire, and other popular shareware Web sites.

In March 2004, antivirus supplier McAfee detected 14 million unique instances of spyware and adware at work, up from 2 million just eight months earlier. A second rank of adware distribution companies, led by DirectRevenue, 180 Solutions, and LoudCash, subsequently emerged with grand plans to jump on board the pop-up gravy train. They precipitated the gelling of an extensive network of "affiliate distributors" by offering 20 cents to 70 cents for each installation of a delivery program that would let them push pop-ups onto an Internet-connected PC. Because these new adware distributors weren't terribly particular about how their pop-ups got implanted, hackers began to use bots to carry out that task.

"They came in using really aggressive means to get adware on people's computers," says Ari Schwartz, deputy director of the Center for Democracy and Technology and cofounder of the Anti-Spyware Coalition. "It was basically, 'How can we compete with Claria and WhenU, who do music sharing;' and the answer was, 'We're just going to get as broad a distribution network as we can. So we're going to go out there and pay people to install this stuff.'"

By the summer of 2004, spyware and adware had become such a public nuisance that consumer groups, FTC regulators, and state consumer protection officials were beginning to stir into action. Congress, led by Representative Mary Bono (R-CA), threatened restrictive legislation. (Spyware and adware endure as problems. However, their impact has been tempered by the efforts of groups like the Anti-Spyware Coalition and StopBadware.org, as well as by the wide availability and increasing use of improved antispyware scanners and filters.)

At the same time, the larcenous twist on spam, phishing, was coming on like gangbusters. It got started in the early 1990s, when scammers discovered they could use an AOL online account for free by e-mailing an unwitting AOL account holder and tricking him or her into divulging his or her user name and password. One wag sharing AOL scamming tips on an Internet bulletin board referred to this practice as phishing, in homage to the "phone phreak" hackers who broke into telephone company dial-up modems in the 1980s for sport.

As Internet commerce advanced, so did phishing. Fraudsters soon began phishing Yahoo, eBay, and Microsoft MSN account holders, directing victims to type in their user names and passwords at bogus Web sites with names like yahoo-billing.com, ebay-fulfillment.com, and Microsoft.checkinfo.com. Soon phishers began to use powerful graphic arts tools such as Adobe Photoshop to improve the artistry of mimicked Web sites.

Then, in November 2003, the self-replicating e-mail virus Mimail.I began spreading. It purported to come from eBay's online payment service, PayPal, and used the ruse that PayPal was "implementing a new security policy." Recipients were asked to click on a Web link that opened an official-looking PayPal page where they were asked to type in a credit card number, PIN, expiration date, and CVV (card verification value) code. Subsequent variants of Mimail asked for a Social Security number, date of birth, and mother's maiden name, as well. The Web site where the data was sent resided on a zombie PC controlled by the phisher.

At the high end, Mimail.I marked the cross-pollination of self-replicating viruses and phishing. At the low end, Web sites began appearing where anyone could download free by-the-numbers tools, called "phishing kits," to construct counterfeit Web pages. All an aspiring phisher needed to supply was a range of e-mail addresses and a spamming program, easy enough to get for free elsewhere on the Web.

In the summer of 2004, one of the many young technophiles who took heed of this was an avid Counter-Strike gamer named Socrates, who had just fallen in with a crowd of meth addicts in Edmonton, Alberta.

Through the course of 2004, phishing skyrocketed in volume as attacks shifted from Internet portals such as Yahoo and MSN to where the real money lay: online banking Web sites. Banks, stock brokerages, auto lenders, and mortgage companies charging aggressively into online delivery of financial services became juicy targets for the phishers.

In the first month of the year, e-mail management company MessageLabs intercepted 337,050 phishing e-mails. By July, the count had jumped almost eightfold to 2,493,734, and continued climbing to an October peak of 4,838,962. Total phishing e-mail blocked by MessageLabs for the year would ring in at over 18 million, with nearly 60 percent of the attacks aimed at Citibank or U.S. Bank account holders, according to the Anti-Phishing Working Group (APWG), a consortium of financial service institutions and tech companies that banded together to battle phishers.

Despite the full-time, concerted efforts of APWG, and widespread publicity warning PC users to be wary of phishing scams, the number of successful attacks continued rising. Virtually every major bank around the world would be hit by phishing. Research firm Gartner estimated that the number of adult Internet users who received phishing e-mail climbed relentlessly from 57 million in 2004 to 79 million in 2005 to 109 million in 2006.

Gartner analyst Avivah Litan observed in late 2006 that the deployment of antiphishing filters and detection services was still "not widespread or effective enough to stop the onslaught of phishing attack e-mails, and more people than ever are clicking on dangerous links embedded in these authentic-looking e-mails." While Litan credited banks for installing stronger authentication systems, she noted that "crooks who manage to evade them are stealing larger sums from wealthier victims."

Internet defenders would hunker down to protect the fragile integrity of online commerce. But in 2004, the bulk of their efforts went to repel the onslaught of underemployed technophiles and precocious script kiddies (unskilled teenagers using free hacking tools) who were rushing in to get some of the easy money to be had at the ground floor of cybercrime.

There were some signs, to be sure, that organized crime rings were starting to probe for fresh attack vectors, as well. One way to put zombie

PCs to work generating illicit profits was to launch extortionist DDoS attacks against gambling Web sites. By the time the NCAA's 2004 March Madness college basketball championship tournament got under way, gambling site operators had been hit by several waves of cyberblackmail. As the field of teams was winnowed down to the Final Four, the gambling sites braced for another onslaught of attacks.

Shadowy crime rings had taken to directing well-organized networks of bots—called botnets—to bombard gambling sites, shutting them down in the days before major sporting events. To avoid going off-line during the height of betting, when online wagers might total in the millions, the gambling sites were required to send payments of $20,000 to $50,000 in U.S. dollars via Western Union wire to parties in Eastern Europe.

"These sites rely on transaction with clients every few seconds," said Michael Caselli, editor of Online Casino News at the time. "You disrupt that and you've got major problems."

DDoS attacks also proved effective against business competitors. Saad Echouafni, thirty-seven, owner of a Sudbury, Massachusetts, home-satellite-TV retail business, hired hackers in Britain and Ohio to pit their botnets against the Web sites of three competitors, causing them more than $2 million in lost revenue and cleanup expenses. After being indicted, arrested, and released on bail in August 2004, Echouafni fled the country, possibly back to his native home, Morocco, says the FBI.

In a similar caper that took place in 2004, Jason Salah Arabo, then eighteen, operated an online business in which he sold sports jerseys from his home in Southfield, Michigan. One day Arabo persuaded a seventeen-year-old Edison, New Jersey, high school student named Jasmine Singh to launch DDoS attacks against two rival online shirt companies. Singh's payment: three pairs of sneakers and a watch. Arabo was sentenced to thirty months in prison; Singh received a five-year sentence.

The use of botnets as an extortion hammer pointed up a profound shift in the cyberunderworld that was lost in the public furor over spyware and phishing: bots, those innocuous programs so easy to implant on Internet-connected PCs, had risen to the fore and become the Swiss Army knife of the hacker's toolbox.

Bots and botnets were a throwback to the early days of the Internet, when techies assigned chores to groups of PCs, sending them simple commands over a designated Internet relay chat, or IRC, channel. In the early 1990s, the techies began to use the IRC channels to communicate in cliques, foreshadowing the use of IRC technology that would one day support instant messaging. Then one day someone got the bright idea to use a botnet to overwhelm the chat channel of a rival clique, and DDoS attacks were born.

Mafiaboy would saunter along in 2000 and forever alter the rules of engagement by aiming his botnet at unsuspecting targets in the outside world, taking out the Web sites of online icons CNN, Yahoo, Amazon, and eBay. Legions of brash hackers would emerge to likewise seek notoriety. Viruses, worms, and bots would begin to converge and blend together. By the time Sven Jaschan came along with his antivirus virus, NetSky, and his voracious worm, Sasser, motives had begun to morph.

By the close of 2004, most spamming, phishing, spyware, and extortionist DDoS attacks shared a common denominator: a profit motive.

CHAPTER 6

Predators and Opportunists

Exploiters

October 26, 2004, North Hollywood, California

Traffic was heavy and it was raining hard. Detective Duane Decker waited patiently in his unmarked police sedan, eyes glued on the entrance to the Copymat at 6464 Sunset Boulevard. Decker watched for a man who looked liked he might have a Caribbean or West African accent.

The sting was about as simple as any Decker had orchestrated in eighteen years of police work. Assigned to the Identity Theft Detail of the Southern California High Tech Task Force, the veteran Los Angeles County deputy sheriff was trying to help ChoicePoint, the giant data-aggregation company, spring a trap to snare a suspected fraudster. Identifying himself as James Garrett, the suspect had called ChoicePoint to inquire about the status of a new account he was trying to set up that would allow his start-up collections agency, Hollywood-based MBS Financial, to access data dossiers on individuals, presumably deadbeat debtors. Bryce Wyburn, the ChoicePoint representative who took the call, noticed that James Garrett sounded an awful lot like John Galloway, of Beverly Hills–based Gallo Financial Services, who had called earlier with a nearly identical query.

Decker advised Wyburn to ask Garrett to supply a fax number and stand by to receive a document that needed to be filled out to open the MBS Financial account. Wyburn did as advised, and Garrett obliged, giving Wyburn a fax number, which Decker then traced to the Copymat on Sunset Boulevard. All Decker had to do was sit tight and wait for "Mr. Garrett" to show up at the Copymat to pick up his fax.

At 11 a.m., a tall black man with a thin mustache and close-cropped hair entered the Copymat. The man wore a blue jacket as protection against the pelting rain. He walked with a limp. Decker followed him in and stood off to the side. The detective observed the man request, receive, and pay for a fax addressed to James Garrett. He spoke with an accent Decker recognized to be West African. Decker identified himself and asked the man to step into a nearby hallway.

Panic etched the suspect's face. In the hallway he dropped a sheaf of papers: the fax he'd just picked up, plus the original ChoicePoint account applications for MBS Financial, signed by James Garrett, and Gallo Financial, signed by John Galloway. Within minutes, the man divulged his true identity, Olatunji Oluwatusin, forty-three, an expatriate of Nigeria. Oluwatusin claimed he was picking up the fax for a white man named "Bobby." But he couldn't describe Bobby or say where Bobby lived or what Bobby did for a living. Upon patting down the suspect, Decker found Oluwatusin in possession of five cell phones and three credit cards in other people's names.

Using his own cell phone, the detective dialed 818-261-3063—the number Mr. Garrett had used to speak to Wyburn. One of Oluwatusin's five phones began ringing. Decker advised Oluwatusin of his rights. The tall man who walked with a limp began whimpering. "He didn't want to go to jail," Decker says. "He had never been in jail."

Oluwatusin complied with Decker's request to take police to his apartment in a sprawling, upscale complex near the intersection of Magnolia and Lankershim boulevards in North Hollywood. The apartment was tastefully furnished, the living room dominated by a plasma TV, at the time a $5,000-plus luxury item. On the kitchen counter Decker found a printout of a data dossier, freshly downloaded from ChoicePoint, for someone named Anthony Munrue, along with a receipt for storage unit B-245 at a nearby Public Storage facility. Oluwatusin agreed to take police to the storage unit. There Decker found two electricity generators, three laptop PCs, a half dozen television sets, and several printers. The detective noted that the shipping labels were cut off each box, making it impossible to trace them back to where the property was purchased.

This wasn't a first-of-its-kind case for Los Angeles County. In September 2002 Bibiana Benson, thirty-nine, a Nigerian expatriate living in Sherman Oaks, pleaded guilty to unlawful use of identification and was sentenced to fifty-four months in federal prison. Her brother, Adedayo Benson, thirty-eight, of Encino, later pleaded guilty to conspiracy charges and received a sixty-six-month sentence.

Bibiana had obtained sensitive information about people by opening accounts under false pretenses with ChoicePoint, Advantage Financial, and Equifax. With help from Adedayo, she sold identity profiles for $40 to $60 apiece. Such profiles typically consisted of names, Social Security numbers, addresses, phone numbers, dates of birth, and other personal data. The Bensons also used identity profiles to hijack funds from existing bank accounts, and to open new accounts. According to court records, Bibiana Benson controlled identity profiles for 10,000 individuals, which she used to tap into credit and payment systems at twenty-three financial institutions, from which she stole more than $935,000.

Oluwatusin picked up where the Bensons left off. Investigators who pieced together his wide-ranging criminal activities took to calling him Tunji or Mr. O. "He was the CEO of an illegal business," says Detective Sergeant Josh Mankini. Ensconced in his plush North Hollywood apartment, Mr. O ran a lean operation. In the ninety days prior to his capture, he had made and received some 12,000 cell phone calls to a serpentine network of data suppliers and data buyers in Canada, Germany, and Holland and throughout the United States. "When I saw the data on this case, my head nearly exploded," says Decker, shaking his head in disbelief.

To get basic identity information, such as names and billing addresses, Mr. O relied on a specialist who controlled insider thieves working at U.S. Postal Service mail-sorting centers. The postal workers "would grab envelopes with credit cards, which are easy to spot, by the hundreds," says FBI Special Agent Alice Tsujihara, who worked on the case. With names, billing addresses, and credit card numbers thus supplied, Mr. O had everything he needed to set up a matrix of shell collection companies, like MBS Financial. He would then order fuller data dossiers from ChoicePoint. He used copy centers, such as Kinko's and Copymat, as bases of operation, routing e-mail, regular mail, and faxes through such places. Mr. O shuttled among at least fifteen copy centers in the Los Angeles area. He paid for everything with stolen or fraudulently set-up credit card accounts.

Mr. O and the Bensons may be off the street; but law enforcement officials fully expect the data they and others stole from ChoicePoint to continue surfacing in scams indefinitely. Jane Robison, spokeswoman for the Los Angeles County district attorney's office, says of Mr. O: "He was just a small piece of it. We honestly don't know how many are involved in this."

Detective Decker commends credit bureaus and data brokers for erecting ten-foot walls to protect their databases. Trouble is, he says, the crooks have eleven-foot ladders. Scammers, like Mr. O, "are so smart, they could make a lot of money in whatever they do," says Decker. "But they don't want to work a forty-hour week. They'd rather drive around in Escalades with a ton of cash."

Enablers

Predatory Banking Fees

Financial industry lobbyists and banking spokespersons love to herald the benefits of easy credit. But they are far less effusive when it comes to outlining the many ways financial services companies profit from the nation's rising dependence on household debt. Yet the financial industry was recently forced to do just that by the Government Accountability Office. Founded in 1921 as the investigative arm of Congress, the GAO is often referred to as the Watchdog of Congress and the Taxpayers' Best Friend. Called upon to make nonpartisan recommendations "for the benefit of the American people," the agency is tasked with uncovering examples of government profligacy, but also with drawing attention to questionable business practices in the commercial sector.

In a report issued in September 2006, titled Credit Cards—Increased Complexity in Rates and Fees Heightens Need for More Effective Disclosures to Consumers, the GAO unraveled the complex matrix of interest rates and penalty fees that are part and parcel of the built-for-speed credit-issuing and payments system. The report exposed industry practices that baffle all save for the financial companies profiting from the system—and criminals grateful for the chance to test the system for security holes.

It used to be that credit cards were fairly easy to understand. They came with an annual fee, a fixed interest rate, and modest penalties. Today, the annual fee has been replaced with promotional interest rates for opening an account spring-loaded to trigger a dizzying array of higher rates and onerous penalty fees. That single-digit or zero interest rate you get by responding to an introductory offer is full of trip wires. Cash advances and balance transfers not covered by the promotion come at steep rates. Miss a payment by one day or spend slightly over your credit limit, and your base rate can double or triple, along with triggering a penalty fee of up to $30.

Banks refer to maximum credit card interest rates as the "default penalty rate." The GAO found that the default penalty rate for twenty-eight popular credit cards was 27.3 percent in 2005, up from 23.8 percent in 2003. Seven cards charged default penalty rates over 30 percent. The system is skewed toward guiding the consumer into paying a tier of different rates and keeping high-rate balances on the books as long as possible.

The most common way banks do this is by allocating payments to the chunk of outstanding balance generating the lowest interest income. So a payment of $100 sent to pay down a balance of $1,000 in store purchases carried at 13 percent and $1,000 in cash advances at 21 percent goes entirely to pay down the lower-rate portion. Interest of 21 percent continues to accrue against the cash advances until such time as the lower-interest chunk is paid down to zero, which could be months or years.

To trip up card users who routinely pay off all or most of their balances each month, some banks resort to "double-cycle billing." Normally, paying off $990 of a $1,000 bill means the consumer got to use $990 of the bank's funds interest free for a month. But some banks treat the $1,000 charge as if it exists across two thirty-day billing cycles. The card user gets billed for interest on $1,000 for the first cycle—even after sending in the $990 payment—then gets billed interest on $10 for the second cycle.

Using the more conventional single-cycle method (and assuming an interest rate of 13.2 percent), the bank would have been able to bill the card user just eleven cents for a two-month loan of $10. However, a double-cycle billing allows the bank to charge $11.02 at the end of the second cycle. In examining twenty-eight popular cards from the six largest credit card issuers, the GAO found that two of the six resorted to the double-cycle billing method between 2003 and 2005.

Then there are the hidden fees. It would be a simple thing for banks to decline transactions that put a consumer over his or her credit limit, a common occurrence during the Christmas shopping season. Instead, the system is programmed to approve transactions that exceed an individual's credit limit, then assess a penalty and jack up the interest rate as a consequence. Fee trip wires lurk everywhere. A card user hustling to avoid a late payment fee by paying by phone or computer runs into fees for phone and online payments. Cash advances, balance transfers, and overseas transactions trigger fees of 3 percent of the amount dispersed. Stopping a payment, requesting rush delivery of a credit card, and asking for a duplicate of records all trigger fees.

Exactly how much banks profit from such practices is unknowable since banking regulations do not require such detail in public disclosures of banking operations. The GAO estimates that about 70 percent of credit card industry revenues comes from interest charges and that "the portion attributable to penalty rates appears to have been growing."

None of this is clearly delineated to the average consumer. The GAO found that disclosures published by four of the largest credit card issuers were "poorly organized, burying important information in text or scattering information about a single topic in numerous places. The design of the disclosures often made them hard to read, with large amounts of text in small, condensed typefaces and poor, ineffective headings to distinguish important topics form the surrounding text."

The predicament of René Rodríguez of Juana Diaz, Puerto Rico, as reported by USA Today banking reporter Kathy Chu, has become all too common. In August 2006, Rodriguez misplaced his Citibank credit card statement and for the first time in years sent in a late payment. Citibank slammed him with a $39 late fee, eliminated his interest-free grace period, and raised his interest rate to 24 percent. All told, the slipup cost Rodriguez nearly $100.

The policy "is perplexing," Rodríguez told Chu. "It's probably somewhere in the contract, and whether it's fair or not, once the company puts it there, you're stuck."

Citibank spokesman Samuel Wang told Chu that the information about the bank's billing policy "is clearly described in the terms and conditions provided to the card member." The bank "encourage(s) our card members to carefully review all communications that we provide."

Despite Wang's inference that Rodriguez was oblivious, the GAO found that he wasn't alone. In a survey of 112 credit card users, the agency found that "many failed to understand key terms or conditions that could affect their costs, including when they would be charged for late payments or what actions could cause issuers to raise rates."

Expediters

"The money makes it right."

Take an impulsive young male with too much time on his hands and a warped sense of right and wrong. Give him a computer and Internet access.

Watch what happens. Socrates gravitated to phishing scams and money laundering. Here's what happened to three other young men of his generation, none of whom had any ties to organized crime. Each simply acted on his own initiative, taking advantage of free technology and free guidance widely available on the Internet.

Jeanson James Ancheta flunked out of Downey High School near San Diego in December 2001. He briefly tried an alternative program, then a private school, before quitting high school altogether, eventually earning a high school equivalency certificate. He took a job as an attendant in an Internet café, and expressed an interest in joining the military reserves.

Instead, in June 2004, Ancheta discovered Rxbot, one of more than 12,800 variants of the Sdbot family. Rxbot, which can be downloaded for free from numerous Web sites, does the basics: It scans the Internet for Windows PCs with unpatched vulnerabilities. When it finds one, it implants itself and begins scanning for others, with no action required by the PC user.

Ancheta quickly figured out how to use Rxbot to gain control of tens of thousands of PCs. With the drive of an entrepreneur spurred by a ripe opportunity, he began offering his bots for sale on a private chat channel he called #botz4sale. Over a period of about three months, Ancheta completed more than thirty transactions, selling up to 10,000 bots at a time to at least ten different clients, who paid him modest amounts via his PayPal account. His buyers indicated that they planned to use the bots in DDoS attacks against rival bot masters, or to disrupt and harass business rivals. His total revenue from bot sales rang in at about $3,000.

By August 2004, Ancheta was ready for a bigger challenge—and bigger profits. He signed up as an affiliate of adware distribution companies Gammacash Entertainment and LOUDcash, both based in Quebec, Canada. (LOUDcash would be purchased in 2005 by adware giant 180solutions, based in Bellevue, Washington; 180solutions now does business as Zango.)

As an adware affiliate, Ancheta could earn twenty-five cents or more each time he installed one of Gammacash's or LOUDcash's adware installer programs on a PC. He was required by the terms of his affiliate's contract to make sure he had the permission of the PC owner to do so. But it was widely known at the time that adware distributors rarely enforced this requirement.

Ancheta shifted his focus to marshaling botnets for his own personal use—to spread adware. He shut down #bots4sale and told past clients he had no bots to sell. In actuality, Ancheta had set up a new chat channel—#syzt3m#—known only to himself. He also began to rent space on computer servers from several Internet hosting companies including EasyDedicated International, The Planet, and Sago Networks. Each time Rxbot infected another PC, it planted a bot instructed to report over #syzt3m# to a command-and-control program running on one of Ancheta's rented servers.

Soon, Ancheta had ready access to several botnets; each reported back to, and awaited instructions from, one of his command-and-control servers. Ancheta kept the adware-installing program stored on a completely separate rented server. The crucial moment came when he would direct a command-and-control server to grab copies of the adware program and download them onto each of the bots in a given botnet.

Manipulating tens of thousands of bots aligned in separate networks took constant monitoring. Subsisting on junk food, the rail-thin Ancheta usually began his workday shortly after waking around 1 p.m. and continued nonstop until 5 a.m. the next day. He soon took on an apprentice, an admiring juvenile from Boca Raton, Florida, nicknamed SoBe, who was fourteen at the time.

Communicating via AOL's free AIM instant messaging service, Ancheta trained SoBe to manage his portfolio of botnets over command channels assigned innocuous names, like #honda and #imports, to fool security officers monitoring traffic for the Internet hosting companies. He once bragged to SoBe that hacking Internet-connected PCs and loading them up with adware was "easy, like slicing cheese."

But it was slightly more complicated than that. To make steady cash implanting adware, Ancheta had to be careful not to assign too many bots to a particular server, lest he overpower the server. The command-and-control servers he rented usually topped out at about 20,000 bots. Ancheta paid SoBe to manage several botnets of between 17,000 and 23,000 compromised PCs, and to moderate the downloading of adware so as not to raise security officers' suspicion. PC users botted by Ancheta would see a rash of pop-up ads and might notice a drop-off in computer performance.

Sometimes the traffic flow got away from SoBe. Once an administrator from the hosting service contacted Ancheta to notify him that suspicious traffic was moving on chat channel #syzt3m. The accurate name of the channel was actually #syzt3m#. That gave Ancheta and SoBe a good laugh. Ancheta messaged SoBe,

> they forgot the # rofl [rolling on the floor laughing]
> so we are cool. I'm gonna msg them saying 'this irc
> network was investigated by my staff and we have
> removed the suspicious channel related to this' hahaha
> always works.

Ancheta regaled SoBe with stories about his tricked-out 1993 BMW 325is and his extensive wardrobe:

> my average spending is $600 a week, every friday I buy
> new clothes and every week I buy new parts for my car.

A few weeks later, during a discussion about doing affiliate work for adware companies other than Gammacash and LOUDcash, Ancheta advised SoBe,

> it's immoral but the money makes it right.

By then SoBe was helping Ancheta cash regular checks, as much as $7,996 from Gammacash and $2,305 from LOUDcash; in six months they would pull in $58,357.86, according to a federal indictment. SoBe inquired in an instant message chat about their earnings,

> i wonder how long itll last?

Ancheta, his sage mentor, replied,

> i'm estimating 6 more months to 8 months, hopefully a
> year.

Ancheta's undoing came sooner than that—at the hands of a client he once sold bots to. The client turned FBI informant. Federal agents raided Ancheta's home on December 10, 2004, and confiscated a generic desktop PC and an IBM laptop. Yet Ancheta continued to receive adware payments through March 2005. In a second raid on May 25, 2005, agents confiscated a Toshiba laptop. Still, Ancheta continued his activities through August 2005.

Ancheta pleaded guilty in January 2006 to federal charges of hijacking hundreds of thousands of computers and selling access to others to spread spam and launch Web attacks. U.S. federal judge Gary Klausner in Los Angeles sentenced Ancheta to fifty-seven months in prison, with this admonishment: "Your worst enemy is your own intellectual arrogance that somehow the world cannot touch you on this."

* * *

On Sunday afternoon, January 9, 2005, the tech-services desk phone at Seattle's Northwest Hospital and Medical Center began ringing incessantly. Computers throughout the 187-bed hospital had become unusually balky. By the next morning, the hospital was in full crisis mode: doctors' pagers fell silent; patient records were inaccessible; key cards failed to open the operating room doors; PCs in the intensive care unit shut down; lab tests ground to a halt.

"I could see everybody was very frightened," Robert Steigmeyer, Northwest's chief financial officer, later told *Baseline* magazine. "You saw the worry and concern in everybody's eyes."

A bot had run amok through the hospital's computer system. This one was being controlled by Christopher Maxwell, then an eighteen-year-old community college student living with his parents in Vacaville, California. From July 2004 to July 2005, Maxwell and two juvenile partners living in other states would earn more than $100,000 using botnets to spread adware, according to indictment papers.

The bot Maxwell used was a close cousin to Sven Jaschan's Sasser worm, the virus killer that had stormed the globe just a few months earlier in May 2004. Like Sasser, Maxwell's bot aggressively searched the Internet for any Windows PCs with the LSASS security hole not yet patched. Maxwell directed newly infected PCs to report to a command-and-control server over the #test chat channel. But instead of renting servers, like Ancheta, Maxwell and his underaged partners hijacked servers from the Department of Defense and California's Colton Joint Unified School District in California.

Maxwell's downfall was that he used a sledgehammer instead of a scalpel to break into PCs. Upon infecting computer number one at Northwest Hospital, his bot took note that the PC's Internet Protocol, or IP, address—its location on the Internet—began with the prefix 172.16. The bot then began sending out repeated requests to connect to any PC whose IP address began with 172.16; all of the hospital's 1,100 PCs did. However, across the Internet some 65,000 IP addresses began with 172.16. Infected PC number one soon found others nearby to infect. Those others, in turn, found others to infect. Soon 150 hospital PCs were infected, each reaching out to the 65,000 other PCs whose IP address began with 172.16. By the time 150 hospital PCs were infected, the simultaneous, overlapping requests overwhelmed the local network.

"This scanning configuration caused each infected computer to repeatedly send millions of network packets across the hospital's network indefinitely," FBI special agent David Farquhar wrote in a report. "The inefficient scanning was so detrimental to network performance that it prevented the IRC bots from fully infecting every vulnerable computer on the network. In addition to disrupting the botnet's ability to spread within the hospital's network, the scanning also caused widespread disruptions to legitimate network programming used by the hospital."

Farquhar, a member of the FBI's Northwest Cyber Crime Task Force, traced the original infection to a NetZero dial-up Internet account using the home phone number at Maxwell's parents' home. Appearing before U.S. District Court Judge Marsha J. Pechman in Seattle, Maxwell, holding back tears, asked for probation in lieu of prison time. "I am a twenty-one-year-old boy with a good heart and I made a mistake," Maxwell told the judge. "I never realized how dangerous a computer could be. I thank God no one was hurt." Maxwell received a thirty-seven-month prison sentence, plus three years of supervised release. Pechman said she hoped to deter "all those youth out there who are squirreled away in their basements hacking."

★   ★   ★

Farid Essebar, a skinny Russian-born resident of Morocco, lived a world apart from Jeanson Ancheta and Christopher Maxwell. Yet thanks to the built-for-speed global payments system and the budding business of online advertising, he could avail himself of the same source of mad cash as the Americans: Canadian and U.S. adware distributors in 2005 were chomping at the bit to pay affiliates to spread adware, wherever they were located, no questions asked.

Essebar surfaced in hacking circles in the spring of 2005 at about the same time a hot new e-mail virus family, called Mytob, emerged. Mytob combined features of Mydoom with botlike functionalities. Essebar, who went by the online moniker Diabl0, using the numeral zero instead of the letter o, was among dozens of neophyte hackers trying their hands at coming up with improved variants of Mytob.

At the time, David Taylor was on the lookout for Mytob variants in his role as the University of Pennsylvania's information security specialist. As part of his work protecting the university's computer systems, he had set up a test PC to receive infections so he could analyze them. In June 2005, Taylor purposely clicked on a Mytob e-mail attachment. He watched as the virus opened a back door and began trying to self-replicate. Then it did something Taylor had never seen before: it lowered the security settings on the PC's Internet Explorer browser so pop-up ads could get through; then it began installing adware.

Mytob also implanted a bot instructed to report back over a chat channel being controlled by someone using the screen name Diabl0, who happened to be actively monitoring the channel at the time. Taylor struck up a chat with Diabl0:

> **[Diabl0]** wht u think about this new worm? :o [emoticon for surprise]
> **[Taylor]** it is pretty good...the variables using the domain from e-mail and then adding the 'www' in front is good. i would imagine you will get a lot of bots
> **[Diabl0]** soon adding logo of domain :p [emoticon for blowing a raspberry]
> **[Taylor]** really?
> **[Diabl0]** yes
> **[Taylor]** that would be interesting...just curious how you could do that...would be hard
> **[Diabl0]** i got more than 200 complaints in last dedicated server :p i guess you too sent complaints
> **[Taylor]** they are probably not going to send you any Christmas presents. it is hard work cleaning up after getting infected with worm like this. it costs money
> **[Diabl0]** no very easy. that worm spread only for money

[Taylor] you should think about joining the other side of this...lots of fun fighting hackers...the thrill is even better
[Diabl0] no

Taylor archived his chat with Diabl0 and thought little of it, until a startling series of events unfolded three months later. Because vulnerability researchers were turning up so many security holes in Windows, Microsoft had taken to issuing patches on the second Tuesday of every month. When Microsoft issued a patch for a particularly worrisome vulnerability on Patch Tuesday, the clock started ticking. The security community would take bets on how long it would be before a hacking group reverse engineered the patch to create a proof-of-concept exploit for the new hole in PCs that didn't apply the patch—and how long after that before someone began using the exploit to infect Windows PCs.

The gap had been steadily closing. In the summer of 2003, the MSBlast worm started spreading twenty-six days after Microsoft issued the patch for the RPC hole, and in the spring of 2004, Sven Jaschan's Sasser worm hit just thirteen days after the LSASS patch was announced. On August 9, 2005, Microsoft issued a patch for a critical vulnerability in the plug-and-play feature that allows peripheral devices to connect quickly to Windows 2000 servers, widely used in corporate settings.

Within ten hours, an Austin, Texas, white hat research group calling itself the Metasploit Project posted a proof-of-concept exploit for the plug-and-play vulnerability. In the tech-security community, Metasploit was something of a lightning rod. Founded by HD Moore, a tech-security prodigy who's now about twenty-five, Metasploit often posts proof-of-concept exploit code faster than anyone else.

Moore insists that his intentions are altruistic. He says his aim is to provide technicians with information in real time, so they can accelerate the process of stiffening their defenses. The underlying assumption is that black hats are working just as fast to break into newly discovered holes. But Moore acknowledges the obvious. "Some people will use it to test their defenses; some will use it break into systems," he says.

Sure enough, the following Saturday—just four days after Patch Tuesday—the first plug-and-play worm, dubbed Zotob, emerged. Besides rapidly spreading itself to unpatched Windows 2000 servers, Zotob did exactly what Mytob did: it lowered the infected PC's browser security setting, installed a mechanism to download adware, and connected to a chat channel controlled by none other than . . . Diabl0.

"To the untrained eye Mytob and Zotob can appear quite different: one travels via e-mail, the other mostly by exploiting a Microsoft security hole," Sophos senior virus analyst Graham Cluley said. "But when closely examined, the similarities become clear. It appears whoever wrote Zotob had access to the Mytob source code, ripped out the e-mail-spreading section, and plugged in the Microsoft exploit."

For a few days Zotob spread slowly and largely unnoticed, planting adware on newer Windows 2000 servers. But by the start of the next work-week, Zotob began to snake into older servers lacking the latest upgrade service pack. Corporate machines at Canadian bank CIBC, American Express, and Daimler Chrysler began to reboot repeatedly. The same thing began to happen at ABC News, the *New York Times*, and CNN. Anyone watching CNN's afternoon anchor Wolf Blitzer that day might have thought a digital Armageddon was under way. Blitzer reported excitedly that a mysterious computer worm had taken out many of the news network's computer systems in Atlanta, New York, and other bureaus around the country. The newscast showed a CNN computer constantly rebooting.

Diabl0 had failed to craft Zotob to work with Windows 2000 servers not equipped with the latest service pack, says Peter Allor, director of intelligence at IBM Internet Security Systems. "Zotob had a quality assurance problem," says Allor. Diabl0 "neglected to test it adequately."

As part of Bill Gates's Trustworthy Computing initiative, Microsoft had assembled a crack group of sixty-five virus hunters, paralegals, and lawyers, called the Internet Safety Enforcement Team, or ISET. The ISET virus hunters reversed engineered Zotob and flushed out a trail to a hacker named Diabl0 in Morocco. Microsoft took the information to the FBI, whose agents collaborated with local authorities to arrest Essebar in his home. An alleged coconspirator, Atilla Ekici, twenty-one, nicknamed Coder, was captured in Turkey. The arrests took place on August 25, just twelve days after Zotob first appeared.

Ekici had paid Essebar with stolen credit card numbers to create the Mytob variants and Zotob worm primarily to spread adware, perhaps also to use later in other profit ventures, such as spreading phishing e-mail or launching extortionist DDoS attacks. Later, a third suspect, Achraf Bahloul, twenty, a friend of Essebar, was arrested in Morocco. Bahloul was sentenced to a year in jail, while Essebar received a two-year sentence.

When news broke of Diabl0's arrest, David Taylor, the college security specialist, stepped forward to supply the FBI with a copy of the transcript of the little chat he'd had with Diabl0 a few months earlier. "I really thought that he was immature," says Taylor. "He was asking me what did I think about his new bot, with all these smiley faces. Maybe he didn't realize what he was doing was so bad."

CHAPTER 7
Perpetuating Errors

Exploiters

December 2004, Edmonton

Police work doesn't always go as smoothly in real life as it does on TV cop shows. Businesses don't always snap to attention and hand over key pieces of evidence upon request so the investigation can reach a denouement by the end of the episode. In real life, official channels often bog down; bureaucracies and other pressing priorities can get in the way.

In pursuing Edmonton's drug traffickers and petty thieves, Detectives Vonkeman and Gauthier often confiscated cell phones activated by means of stolen credit card numbers. It seemed like everybody was out to scam the phone companies, which had a tendency to make themselves easy targets. One service provider once offered three months of free cell phone service for a $5 setup fee. Scammers opened half a dozen accounts at a crack, throwing in a prepayment for three additional months of service, paid for, of course, with a stolen credit card number. They scored untraceable cell phones, street value $200 to $250, guaranteed to work for six to seven months before the phone company would shut them down.

When Vonkeman and Gauthier confiscated such fraud phones, instead of stashing them in the evidence hold, they made it a practice to alert the phone company. That way the company could check for other phone accounts opened about the same time with the same credit card number and shut them down. "We helped them informally because if we go through official channels, nothing gets done," says Gauthier.

By going out of their way to help the phone companies tighten down their operations and save money, the detectives were also creating a chit they could call in later. "We try to have a good working relationship and help them cut off their losses," says Vonkeman. "Then we take the opportunity to educate them. A lot of businesses think because of privacy laws they can't give us anything. But if fraud is involved privacy laws don't apply and they're allowed to give us everything."

When Vonkeman alerted his contacts at the Canadian telecom giant Telus that one of its employees had come forward to admit that he had set up a dial-up Internet account for free use by unknown parties, probably associated with drug trafficking or fraud, the phone company dug a little deeper. It discovered an associated e-mail folder containing 500 PayPal log-in names and passwords. The phone company sent a printout listing the data to police. Vonkeman asked Telus not to shut down the account, but to keep it open and alert him anytime anyone logged on. The phone company readily agreed to do so.

On Friday morning, December 10, 2004, Vonkeman got a call from Telus advising him that someone had just logged on to the account from the Ramada Crowchild Inn, an upscale sixty-unit establishment in the Rocky Mountain city that hosted the 1988 Winter Olympics, located 200 miles due south of Edmonton. Vonkeman called some police contacts in Calgary and asked them to check it out. But by the time the investigators got to the Crowchild and sorted out which of the sixty rooms the call had come from, the occupants had checked out.

The following Tuesday, Vonkeman heard from Telus that the dial-up account had been accessed a couple of times over the past weekend from an apartment in north Edmonton. The phone company employee put Vonkeman on hold to run down more details, then returned to advise the detective that someone had just logged on to the account from the Beverly Motel, a cinder-block establishment, painted peach and turquoise, a few blocks northeast of downtown.

Vonkeman and Gauthier hustled down to the corner of 118th Avenue and Forty-fourth Street in the heart of the city's seedy northeast corridor. At the Beverly, you can rent rooms by the hour. The phone company could tell the detectives only that the Internet connection was being made via a phone somewhere on the motel property. It could be a phone in the manager's office or one of the rooms. Upon checking with the property manager, the detectives were advised that only one phone on the property was in use, the one in room 24, just around the corner from the office, two doors down. At approximately the same moment Vonkeman and Gauthier thanked the manager and turned the corner, Biggie strolled out of room 24, followed a few seconds later by Socrates.

The detectives instantly recognized Biggie, whom they had arrested before, but this was the first time they had laid eyes on Socrates. "We had heard there was a new guy running around out there with access to thousands of accounts, but previous to this he had so little involvement with the police, and we had nothing on him to relate him back to this crowd," says Vonkeman.

Inside room 24 the detectives found meth pipes, stolen credit cards, notebooks with handwritten notations about fraudulent transactions, and printouts of stolen identity data. The acrid stench of crystal meth pervaded the air. Gauthier walked over to the bed to examine a Toshiba laptop computer connected to a wall phone jack. It was downloading something: a level upgrade for the video game Counter-Strike, arriving at an agonizingly slow rate via the Telus dial-up Internet connection.

Socrates was carrying a fake ID, and the detectives found receipts for a cash transfer made for a Western Union money order issued to Biggie, along with receipts for first-class travel on the Red Arrow bus line between Calgary and Edmonton. Red Arrow coaches feature tray tables with power outlets to plug in laptop PCs. They also confiscated a receipt of a room at the Crowchild Inn in Calgary on the previous Friday, the same room visited by the Calgary constables.

Enablers
Rife with Inaccuracies

Lending is the art of hedging your bets. The basic model for doing it profitably is simple. Whenever possible, make loans only to borrowers of good repute likely to repay you as agreed, with reasonable interest. Should you choose to lend to folks who might be late with a payment—or worse, default on the loan—simply charge a higher interest rate to reflect your increased risk.

The art comes in differentiating reliable borrowers from risky ones; in short, profiling. When it comes to profiling prospective borrowers, lenders have a key accomplice: the big three credit bureaus, Equifax, Experian, and TransUnion. The big three comprise a singularly powerful and essential component of our built-for-speed credit-issuing and payments system. Together these giant data-handling companies keep close track of every loan, every installment payment, every credit application for every consumer. Each bureau maintains more than 210 million files and updates more than 4 billion pieces of data each month.

This intelligence is distilled down to individual credit reports, which form the basis for calculating interest rates and dictating repayment terms for all forms of consumer credit: bank loans, credit card accounts, auto loans, mortgages, stock portfolio margin loans—you name it. What's more, insurance companies use credit reports to determine one's policy premiums, landlords use them to decide whether to rent to someone, and employers sometimes use them to determine whether to hire a potential employee.

To consumers, credit reports loom as a cornerstone of financial life. Over a lifetime, your credit report will determine how much you'll pay in interest rates and insurance premiums and could factor into where you are able to live and whether you qualify for certain jobs.

To lenders—banks, credit card companies, mortgage brokers, and others—credit reports are the magic profiling tool that enable them to hedge their bets and push out fresh credit very rapidly on a mass-market scale.

To the big three, credit reports are like flakes of gold. Each credit report issued brings in revenue ranging from 50 cents (as when delivered in bulk to large banks) to $15 (as when a report is sold to an individual consumer). Experian reported revenues of $3.1 billion in the year 2006, Equifax reported $1.6 billion, and Hoover's Company Reports estimated private TransUnion's revenues at $1.2 billion.

The trouble is that credit reports are typically rife with inaccuracies. It turns out that the computer-to-computer exchange among the credit bureaus, keepers of payment behavior data, and lenders, who assign rates and terms based on that information, is quick to incorporate errors and yet highly resistant to correction.

"The goal is to try to deliver as many credit reports to lenders as possible and this requires a largely automated file identification and delivery system," says John Ulzheimer, president of Credit.com Educational Services, which advises consumers on credit management. Ulzheimer is also a former Equifax and Fair Isaac customer service manager.

Once the credit bureaus' automated systems add erroneous data to an individual's credit history, it can be next to impossible to clear the inaccuracies. A 2005 survey by the U.S. Public Interest Research Group (PIRG) found that a whopping 79 percent of credit reports contained errors, and 25 percent contained mistakes serious enough to prevent the individual from obtaining credit.

The PIRG survey stands out among myriad surveys and anecdotes confirming how routinely strangers' names, wrong addresses, payment history falsehoods, erroneous judgments, and even aberrant Social Security numbers get molded into credit reports.

Yet any consumer who attempts to get errors corrected is in for an Alice in Wonderland experience. Perseverance is a must, and a satisfactory resolution often requires assistance from the cottage industry of credit repair consultants and lawyers expert at bringing Fair Credit Reporting Act (FCRA) lawsuits against the big three. "Basically you've got to get a lawyer and hit them between the eyes with a two-by-four to get their attention," says Richard Feferman, an Albuquerque, New Mexico–based attorney, who represents plaintiffs in FCRA lawsuits.

The bureaus typically respond to complaints by reducing each one to a two-digit code forwarded in a document called a CDV, or consumer dispute verification, to the lender. Often the CDV gets routed through a series of intermediaries working in sweatshops in third world countries. One such employee testified that the bureau she worked for received up to 8,000 CDVs per day and that each worker was required to handle one dispute every four minutes to meet quotas, says Anthony Rodriguez, staff attorney for the National Consumer Law Center.

In a 2006 FCRA lawsuit filed in New Mexico by Feferman, U.S. District Court Judge M. Christina Armijo ruled that "a rational factfinder could conclude that Equifax knew that the pointless repetition of the cursory CDV procedure by its various agents and contractors was not going to resolve Plaintiff's dispute in a timely manner and only served to delay the matter until Plaintiff tired of the process or proceeded to litigation."

Lenders typically respond to a CDV by referencing the document containing the error in question, and going no further, says Blair Drazic, a St. Louis–based FCRA attorney "When you apply for a loan, there's supposed to be a paper with your name on it. They never have that. They'll say you're in our files as owing it [the disputed loan balance], and the investigation consists of checking the same computer that reported you to start with," says Drazic.

Testifying before Congress in 2003, Rodriguez, the National Consumer Law Center attorney, delineated the economic incentive to perpetuate errors: "So long as the mistakes about consumers generally make the consumers appear to be a worse credit risk than they really are, rather than better, the credit industry has no incentive to improve the system, especially where the current system covers additional risk by charging more for riskier borrowers wrongfully identified as being a greater risk by the credit reporting system."

Stuart Pratt, president and CEO of the Consumer Data Industry Association, the powerful lobbying group that represents the credit bureaus, says CDVs make the process more convenient for consumers because they can report problems at any time of the day or night. Pratt notes that under federal law, consumers who are unable to resolve errors can ask the credit bureau to include a statement about the dispute in their file. But such dispute letters are widely disregarded by lenders.

"This is all designed to save them [credit bureaus] money," says Feferman. "They just don't have the will to fix errors. They get the same amount for a credit report whether the credit report is accurate or not, and the costs of investigations are a drag on profits."

Pratt insists mistakes are rare. He contends the greater good is compelling. After all, an automated, wide-ranging credit-approval system perfectly complements a card-based payments system that can process transactions in as little as 1.4 seconds. And this acceleration has been crucial to expanding consumers' buying power. Meanwhile, revolving and nonrevolving household debt climbed 580 percent to $2.4 trillion by 2007, up from $352 billion in 1980, while the median household income of young families rose just .08 percent to $45,485 over roughly the same period, according to the Federal Reserve and U.S. Census Bureau.

That ability to extend credit to virtually everyone from teenagers to first-time business owners to any consumer desiring a new SUV or high-definition television, Pratt argues, far outweighs what he characterizes as comparatively minor glitches in the system. "Credit has been democratized," says Pratt. "Credit has facilitated economic growth in this country and it has saved consumer money on an individual basis." Pratt makes such statements with a practiced earnestness honed during years of defending the status quo in the halls of Congress.

But what Pratt won't ever volunteer in public discourse is that no law or decree ever gave the credit bureaus exclusive rights to handle credit records. The bureaus simply grabbed that power. And the imperfect data-handling systems the bureaus have put in place make no profit offering transparency to individual consumers. The credit bureaus' data-handling systems have proved to be supremely efficient and productive at a singular task: keeping our credit-issuing and card-based payments system running full tilt.

Expediters

Low-Tech Spree

Among those who most appreciate our credit-issuing and payments system, as is, are the identity thieves who fully grasp its weaknesses. One such rogue put Matthew and Lisa Kirkpatrick, of Portland, Oregon, through five years of hell. In February 2001, the Kirkpatricks were getting desperate because they couldn't get a loan to finish a remodeling project to make room for their third child, who was on the way. The loan should have been a slam dunk. After all, Matthew earned a good living as a union carpenter, and the couple had always maintained a credit score of around 750, good enough to get favorable loan rates and terms.

But a couple of years earlier, a scam artist in Coeur d'Alene, Idaho, had started probing soft membranes in the credit-issuing system. Somehow the crook had gotten hold of—and renewed—Kirkpatrick's Washington state driver's license, though Matthew hadn't lived in Washington for a dozen years. He also somehow obtained Kirkpatrick's Social Security number. With those two items, the crook had all he needed to go on a low-tech crime spree.

On the Friday before the 2000 Super Bowl, the imposter opened a Wells Fargo banking account in Spokane, Washington, depositing a bad check for $5,000. Two days later, on Super Bowl Sunday, he went on a shopping spree writing checks for up to $2,000 at various Spokane retailers. When the store clerks called to verify sufficient funds to cover the check, the automated systems showed a $5,000 balance. After the checks bounced the following week, a dozen merchants were looking for Matthew Kirkpatrick to make good.

The thief wasn't done. Over the next several months, he used Kirkpatrick's data to open a series of cell phone accounts and obtained credit cards, which he used to stay in hotels and go on shopping sprees. He also made several trips to hospital outpatient clinics across Washington seeking treatment—and medication—for earaches, backaches, and joint pain. None of the bills ever got paid, and each one eventually got turned over to collections. A lot of creditors were looking for Matthew Kirkpatrick.

Kirkpatrick first got wind in early 2000 that a small army of collections agents was hunting for him. He knew there had been some kind of horrible mistake, but believed the mix-up was easily correctable. In a positive frame of mind, he immediately set out to definitively prove that he was the victim of fraud.

He compiled a package of documents with police reports, letters from lenders stating he was not at fault, a copy of his signed Social Security card, a copy of his Oregon driver's license, and a detailed cover letter summarizing the circumstances. He mailed it to Equifax in February 2001. He resent another copy of the package in March, in April, and twice more after that, the last time by registered mail, return receipt both requested and received. Each time, Equifax representatives refused to confirm receipt of the documents, much less advise Kirkpatrick of the status of his corrupted files.

"We were living in this construction zone with a new baby and growing family for two and half years," recalls Kirkpatrick. "It was very stressful calling Equifax and saying, 'What happened to all the police reports and all the documents I sent you?' and them saying, 'We shredded them. We didn't get them. We get a thousand of these every day.'

"It was stressful knowing they had this power over me and my family. And their business decision was that it was cheaper for them to deal with you in litigation, if you end up being stubborn enough to take it that far."

The Kirkpatricks did get their day in court in January 2005. They were awarded $210,000. As he has done numerous times, Mike Baxter, the Kirkpatricks' attorney, directed the jury's attention to provision 1681 I(a)(2)(B) of the Fair Credit Reporting Act, which requires credit bureaus to promptly forward documentation of a dispute to the lender. That federal rule was one of the hard-won proconsumer protections hashed out in congressional subcommittee meetings between industry lobbyists and privacy advocates. It was intended to spur a process by which the creditor is compelled to evaluate the validity of dispute in a timely manner.

However, Baxter and other FCRA attorneys say the credit bureaus and lenders have long since established a practice of dispatching dispute documents into limbo. "I have never seen a credit bureau send supporting documents to the creditor; in fifteen years, I can't recall a single instance," says Baxter. "They never send those documents because it's more profitable for them to not follow the law than it is to actually follow the law, as far as I'm concerned."

CHAPTER 8

Cost of Doing Business

Exploiters
March 2005, Edmonton

In the year and a half Yolanda and Jacques were a couple, they had lived in three different places. The apartment they currently occupied, a two-bedroom, third-floor walk-up in the middle-class Mill Woods neighborhood south of the city, was by far the nicest.

Yolanda, twenty-three, was a functioning addict. Her drug of choice: crystal meth. Yolanda held down a decent job as a clerk for a courier company and earned enough to afford a car—she drove a white 1995 Chevy Cavalier—and cover rent and living expenses. Her apartment complex was done in a Hansel and Gretel motif with black trim and faux white stone walls. The rooms were compact. The living room opened via sliding glass door onto a small deck overlooking the street with a territorial view to the northeast of an expansive, undeveloped tract of land.

Prior to moving to Mill Woods, Yolanda and Jacques, twenty-four, a crack cocaine dealer, had lived in an apartment in the run-down Stadium neighborhood near the provincial courthouse, and before that they had lived for three months with Jacques's father, a crack addict. It wasn't very long into their relationship before Jacques hit Yolanda for the first time. Jacques had grown up watching his father strike his mother countless times. If his mother cried, the beatings would intensify. Jacques vividly remembered the beating his father administered that culminated with an ambulance rushing his mother to the hospital and cops hauling his father to jail. He was eight years old at the time.

Though Yolanda lived in constant fear, that didn't stop her from mouthing off to Jacques—or making excuses to others for how he treated her. She spoke often to acquaintances about "Jacques's psychosis" and "Jacques's post traumatic stress syndrome." Yolanda realized she, herself, probably needed mental health therapy. "I cried all the time, which induced Jacques's psychosis, which made him beat me more," she says. Yet, Yolanda stuck by Jacques, even after the couple was evicted from the

Stadium apartment because Jacques, in a jealous rage, broke the front window and smashed all the closet doors.

In December 2004, Jacques was doing jail time, sharing a cell with another prisoner in the overcrowded Edmonton Remand Centre. A third prisoner was soon assigned to sleep on a floor mattress in their two-bunk lock-up. It was Socrates, fresh from his arrest at the Beverly. Through his connections in the drug-trafficking community, Jacques knew a little about Socrates. He knew, for instance, that Socrates owed another drug dealer some money, so he took it upon himself to step forward as a self-appointed collections agent.

"He says, 'I'll light you on fire if you don't pay me,'" Socrates recalls. "I was, like, 'OK.' I was scared of him. But I was scared of most people back then. That's what meth does to you."

Jacques backed off after he learned from another inmate that his new cell mate possessed the skills to scam-order new PCs. Jacques got Socrates to agree to supply him with a new laptop computer. After about a week in jail, Socrates was released. He reconnected with Biggie and slipped back into meth use and financial scams. When he skipped out on a scheduled court appearance, a warrant was issued for his arrest.

Socrates returned to the pattern of flitting among different sketch pads, including a brief stay with Jacques and Yolanda at Yolanda's Mill Woods walk-up. In early 2005, he began building a reputation for himself in #cchouse, #carderz, and #carder—the IRC chat rooms where he befriended the Oklahoman who gave him the phished PayPal log-ins. Partnering with Biggie, Socrates began offering access to Edmonton drop accounts as a service to fraudsters, like the Oklahoman, who needed a way to extract cash from hijacked online accounts they controlled. The idea was to have the outsiders transfer funds into Edmonton drop accounts. Biggie would orchestrate the withdrawals. If the hijacker transferred, say, $2,000 into an Edmonton drop account, Biggie would make a withdrawal happen, then send $500 via Western Union wire to the source. After paying off the drop-account mule, Biggie would split $1,200 with Socrates.

Socrates was happy to leave such details to Biggie and stay immersed online. He caught a fascination with trying to crack the Web sites of medium-sized companies selling products or services on the Internet. He knew from chat room chatter that such companies often had weak Web security and that many linked their customer databases to their public-facing Web pages. He began hacking URL addresses—the http//:www.etc. line that appears in the top window of a Web browser and loads up the Web page. He struck it rich when he was able to break into the customer data-base of a Michigan retailer that sold work uniforms online. He was able to copy the company's customer list with names, addresses, credit card numbers, and purchase histories for its 3,000 online customers.

Socrates's stature as a brilliant techie hacker and scammer soon began to eclipse Frankie's in local circles, which wasn't necessarily a good thing. One day, two drug dealers showed up at the sketch pad where Socrates was holed up, muscled him into the trunk of their car, hauled him to another sketch pad, sat him down in front of a computer, and ordered him to get online and make them some money. When one of the drug dealers left to get some food and the other went to the bathroom, Socrates took off like a scared rabbit.

Not long after that, Hula Girl, the gutsy fake ID specialist, whom Socrates had long admired, began flirting with him and invited him to move into her west end apartment, a few blocks from the gigantic Edmonton Mall. Socrates was making enough money to keep himself and his friends continually high and buy components to build his dream PC, which he began doing.

"He says she was his girlfriend, but she said she never really was," says Detective Vonkeman. "She basically used him to whatever extent because she saw his talent and fully exploited that."

Socrates gave Hula Girl a copy of everything he had, including the 3,000 profiles from the Michigan uniform company whose Web site he had hacked. Alone in Hula Girl's apartment one day, he answered a knock at the door. In burst two assailants, one with a shotgun. Socrates would later say what happened to him next had no rhyme or reason. But his acquaintances passed along the story that another of Hula Girl's beaus, a drug dealer, got jealous about Socrates moving into her apartment, and hired goons to put the fear of God in him.

"They smashed me with the back end of the shotgun five or six times in the head. Knocked me out. There was blood everywhere. On the ceiling of the apartment. And then they put zip ties around my hands and feet. Put me in the closet. Threw a bunch of blankets and stuff on me.

"I had to crawl out of the closet, doing this little worm-wiggle thing, all the way to the front door. Had to drag a chair across the kitchen with my teeth and prop myself up on the chair and unlock the door with my mouth. I went out into the hallway to the neighbor's house and knocked on the door with my head, and he came to the door and he was, like, 'What happened to you! What's going on?'

"He's, like, 'In my thirty-two years of being alive, this is the scariest thing I've seen. Why don't you call the cops?' I was, like, 'I can't.' I didn't tell him it was because there was a warrant out for my arrest."

Instead, Socrates made a phone call to Biggie, who whisked him across the city to Yolanda's Mill Woods walk-up in the south end. With them went the powerful new dream PC Socrates had just finished assembling.

Enablers
Sweeping Immunity

Credit bureaus began humbly enough more than 100 years ago. Brothers Cator and Guy Woolford launched Retail Credit Company in Atlanta in 1899 by publishing the Merchant's Guide for a $25 annual subscription. The Woolfords gained intelligence on prospective borrowers by sending out inquisitive Welcome Wagon women with baskets of goodies—and keen powers of observation. Retail Credit endured, grew, and evolved into Equifax.

Homegrown credit bureaus proliferated steadily through the first half of the twentieth century; their number spiked in the 1950s with Frank McNamara's introduction of the Diners Club card and Bank of America's launch of the BankAmericard. By 1970 the number of credit bureaus in the United States peaked at more than 2,200.

As the financial industry began to apply digital technology to speed up and extend card-based payments, consolidation of the credit bureau industry became inevitable. The process of compiling credit reports needed to be centralized and accelerated to keep pace with the rising distribution of credit cards. By the end of the 1980s, five giant credit bureaus dominated the space, and by 1997 the big three controlled 90 percent of the market.

Experian emerged from the maneuvering of conglomerates TRW and Chilton Corporation and was acquired by Grand Universal Stores of the

United Kingdom. Meanwhile, the credit bureau division of TransUnion, a onetime rail car– and equipment-leasing giant, landed in the portfolio of the Marmon Group, a private conglomerate that includes the Hyatt Hotel chain and is run by the Pritzkers of Chicago, one of America's wealthiest families.

As this consolidation played out, leaders of the credit bureau industry were mindful to defuse rising concerns about inaccuracies and misleading data increasingly turning up in credit reports. In the late 1960s, Senator William Proxmire (D-WI) stepped forward as a vocal advocate for consumer privacy protection. However, in championing the Fair Credit Reporting Act of 1970, Proxmire got outmaneuvered by proindustry senators.

What began as a proconsumer proposal got twisted into a law so probusiness that one observer, Professor Arthur Miller, of the University of Michigan, described the final version as "an act to protect and immunize the credit bureaus rather than an act to protect the individual who has been abused by the credit information flow created by the bureaus."

The FCRA of 1970 required credit bureaus to investigate complaints within a "reasonable" period of time but set no limits. It remained silent on whether lenders had a duty to supply accurate information to the bureaus. And the coup de grâce for industry: it granted credit bureaus and lenders sweeping immunity from state defamation laws by which consumers could seek legal redress for bad data getting integrated into their credit histories. This represented a 180-degree divergence from Proxmire's original intent to create federal liability while preserving state liability, says Evan Hendricks, editor and publisher of the newsletter *Privacy Times* and author of *Credit Scores & Credit Reports: How the System Really Works, and What You Can Do.*

For the next two decades, complaints about inaccuracies and the recalcitrance of bureaus and lenders to fix errors predictably mounted. Crooks figured out how to manipulate the system, and identity theft became a rising concern. By the late 1980s, consumer groups and privacy advocates began to clamor for reform. In the early 1990s attorneys general from some nineteen states won a court injunction mandating that credit bureaus improve accuracy and do a better job of investigating complaints.

Meanwhile, in the nation's capitol, Congress, after several years of debate, finally strengthened the federal rules. Amendments to the FCRA that took effect in 1997 required credit bureaus and lenders to investigate consumer complaints within thirty days and make full credit reports available to consumers. Yet the savvy credit bureau lobbyists didn't come away empty-handed. They scored a valued prize: preemption of state requirements calling for the meticulous handling of credit data and responsiveness to consumers' complaints. The preemption was set to expire in 2004.

"Industry lobbyists claimed it would be too expensive to deal with fifty different state laws, but actually, most states pass very similar laws and the easiest and cheapest way to comply is to comply nationwide with the strongest one," says Ed Mierzwinski, consumer program director of the U.S. Public Interest Research Group.

With the states' preemption about to expire in 2003, the horse trading between lawmakers siding with privacy advocates and those lending a friendly ear to industry began anew. When the dust settled, the credit bureaus took home the trophy they most coveted: extension of the preemption that cut off states from setting data-handling rules. Consumers' consolation prize: one free credit report per year from each of the big three bureaus.

The bureaus would soon figure out how to turn this seemingly trivial concession into a fresh source of profits. But what they did not see coming was the impact of provisions that allowed states to enact rules to mitigate identity theft. The battle lines in 2006 and 2007 would be drawn over data-breach notification laws, requiring companies to notify consumers if sensitive data is lost or stolen, and credit freeze laws that empower consumers to ban the bureaus from compiling and issuing a credit report without the consumer's consent.

"The real reason industry doesn't want states to protect consumers is because the states are quicker and more responsive than the Congress in passing tough laws, and more immune to their lobbying and donation excesses," says Mierzwinski. "By the time Congress took its first identity theft baby steps in 2003, California had already invented the security [credit] freeze and seven other states had given consumers the right to a free credit report."

As this wrangling over regulation unfolded, the credit bureaus continued issuing credit reports using essentially the same processes honed in the 1970s. The bureaus jealously guard details about how this process works. TransUnion spokesman Steve Katz cites the danger of divulging "an unintentional instruction manual" for crooks.

But criminals long ago triangulated how the bureaus verify the identities of loan applicants and decide which records to pull into a credit report. And they've devised countless scams that take advantage of the system's propensity to readily accept and amalgamate close-enough data.

A prospective borrower filling out an online loan application can submit less than nine correct digits of Social Security number and just three matching letters of the first name of someone of good credit standing. Often that's often enough to trigger the delivery of a credit report and subsequent approval for a new cell phone account or credit card, says David Szwak, a Shreveport, Louisiana–based FCRA attorney.

"The three letters of the first name don't even have to be in the same order or sequence. Marsha and Mark would be the same person; David and Diana would be the same, as far as the credit bureaus are concerned," says Szwak. Last-name matches aren't necessary, he says.

One of Szwak's clients, Cynthia Comeaux, a native of Laplace, Louisiana, now living in Dallas, had her credit history deeply entangled with that of Cindy Carr, a military wife, living in New Orleans. "Their Socials were within 7 of 9 digits, and both of them had a C and I and N in their first names, though not in the same order," says Szwak. "They were repeatedly blended together for years; Experian never could get it unwound, had no desire to unwind it; the other two bureaus eventually fixed it."

The bureaus also ignore the applicant's date of birth and employment history; this makes it easy for thieves to create fraudulent new accounts by submitting a slightly tweaked name and Social Security number—or even using a dead person's or juvenile's personal data. Since the bureaus also accept any address submitted by a loan applicant, a crook can easily divert delivery of credit cards and billing statements into his or her own hands, says Szwak.

Perhaps most galling to consultants and attorneys who help consumers correct errors in their credit records is the fact that when a consumer requests a copy of his or her own credit report, the bureaus suddenly become sticklers for accuracy. The bureaus supply consumers with a report that includes only those loan and payment records with a perfect match of name, address, Social Security number, and date of birth, disregarding potentially fraudulent records with any of these items awry.

"When you order your own credit report, it may not contain derogatory information from someone with a similar name or Social Security number, but that data would appear on the credit report the bank or mortgage company orders, which is a huge problem," says Mike Baxter, a Portland, Oregon–based FCRA attorney.

Consumers who go to court to get the bureaus to correct errors occasionally get big awards. Baxter was cocounsel for Judy Thomas, of Klamath Falls, Oregon, who spent six years trying to get TransUnion to correct her credit history. In 2003, a Portland, Oregon, jury ordered TransUnion to pay Thomas $5.3 million, but a federal judge later reduced the award to $1 million.

Most successful lawsuits bring only modest awards, and the vast majority of cases settle out of court for less than $25,000. Thanks to the skills of manipulative lobbyists, kid-glove treatment from regulators, and the absence of a unified constituency of aggrieved consumers, the credit bureaus remain insulated and haven't had to change their practices much over the past three decades, says Hendricks, of *Privacy Times*. Nobody ever died from an error-riddled credit report. In fact, damages to consumers, such as losing sleep over credit history errors or having to pay higher interest rates, are difficult to quantify, much less prove in court.

"They've never been hit with tobacco-sized litigations, and the Federal Trade Commission has been very soft on the credit reporting agencies, especially in recent years," says Hendricks. "They've been able to contain it all, and just write it all off as a cost of doing business as usual."

Expediters
Multiheaded Hydra

In late 2005 and 2006, the aftermath of Hurricane Katrina, escalating mayhem in Iraq, and the fate of contestants on the popular TV program American Idol arrested the attention of the mainstream media and the wider U.S. populace. Hardly anyone picked up on a 335-word story that moved across the Reuters world newswire on November 29, 2005, dateline Riyadh, Saudi Arabia, noting that cybercrime had surpassed illicit drug sales as a global economic force.

Veteran Reuters reporter Souhail Karam had cornered U.S. Treasury consultant Valerie McNiven at an unusual setting: a two-day security conference put on by the Saudi central bank.

"McNiven was the only female speaker invited to speak at the conference in her quality [capacity] as an adviser to the U.S. Treasury and expert on e-finance and e-security for the World Bank," recalls Karam, a thirty-three-year-old Moroccan. "Like any female foreign visitor, she had to wear a black dress covering her from head to toe."

McNiven addressed a ballroom packed with male bankers and tech-company executives from the Gulf region, Asia, and Europe; she spoke at the top of the agenda, just after the Saudi central bank governor's opening keynote address. The essence of her speech, Karam says, revolved around the rapid growth in cybercrime and the need to help developing nations catch up with developed peers in cybersecurity.

During a break, McNiven told Karam, "Last year was the first year that proceeds from cybercrime were greater than proceeds from the sale of illegal drugs, and that was, I believe, over $105 billion. Cybercrime is moving at such a high speed that law enforcement cannot catch up with it."

The disclosure was noteworthy because it came from a banking industry insider. Banking officials are notoriously loath to publicly discuss security issues, yet among themselves they are known to keep very close tabs on how money flows. McNiven's estimate of cybercrime's global impact meshed with three surveys done at the time: the FBI and Computer Security Institute found that 639 of 700 U.S. companies and government agencies had lost $31 million worth of proprietary data and spent $43 million cleaning up computer viruses in 2005; the Conference Board Research Center estimated that 41 percent of Internet users had begun to shy away from online purchases because of security threats; and payments consultant CyberSource reported that 400 U.S. and Canadian online merchants lost nearly $3 billion to fraud in 2005, up from $1.5 billion in 2000.

Legions of video game–obsessed, ethically immature young males with moderate tech savvy—wastrels typified by Socrates, Ancheta, Maxwell, and Essebar—were flocking into a teeming cybercrime market every bit as interactive and user-friendly as Amazon. The criminal virtual underworld had began to hum with the efficiency and responsiveness of eBay. The tools, the training, the support services—everything necessary for cybercrime to flourish—were rapidly becoming commoditized. Supply and demand dictated prices.

As in the legit business world, a good reputation was important and trusted partners were essential. Tapping away at his keyboard in Edmonton,

Socrates could easily sweet-talk an Oklahoma phisher into sending him a handful of eBay log-ons on a trial basis. But more log-ons would come his way only after he proved he could really access drop accounts from which to withdraw cash, and could truly be relied on to wire a share of the proceeds back to the phisher via Western Union in a timely manner.

In true capitalist tradition, advancement in this virtual underworld was restricted only by one's drive. Unsatisfied earning just $3,000 selling his hard-won botnets at the market price, Jeanson Ancheta advanced to earning $60,000 in six months—by deploying his botnets to distribute pop-up adware. Christopher Maxwell, meanwhile, trimmed his overhead by using compromised PCs as command-and-control botnet servers instead of renting them. And Farid Essebar became a specialist, hiring out his services as an expert at concocting cutting-edge infections that turned off browser security and installed pop-ups in one fell swoop. The self-starter's enterprise and cheater's mind-set nurtured in the world of video gaming translated well on cybercrime's main trading floor.

Yet it was most fitting that Zotob, Essebar's brainchild, began with the final letter of the alphabet. After Zotob, there would be no more crudely crafted e-mail viruses or self-replicating worms grabbing global attention. CNN's Wolf Blitzer would never again breathlessly report a breaking news story about a mysterious computer ailment appearing out of nowhere to mindlessly crash corporate systems. This was not because defenders of the Internet had suddenly found a silver bullet for security; it was because, after the summer of 2005, cyberattacks systematically became much more carefully drawn to fly under the radar in pursuit of illicit profits.

An expansive market for stolen account and personal identification data soon took root in private IRC chat channels, and on slick "carding forum" Web sites, with names like CarderPlanet, Shadowcrew, StealthDivision, and DarkProfits, dedicated to cybercrime topics. Everything was available for a price: user names, passwords, account numbers, PINs, CVVs and CVV2s, Social Security numbers, birth dates, mothers' maiden names. Sensitive information—whether phished or hacked or physically stolen—came to have intrinsic value correlating to the data's usefulness for committing fraud.

"It's like the Wal-Mart of the underground," says Dan Clements, CEO of the security firm CardCops. "Anything you need to commit your crimes you could get in the IRC chat rooms or the carding forums."

In the burgeoning cybercrime underworld, the script kiddies and novice scammers tended to cause the most obvious disruptions, drawing an inordinate amount of law enforcement attention. This provided welcome cover for seasoned black hat hackers and well-financed cybercrime gangs, who increasingly formed partnerships to probe for fresh attack vectors and carve out novel ways to put zombie PCs to work going after the big payoffs.

In these endeavors, the versatility of bots stood out. "A bot is like a worm on a leash," says Chris Rouland, chief technology officer of IBM Internet Security Systems. "The bot master can walk the worm to wherever he wants it to go, and then he can stop it, and let it off the leash and tell it to do whatever he wants it to do."

While waiting for instructions from a command-and-control server, bots didn't sit idle; well-crafted bots continually scanned the Internet for PCs with security holes through which they could infect more machines, propping open a back door on each one. Through the back door, the bot master invariably set up a proxy server for relaying spam and DDoS attacks and for masking the true routes of data exchanges, and installed tools to harvest sensitive personal data, such as user names, passwords, addresses, PINs, CVVs, birth dates, and, especially, Social Security numbers.

The data-harvesting tools planted with the help of bots included "packet sniffers," which captured and analyzed all Internet traffic; "keyloggers," which collected data typed into online banking and shopping forms; and "man-in-the-middle attacks," which waited until the user logged on to an online account before stealing data or funds.

Seasoned bot masters did not make silly newbie mistakes. "We're not talking about script kiddies with this stuff. We're talking about professional programmers, people who have been writing malicious software for the past five to ten years and are pretty good at it," says Martin Overton, security specialist at IBM Global Services. "Now they were being recruited by organized crime syndicates to create botnets and malicious software to order."

Cutting-edge botnets became ever more nimble. To overcome having one of their botnets crippled when the good guys managed to knock down a command-and-control server, bot masters began enabling multiple bots in a given network to standby as backup command servers. "It's like deploying a multiheaded hydra," says Overton. "You cut off one head, and there are seven or eight more at the ready, and you can regrow new heads as required."

Botnets proliferated at an astounding rate, in spite of the best efforts of white hat researchers, virus hunters, and corporate security managers. Top researchers began hashing out defense strategies as part of a body called the Messaging Anti-Abuse Working Group. At MAAWG meetings, the experts referred to a consensus bot infection rate of 7 percent. That meant by the end of 2005 as many as 47 million of the 681 million PCs connected to the Internet belonged to a botnet. CipherTrust (since acquired by Secure Computing) estimated that more than 200,000 PCs got turned into bots on a typical day.

So who controlled the high-end botnets and what were they doing with them?

In April 2005, investigators at Microsoft made note of a distinctive piece of e-mail that arrived in a Hotmail account set up to receive and analyze spam traffic. The e-mail message stood out because it was copied to a list of other Hotmail addressees, each with the same first name but different last names. It directed the recipients to a pornographic Web site, part of a series of such sites. Upon tracing one of the Web sites to two persons based in the Netherlands, the investigators reported the case to OPTA, the independent post and telecommunications authority in the Netherlands.

On November 1, 2005, Dutch authorities arrested a suspect in Amsterdam for sending at least 9 billion pieces of spam pitching erection remedies, porn Web sites, and sex products since May 2004. The unidentified suspect used botnets equipped with spamming proxies. "In this way the spammer managed to conceal his real identity," OPTA said in a statement.

OPTA fined the spammer a record $97,000. In his defense, the man claimed he had stopped spamming by the time he was caught, "not because he realized that what he was doing was a violation of the law, but because he simply wasn't earning enough money by sending the messages," OPTA said.

Indeed, a couple of other Dutch hackers, aged nineteen and twenty-seven, active around this same time, were more representative of bot masters who were fast becoming attuned to the diversified earning capabilities of botnets. From June to October 2005, the pair infected 2.5 million PCs, earning quick paychecks spreading adware, just as Ancheta and Maxwell had done.

But they also planted keystroke loggers and sent out phishing e-mail crafted to collect account log-in data from PayPal and eBay patrons. They kept some of the sensitive data to acquire iPods, digital cameras, and video game consoles from online merchants, and sold the rest on IRC chat channels and carding forums. Their total take over the course of four months tapping away at their keyboards: close to $80,000.

When U.S. adware supplier Zango, then called 180solutions, began to balk at paying the Dutch bot masters, and then cut them off as affiliate adware distributors, the pair asked to be reinstated. When the company refused, they used their botnets to launch a retaliatory DDoS attack on Zango. The company reported the attack to the FBI, and the bot masters, along with a third suspect, shortly thereafter were tracked down and arrested in Amsterdam. The two men received eighteen-month prison sentences and were fined $11,800 and $5,000, respectively. The third suspect was released.

The fact that the Dutch pair was caught so easily (the attack was reported in August; the arrests followed in early October) suggested that the young bot masters, for all their diversified activities, played in the shallows of the cybercrime market. Botnets continued right on proliferating. Virus hunters and law enforcement could see the footprints of big-time bot masters on the move and obviously controlling the most sophisticated botnets. They just couldn't do much to stop the high-level bot masters from collaborating with organized crime rings. To dodge good guys monitoring the IRC chat channels, which most bot masters used to communicate with their bots, elite bot masters began directing their bots to report for instructions by clicking to obscure Web pages running on compromised servers.

"It looked just like regular Web traffic," says Rob Fleischman, chief technology officer at Denver-based tech-security company Simplicita. "They [bot masters] know the Web is like a giant haystack and that hiding their command-and-control servers on the Web makes them much harder to spot."

Clever bot masters also began using proxies—the favored mechanism to spread spam and launch DDoS attacks—to handle all routine communications. So a chat between a spammer and his hired bot master, for instance, would zigzag among a series of proxies; an investigator tracing communiqués between coconspirators would end up in a cul-de-sac of zombie PCs.

Dmitri Alperovitch assiduously mapped out this evolution as a principal research scientist at Secure Computing. As a youth growing up in

Moscow in the late 1980s, Alperovitch learned how to program computers from his father, Michael, a Russian nuclear physicist, who instructed him on paper since personal computers were not widely available in Russia at the time. Young Dmitri's lessons accelerated in the early 1990s, when Michael Alperovitch returned from a trip to Maryland, where he had worked on a nuclear power plant simulation project, and brought back the family's first home computer; Dmitri was eleven at the time and became intrigued with the mathematics behind breaking cryptographic algorithms.

Raised by a nuclear physicist father and a mother, Tatiana, who was a health-care information technology specialist, Alperovitch took the route bypassed by so many other bright Russians of his generation: he became a white hat. When a cybercriminal defrauded a close family friend, Alperovitch says he was repulsed. "Nothing would please me more than to see them go to jail," he says of the culprits. "The victim was very sick; she had had a stroke and wasn't completely functional in terms of her brain capacity. She was very easily defrauded."

In college he studied international affairs and emerged in the vanguard of virus hunters who began piecing together the nexus of cyberconflict and international policy. Out in the deeper waters, crime rings had begun hiring specialists to write viruses, manage botnets, and carry out various scams.

"Guys were making $20,000 to $30,000 a month. The top guys might make $100,000 a month," says Alperovitch. "These were the guys doing the full-scale attacks, sending out phishing e-mails, collecting bank accounts, logging in to accounts, doing interbank transfers, wiring the money out, and collecting the money, all while sitting comfortably in an apartment in Moscow."

Vardan Kushnir had such an apartment in downtown Moscow, out of which he ran the Centre for American English, the New York English Centre, and the Centre for Spoken English. These were front businesses for sending out spam. Kushnir was widely reviled as the Spam King of Russia, where, unlike Europe and the United States, spamming remained legal.

Retaining the services of top-level bot masters, Kushnir sent out so much spam that he angered legit system administrators, some of whom took it upon themselves to bombard his English centers with repeated retaliatory DDoS attacks. Even his business phones came under assault after someone posted the centers' phone number on the Web as a contact number for cheap sex services.

On July 25, 2005, Kushnir, thirty-five, was found dead, his head repeatedly smashed with a blunt object, his apartment ransacked. The next day an editorial on mosnews.com (which would shut down in June 2007) noted that the murders of 1,935 Muscovites in a recent five-month period would likely never be solved. The publication made this observation about Kushnir's murder: "There is no reason for Moscow's law enforcement officials to give Kushnir's case any special treatment, so they most probably won't. But the Moscow-based media is awash with comments and speculations, expounding one simple, albeit largely irrational, theory: someone (ranging from God almighty to an irate IT office worker) finally punished Vardan Kushnir for his seemingly unstoppable spamming activities."

Chris Rouland, IBM Internet Security Systems' chief technology officer, has a different theory. By the summer of 2005, botnets had become big business. Tens of millions of compromised PCs were being put to systematic daily use generating revenue through a matrix of scams. Bot masters in control of the most sophisticated botnets had become all-powerful, even untouchable. Rouland believes Kushnir may have crossed his bot master.

"My theory is he got murdered because he didn't pay his bill to the botnet guys," says Rouland.

CHAPTER 9

Vulgar Cheats and Swindles

Exploiters
2007, Chicago

A year after graduating from Dwight D. Eisenhower High School in Blue Island, Illinois, David Joe Hernandez joined the U.S. Air Force. He spent the next three years stationed at Cannon Air Force Base in Clovis, New Mexico, working his way up the ranks, and in March 2003, shipped out to Misawa Air Force Base in Japan. Hernandez became a staff sergeant and served as a jet fighter crew chief. In June 2004, he returned stateside and was honorably discharged.

Upon returning to Illinois, Hernandez would personally experience how some fraudsters prefer to work as lone wolves. His trials began in the fall of 2004 while living in his parents' home in Oak Forest, Illinois. First National Bank of Chicago called him seeking repayment for a delinquent $4,500 loan.

"I said, 'That's kind of impossible. I've always banked with Bank of America, never with anybody else, and I haven't even been in the states.'"

Hernandez pulled his three credit reports from Equifax, Experian, and TransUnion and discovered that a Chicagoan named David Hernandez, listing home addresses at 7219 South Hamlin Street and 6242 South Knox Street—but using his Social Security number—had opened some twenty accounts for cell phones, credit cards, utility payments, and hospital bills that had all gone delinquent.

"All of the billing addresses were to places in Chicago—places I'd never lived," he says.

Hernandez dedicated many hours over the next year and a half trying to clear up the mistakes. But things only got worse. He discovered he was linked to a string of felonies in Maricopa County, Arizona, where there was a warrant out for his arrest for driving on a revoked license, and where he had a criminal record for auto theft, evading law enforcement, making wrongful statements to law enforcement, wrongful use of a weapon, and driving on the wrong side of the road.

In July 2006, about a week after Hernandez started working at Best Buy, his manager informed him that he was being let go because a criminal record check came back showing a felony drug conviction. Hernandez pleaded that he'd never been in trouble with the police. He would get reinstated at Best Buy, but only after appearing before a judge and prosecutor to get a new driver's license and expunge the criminal records that followed him around.

"I had to go to court to prove I wasn't in the states during the time of these incidents," he says. "I had to show them all my military papers and time frames in sequence."

His problems weren't over yet. In August 2006 state regulators began garnishing wages Hernandez earned as an Air Force reservist to cover child support payments to a woman in Chicago he'd never heard of. The money was earmarked for a baby boy born March 2006 to a twenty-nine-year-old Puerto Rican woman at Chicago's Christ Hospital. At his wits' end, Hernandez searched for help on the Internet and found Rick Lunstrum at ID Watchdog, a Denver-based identity theft prevention and mitigation consultancy.

ID Watchdog determined that a couple of things had gone awry. First, the criminal records actually belonged to a David Hernandez from Mesa, Arizona, five foot ten, 295 pounds, born on the same day in 1981 as the Oak Forest David, who was five foot nine, 200 pounds. The Mesa David had an entirely different Social Security number than the Oak Forest David. There was no reason to confuse the two men.

But Lunstrum says data broker Lexis-Nexis had circulated a data dossier for the Oak Forest David that included the criminal records for the Mesa David—overlooking the differences in physical descriptions, not to mention the disparate Social Security numbers. Although he indeed had an extensive criminal record, it was clear that the Mesa David had nothing whatsoever to do with the delinquent accounts in Chicago, says Lunstrum.

The matter of mixing up criminal files so blithely highlighted how data brokers act much like credit bureaus. Each makes money by issuing identity profiles, be they data dossiers or credit reports. Each uses automated systems tuned to accept close-enough data in assembling such documents. Data brokers, like credit bureaus, "are in the business of selling information," says Lunstrum. "If they start putting filters on, then maybe they won't have as much output to sell."

As for the lone wolf—the Chicago David—he very likely took advantage of the convenience of the Internet. Lunstrum says that a person in Chicago whose name was also David Hernandez obtained the Oak Forest David's Social Security number and used it to open new accounts and ring up balances he never intended to pay. The fraudulent activity began after Hernandez arrived in Japan, suggesting that his data was swiped while he was in the military, Lunstrum says. Someone in the military might have copied down his information, or Hernandez may have been victimized by data harvesters, who spread phishing attacks or plant keyloggers on Web pages all across the Internet. Once it was stolen, Hernandez's Social Security number could have landed in the Chicago thief's hands by way of Internet chat channels or carding forums, like CardersMarket, where stolen identity data is widely traded.

"The Internet factors into a lot of scenarios," says Lunstrum. "Based on current trends we're seeing in identity theft, it was likely done online."

Among the fraudulent accounts ID Watchdog had helped clear were bills for unspecified services from Christ Hospital, totaling $27,237, and a Visa credit card issued by Elan Financial showing a balance owed of $4,842. An Elan representative disclosed that there was a Chicago woman listed as an authorized user of the Visa account—the same woman who had garnished his wages.

"I kind of flipped out a bit," says the Oak Forest David. "I told him, 'That's the same girl who's taking money from me for child support. She's been the headache of my life right now and I've never met this person.'"

It took the Oak Forest David several weeks and two in-person interviews with state family services regulators to remove the garnishment. Not long afterward, ID Watchdog spotted the lone wolf—the Chicago David—on the move. Public records indicated that he went by another Social Security number and moved from Chicago to Texas in late 2006. In January and February of 2007, ID Watchdog spotted what appeared to be the lone wolf on the hunt. Someone in Texas made three futile attempts to take out online auto loans using the Oak Forest David's name and Social Security number.

Hernandez had placed fraud alerts on his credit records, so the loans were denied.

Still, the continued attempts to use his name and Social Security number to obtain loans hurt his credit rating. "I've done everything I could to keep up good credit," he says. "But no matter what I do, I come up losing."

Enablers

Staying on Message

What exactly is identity theft, anyway? Is it when someone swipes your credit card number and goes on a shopping spree? Is it when someone in possession of your user name and password logs in to your online banking or brokerage account and begins making cash transfers? Is it when your Social Security number and other private information begins turning up in new credit and loan applications you know nothing about?

The answers: "yes" to all of the above. Identity theft, in the broadest sense, takes place anytime someone pilfers nuggets of your personal data and uses them to commit fraud.

Yet banks, credit unions, and other financial service providers caught up in extending the credit-issuing system routinely misclassify identity theft. This creates cover for cybercriminals, making it easier for hackers and scammers to escape detection and prosecution, says Gartner analyst Avivah Litan.

Litan knows whereof she speaks. A former director of financial systems at the World Bank, where she managed online systems that reached bank patrons in more than eighty countries, Litan has conducted scores of surveys of major banks and their customers on banking security issues. She notes that a bank's risk department—the group tasked with stemming fraud—typically operates as a completely independent silo from the collections department, which is responsible for taking in payments. If the collections department can't collect on a loan, it has very little impetus to ascertain if fraud was a factor, she says.

"They just write it off as a bad loan. That way nobody looks bad," says Litan. "The risk people don't look bad, and it kind of gets buried and goes into loan lost reserves, which they already have set aside on their balance sheets."

The ability to report a consistently low measure of fraud activity helps support the banking industry's mantra that consumers are fairly well protected from payment card fraud. However, assuming that fraud accounts for less than 1 percent of the dollar value of all payment card transactions—as the current industry consensus holds—that benchmark is true only in the narrowest sense. Generally speaking, where financial fraud is concerned, a consumer is fairly well protected if a credit card is involved.

Rectifying credit card fraud is relatively simple. Notify the bank, sign an affidavit, and it will suspend the charge, deactivate your card, and issue you a new one. If a thief gets ahold of your debit card number or swipes your online banking log-in and password, you're in for quite a bit more hassle. Now you're dealing with loss of your personal funds, not the bank's, and you may have to fight the bank to get your own money back. Meanwhile, checks bounce, penalty fees mount, and bills go unpaid. And when it comes to your credit history getting mangled because of new-account fraud, you'd better gird yourself for months, even years, of wrangling to get your good name restored.

"Everyone says consumers are well protected, but it's really just in the niche of credit card fraud," says Julie Fergerson, vice president of Emerging Technologies at Debix, an online service that helps consumers protect their identities. "Banks and merchants and really anyone that benefits from commerce wants to keep a consistent message that everything is safe. So banks and merchants are willing to eat the losses on behalf of consumers. The world needs to be a safe place to do commerce, and thus marketing is driving the messaging."

To stay on message that online purchases, in particular, are worry free, payment card consortiums Visa and MasterCard have set an international standard of allowing consumers up to six months to request a refund, known as a charge-back, for any fraudulent transactions. Staying on message is one thing. Divvying up fraud losses is another. In deciding who eats how much of the fraud loss, the biggest gorilla gets the most say. By far the biggest gorilla, in terms of political clout, control of standards-issuing bodies, and sheer self-preservation moxie, is the financial services industry.

Not surprisingly, the rules and practices governing charge-backs tilt decidedly in favor of credit-issuing banks and affiliated card-processing companies. When a cardholder requests a charge-back, citing fraud, the bank has wide leeway to bill back the merchant. The merchant is left out of a payment and out of the product or service delivered to the fraudster. To add insult to injury, the card processor also gets to slap the merchant with a $25 charge-back fee.

Banks impose this practice for all "customer not present" payments, namely, payments made online or by e-mail or fax. This shifts the burden for online fraud losses to the merchants. Card users are assuaged, the public perception of safety stays high, the banks lose nothing, and the card processor makes a tidy profit in fees. Merchants take the hit.

"Right now it isn't painful enough for consumers," says Fergerson, who is also cofounder and a board member of the Merchant Risk Council, an industry group formed to fight online fraud. "It's not fun for merchants, but they write it off as a cost of doing business, and the banks are making money, so they're happy."

For his first few years in business, Brian Mortensen, founder of Njphones.com, a Dover, New Jersey–based online supplier of business telephone equipment, had no trouble taking credit card payments to fill orders sent in by e-mail. It was not unusual for his clients, mainly small business owners, to use multiple credit cards.

"A lot of times a customer might use the company's credit card, find out it's maxed out, so he'll try his own personal card, or his wife's card because he really needs the equipment," says Mortensen. "Everything's legit. I understand how that works."

So Mortensen wasn't suspicious when a customer in Brooklyn, identifying herself as Mrs. Robinson, placed a series of e-mail orders in April 2005 using five different credit cards. The phone equipment purchases totaled $20,000. Mortensen entered information into an automated point-of-sale terminal set up by his bank, PNC Bank. Upon receiving approval, he shipped the orders. The following month, PNC Bank notified Mortensen that his account was being charged back $20,000 because the five credit card numbers Mrs. Robinson had used had been reported stolen. By then, Mortensen had paid his supplier $12,000 for the equipment shipped to Mrs. Robinson.

A bank official told Mortensen that the only way he would be made whole is if he could prove he had confirmed the validity of each card's CVV2 number, the three- or four-digit value printed on the signature strip. CVV2 was introduced in the late 1980s as a security measure so merchants taking phone orders could confirm that the buyer had the credit card in hand, and not just the sixteen-digit card number, which could have easily been stolen off a restaurant or hotel receipt. Today CVV2 is used by online merchants for the same purpose. But its use is not uniform.

Mortensen says the point-of-sale terminal set up by PNC's card-processing affiliate, Direct Merchant Services, prompted him to input three things: the card number, the expiration data, and the sale amount. It never asked for the CVV2. Yet now the bank invoked his failure to verify the CVV2 as rationale for not covering his losses—and charging him penalty fees.

"I was pretty outraged when I found out not only did they not care, but they were actually making money out of all of this," he says. "I called them up, and said, 'This doesn't seem right. I kind of trusted you guys and what you told me to do. You guys should be watching out for me, not profiting from the crime.'"

Mortensen set up a Web site and contacted the news media about his plight. A reporter from Long Island News 12 took a camera crew to the Brooklyn address the phones were shipped to. The reporter found a storefront set up as a UPS mail stop. The camera crew filmed stacks of sealed boxes, filled with unknown goods, ready for shipment to Nigeria.

Merchants, of course, have no choice but to fold fraud losses into their price structure. So in the end, as always, society pays. The hidden cost of charge-backs advances in parallel with the payment system speeding up and e-commerce accelerating. CyberSource pegged merchants' online fraud losses at $3 billion in 2006, up from $2.8 billion in 2005. In an earlier report, the Merchant Risk Council estimated that merchants absorbed online fraud losses of $700 million in 2004, up from $400 million in 2003.

Expediters
Law Enforcement Challenges

That Vardan Kushnir could operate his spam empire with near impunity, subject, perhaps, only to the criminal world's austere self-correcting mechanisms, demonstrated the special set of challenges law enforcement faced in the war on cybercrime.

Law enforcement techniques for catching murderers and bank robbers have long been well understood and proved in the field: recruit informants, surveil the suspects, gather incriminating evidence, haul alleged perpetrator off to jail. But nabbing keyboard crooks was another matter altogether. The Internet afforded criminals an unprecedented level of anonymity, and the smartest crooks were obsessive about keeping a low profile. They used multiple nicknames, or nics, hid behind a forest of misdirecting proxies, and gravitated to locked-down private networks, called virtual private networks, or VPNs. All of these tricks assured that the digital trail ricocheted as far away as possible from the crook's IP address—the unique location on the Internet where he or she taps away at a keyboard.

What's more, the Internet freed criminals from the constraints of time and space. In the physical world, the reach of mafia bosses and drug lords extended only as far as they could dispatch henchmen to complete deals and impose their will. But in the world of cybercrime, communications and transactions could span all corners of the globe and took place in real time, around the clock. Cash and contraband in digital representations could cross multiple geographic boundaries and change hands several times, never once having to sneak past a border guard or a customs agent.

While broadening criminal opportunities, the Internet at the same time exacerbated law enforcement's intrinsic limitations. Investigators often had to deal with cybercrime statutes from several nations, many of which were poorly written, or sometimes didn't even exist at all; language and cultural barriers were the rule. What's more, in the United States, the FBI was charged with enforcing federal law, the U.S. Secret Service kept tabs on financial fraud, and the U.S. postal inspector covered mail fraud. Cybercrime cases routinely overlapped all three jurisdictions, triggering the intense tribalism endemic to federal bureaucracies.

Despite all of those obstacles, law enforcement, nonetheless, has made headway. The year 2004, in fact, turned out to be a bumper-crop year for catching cybercrooks. The quiet arrests of Douglas Cade Havard, twenty-two, an American, and Lee Elwood, twenty-three, a Scotsman, in Leeds, England, and the extradition from Cyprus of Roman Vega, a Ukrainian, in the early summer of 2004, would draw scant attention. Yet these overseas busts foreshadowed a pinnacle crackdown to come on U.S. soil just a few months later.

Havard, aka Fargo, was the son of a well-off Dallas entrepreneur. He began getting into serious trouble with the law at age nineteen. In 2003, Havard migrated to Leeds, a prosperous city in West Yorkshire, England, known for its universities and medical businesses, by way of Belize, where he had fled to escape a series of felony criminal charges he faced back in Texas.

Members of the United Kingdom's National Hi-Tech Crime Unit, or NHTCU, began watching Havard and Elwood, aka Raptor, as part of a crack-down on the carding forum CarderPlanet, headed by King Arthur, a master

Russian credit card scammer. In the top-tier forums—CarderPlanet, Shadowcrew, and DarkMarket—cybercrooks brazenly struck deals and set up partnerships. According to court records, Havard met Elwood online, and the two quickly established their reputations as CarderPlanet's go-to street cashiers.

CarderPlanet operatives, overseen by King Arthur, took to sending Havard and Elwood private instant messages that contained fifty to 120 debit card numbers and PINs. The pair would transfer the card numbers onto the magnetic stripes of blank plastic payment cards—blank cards and a device for transferring account numbers, called a magstripe reader/writer, were easy enough to get from online suppliers—then make stops all around Leeds to withdraw cash from ATM machines. Once they had sent 60 percent of the proceeds back to their handlers via Western Union, another batch of card numbers and PINs would arrive. Havard and Elwood also used stolen bank card numbers to buy laptops and other electronic goods from online merchants, which they in turn sold on eBay. NHTCU estimated the pair stole at least $1.4 million over ten months, and possibly as much as $11 million over a two-year period.

At the time of their arrests, Havard and Elwood each owned expensive Mercedes sedans and had access to several residences from which police confiscated $18,000 in cash and $28,000 in forged traveler's checks, along with fake drivers' licenses and passports and equipment for manufacturing fake credit and debit cards. Havard would get a six-year prison sentence; Elwood, four years.

The same month Havard and Elwood were taken into custody, the U.S. attorney's office for the Northern District of California filed papers to extradite from Cyprus a Ukrainian named Roman Vega, aka Roman Stepanenko, aka Boa, for trafficking stolen credit card numbers. Vega ran a carding forum called BoaFactory. And he was active on the much bigger CarderPlanet and Shadowcrew forums.

The arrests of Havard and Elwood and the extradition of Vega rattled King Arthur. He had guided CarderPlanet to becoming the top forum of its kind, with an estimated 7,000 members, using a cautious approach. On July 20, about a month after CarderPlanet's most productive street cashiers got taken out in Leeds, King Arthur posted a long rambling message, written in fractured English, that sent shock waves reverberating through the carding world. The message began:

> Good time of day, respected and in some meaning dear
> forum members:
>
> It is time to tell you the bad news. The forum should
> be closed. Yes, it really means closed and there are a
> lot of reasons for that.

King Arthur bemoaned the fact that CarderPlanet had become infested with double-crossing rippers, "with their vulgar cheats and swindles," and with undercover agents from the FBI and Interpol, looking to pounce on any lapse in forum security:

> How clever we can be, how much proxies do we use and
> even the most darkest corners of the world where we
> can locate our VPN—all of us are just people and all
> of us can make mistake, we can forget to switch on the
> VPN or probably proxy can be with holes.

A forum member, nicknamed Darker, took the news hard:

> HUH!!!
> you want to close our home!!
> why don't you just list the forum for sale and you
> leave this issue+getting some money for your great
> work.
> its an idea no?

King Arthur could not be dissuaded. He disbanded CarderPlanet at the end of July. Meanwhile, the leaders of Shadowcrew, the second-largest forum, did not share King Arthur's sense of foreboding. They should have. One of their inner circle, Cumbajohnny, had been arrested in April 2003 and immediately volunteered to become an undercover informant in exchange for escaping prosecution. Working for the U.S. Secret Service, Cumbajohnny lured Shadowcrew's most prominent members, including top administrator Anthony Mantovanni, aka Deck, aka ThnkYouPleaseDie; security chief David Appleyard, aka BlackOps, aka BlackBagTricks; and senior moderator Brandon Monchamp, aka Kingpin, aka PVTHC, into regularly convening on a VPN set up and monitored by the Secret Service.

Mantovanni, Appleyard, Monchamp, and most other Shadowcrewers were careful to encrypt their message texts and routinely bounced all communiqués off multiple proxies embedded on zombie PCs around the globe, the better to throw law enforcement off their trails. However, once the top members ducked into Cumbajohnny's VPN, they took fewer precautions, assuming they were on protected turf. As messages pinged through the private network, federal agents captured their IP addresses.

Instead of heeding King Arthur's prescient warning and marking his departure from the carding scene as an omen, Mantovanni, Appleyard, and Monchamp saw only expanding opportunities as leaders of the new top carding forum. Some Shadowcrewers began to bask in their own hubris, openly boasting about forthcoming exploits and taunting law enforcement to catch them, says Scott Christie, a New Jersey attorney and former federal prosecutor with experience in cybercrime.

On the evening of October 26, 2004, Cumbajohnny used a ruse to get thirty members to agree to show up in his VPN. Meanwhile, Secret Service and FBI agents, joined by local police officers and armed with arrest and search warrants, got into position in several states, some armed and wearing bulletproof vests. As the Shadowcrewers logged on to Cumbajohnny's VPN, law enforcement swooped in, arresting twenty-two people.

Most suspects succumbed with no fuss. But not Monchamp. Securing his place in cybercrime lore, he leaped out the second-story window of his Scottsdale, Arizona, home and fled on foot, leaving behind two loaded guns, one of them an assault rifle. Federal agents swiftly ran him down. Twenty suspects would plead guilty and receive sentences ranging from five years' probation to seven and a half years in prison. Mantovanni, who was a Scottsdale community college student at the time of his arrest, received a thirty-two-month sentence.

With officious pomp and circumstance, then-U.S. attorney general John Ashcroft called a press conference two days after the spectacular raid to herald what he characterized as a major breakthrough in the war on cybercrime: Operation Firewall, as the Secret Service had called it, had shattered the largest English-language cybercrime trading board, Ashcroft announced.

"This indictment strikes at the heart of an organization that is alleged to have served as a one-stop marketplace for identity theft," Ashcroft crowed with sufficient gravitas.

It was a public relations triumph for the Justice Department, which had vowed to crack down on the cybercrime wave. But, in the end, like so many law enforcement clashes with cybercrooks, it turned out to be a Pyrrhic victory.

Justice Department officials painted Shadowcrew as an "international organization of approximately 4,000 members" and pegged losses engendered by the forum's criminal activities at $4 million over a two-year period. However, screen shots of the forum's final days showed about 2,700 registered members, many known to use multiple nicknames. And regulators used a generous formula to derive the $4 million loss figure: they multiplied the 1.5 million stolen credit card numbers linked to Shadowcrew's activities by $500—assuming, with no hard evidence to back it up, that every card number was valid and had been put to fraudulent use for at least that amount.

There is no question that knocking out the two top forums was a big win for law enforcement, the fruit of the combined efforts of scores of agencies in Europe and America. It proved that investigators were making strides in use of high-tech forensic equipment and that prosecutors were getting better at bringing the hammer down on cybercrime suspects, says Paul Luehr, a former federal prosecutor of computer crimes who is now a tech attorney in Minneapolis. "It is unfair to portray law enforcement as standing still," says Luehr. "Nevertheless, I think they face a daunting task keeping up with the pace of cybercrime."

Indeed, the effects of Operation Firewall would be fleeting, at best. Thousands of forum members who weren't caught in the crackdowns scattered like cockroaches. Some went deeper underground, while others reemerged in other organizations. While the bad guys would quickly regroup, stronger than ever, the good guys would continue to run into the brick walls of jurisdictional constraints and interagency rivalries, just as before.

Some critics viewed the litany of obstacles as overwhelming. Lacking manpower and training on cutting-edge cyberexploits, federal agents "arrest the easy ones to find," says Richard Clarke, former national cybersecurity czar who is now a best-selling novelist. "It's like arresting prostitutes instead of the johns."

Long-standing rivalries, steeped in the competition for public funding, didn't help. On the heels of Operation Firewall, the FBI broke off to pursue cybercrooks as part of its unilaterally run Operation Cardkeeper. In

November 2006, the FBI announced the arrests of thirteen comparatively low-level alleged data thieves in the United States and in Poland, with additional arrests expected in Romania.

Meanwhile, in a duplicative dragnet, the Secret Service launched Operation Rolling Stone, targeting essentially the same pool of low-level cybercrooks. Through the course of 2006 the Secret Service would arrest some thirty-five suspects in several states and Canada; none of the enforcement actions came close to the Shadowcrew bust for drama and impact.

Rationalizing the parallel federal probes, Secret Service Agent Kimberly Bruce explains, "Because of the nature of the Internet, overlap is inevitable. The Secret Service attempts to de-conflict duplication of effort whenever feasible."

CHAPTER 10
Hungry Sharks

Exploiters
March 27, 2005, Edmonton

Socrates blew five grand in a splurge to build his dream PC. It had an overclocked motherboard, a beefy microprocessor, four hard drives, a massive heat sink, and multiple fans. Through the Plexiglas side panels, the components could be seen processing data at blazing speeds, bathed in the glow of twinkling blue lights. Socrates used two seventeen-inch flat-screen monitors, across which he could spread out his computing desktop, or play Counter-Strike on one screen, while keeping a chat channel open on the other.

Once he recovered from the brutal assault at Hula Girl's apartment, Socrates, ensconced in the guest bedroom at Yolanda's Mill Woods walk-up, buckled down to focus on financial fraud. He got back into supplying drop accounts to the Oklahoman and about ten other online clients who controlled large portfolios of hijacked accounts. Socrates's contacts were from the United States, Quebec, Romania, and Egypt. His reputation was solidified as long as Biggie took care of the withdrawals and wired the agreed-upon split to clients via Western Union in a timely manner.

Socrates also began to pursue a growing fascination with the hacking end of the business. From tutorials and advice in the chat rooms, he learned how to create phishing scripts, and began to specialize in creating e-mail spam messages designed to lure online banking customers from the five Canadian banks to divulge their account log-ins and passwords. From the banks' official Web pages he would copy logos and paste them onto a bogus Web page. He would then send e-mails crafted to entice recipients to click to a Web form and fill out their names, account numbers, and passwords. He mastered the skill of blasting out waves of e-mail carrying these phishing lures to hundreds of thousands of Canadian e-mail addresses.

Out of every 100,000 phishing lures he e-mailed, Socrates calculated that he could trick seventy-five to 100 recipients into responding and supplying him with their online banking account access information. He would spend countless hours going through each phished account, not really to steal anything, but to catalog how the accounts were set up and tally how much cash theoretically could be transferred out of each account. He also kept an eye out for celebrity data. These he would keep as trophies. His top catches: Canadian-born shock comic Tom Green and American sitcom star Bob Saget. "Sometimes the odd celebrity would get caught in a phish and send me their personal information," he says. "I would never use a celebrity's profile. It was like a super collector hockey card."

When certain forces in the cyberunderground, for whatever reasons, put a premium on Canadian accounts, Socrates was able to leverage his data, trading blocks of Canadian accounts for larger blocks of U.S. accounts. Soon the hard drives on Socrates's dream computer stored eight megabytes of compressed text—profiles, including names, addresses, birthdays, Canadian Social Insurance numbers, U.S. Social Security numbers, credit card numbers, passwords, and PINs for several thousand individuals.

He took steps to protect access to this valuable data by setting up multi-tiered passwords. A person would have to know or break the password he set up to start up the BIOS (basic input/output system) page, the black screen that came up immediately upon turning on the PC's power source. Another password was required to start up the Windows desktop, and yet another to open the zipped data files, which in turn were encrypted. Eventually, Socrates began to de-emphasize the labor-intensive process of writing and managing phishing attacks in favor of spending more and more time in #carderz, #carder, and other chat channels. He concentrated on promoting the Edmonton cell's ready access to a matrix of local drop accounts.

This was encouraged in no small part by Jacques, who by force of personality, not to mention the fact that he had more contacts in the drug-trafficking community, soon replaced Biggie as chief handler of the drop accounts. A typical cell transaction now went like this: Socrates would relay the routing numbers of drop accounts to one of his regular contacts, who controlled access to hijacked online banking accounts. The client would make an initial cash transfer of $2,000 into a drop account. Using Yolanda's car, Jacques would accompany a runner to make the withdrawal, or make the withdrawal himself. The runner would get paid $200 to make an ATM withdrawal, or more to do a riskier in-person withdrawal from a bank branch. Jacques would next go to the nearest Western Union office and route $500 back to the partner. The cell would keep the rest. As soon as the partner received the $500, he would make another $2,000 cash transfer, and the process would repeat itself.

Usurped by Jacques, Biggie shifted his attention to learning everything he could about doing business on the chat channels. He took to looking over Socrates's shoulder every chance he got. When Socrates moved away from the keyboard for whatever reason—to go to the bathroom or to crash out for days at a time—Biggie, who had a sharp memory, would log in to the chat rooms using Socrates's nickname and password and set deals in motion, impersonating Socrates.

By mid-March 2005, the cell was pumping out mad cash. When everything clicked, Socrates, Jacques, and Biggie could push as much as $10,000 in twenty-four hours through the drop accounts. Yolanda fed them and kept the apartment clean. And yet the more cash the cell generated, the more drugs its members consumed. Socrates by himself was consuming an eight-ball of ice a day, roughly three to four grams, smoking a bowl at his keyboard every ten to fifteen minutes. Another half ounce, roughly fourteen grams, got consumed communally each day, as the party pipe got passed around Yolanda's apartment.

"I was smoking it all the time, like smoking cigarettes," says Socrates. "I was using the most in a day that you can without killing yourself."

To convert over-the-counter cold medicine tablets into crystal meth, an ice cook tweaks the chemical makeup of the cold medication ephedrine, which has almost the identical chemical structure of amphetamine. The conversion process makes ephedrine more fat soluble, and thus more readily absorbed by the brain. It is the meth in methamphetamine that helps the drug flood across the blood-brain barrier; in so doing it also accelerates the destruction of brain cells.

Methamphetamine causes a wallop of norepinephrine to be released into a person's sympathetic nervous system. This triggers instant, acute anxiety. Norepinephrine is the hormone associated with the fight-or-flight mechanism in humans—that surge of excitement that occurs when a car driver sees the vehicle ahead suddenly slam on the brakes or when an ocean swimmer sees a large gray fin closing in. Ingesting crystal meth continually, as the cell was doing in the spring of 2005, was akin to treading water in a sea of hungry tiger sharks.

Enablers

Gaps in the System

Melinda Scott, thirty-four, a mail carrier in pastoral Bishop, California, rarely travels far from her rural home. She relishes the peaceful life she has with her husband, Greg, and their adolescent son, Jacob, in a quiet hamlet in the shadow of California's Mammoth Mountain. In January 2006, Scott got a phone call from Capitol One MasterCard inquiring about purchases she had made on a replacement credit card the bank had recently sent, per her request, to an address in Ontario, Canada. It was Scott's MasterCard account all right, but Scott told the bank representative that she did not request a replacement card and had never been to Ontario, 2,200 miles away. The bank immediately suspended that account number.

The next statement Scott received showed a flurry of charges in Ontario over the course of the two days prior to the bank rep calling her. It seems a woman had contacted Capitol One, supplied the bank with enough personal data to convince the representative that she was Melinda Scott, and persuaded the bank to issue her a replacement card mailed to an address in Ontario. The bank had cheerfully obliged. When the card arrived, the woman went on a shopping spree until enough red flags went up and Capitol One called the real Melinda Scott.

Within forty-eight hours the woman had bought gas, meals, clothing, furniture, and electronic gear and had taken out cash advances, all totaling nearly $10,000. One online transaction stood out: an online charge to Equifax for $39 for purchasing Scott's credit report. That gave the thief a complete record of Scott's credit history.

Capitol One assured Scott she wouldn't have to pay the Ontario charges, and quickly issued her a new MasterCard with a different account number. Scott reported the theft to police in Canada and resisted the urge to travel to Ontario to confront the woman at the address where the bank had mailed the credit card. The police had talked her out of the trip, and Scott has heard nothing else since then—from the bank or law enforcement. Absolved from having to pay for the Canadian shopping spree, Scott nonetheless continues to fret about the details in her credit history data Equifax so blithely sold over the Internet to the Ontario thief.

"There are a lot of unanswered questions I'd like to know the answers to. But I'm just small potatoes. Nobody cares about what happened to little old me," says Scott. "They took care of all the charges. It didn't cost me any money. But emotionally it's just a sick feeling this could happen to you. It was such a violation. It's such a helpless feeling because you don't know how much more of it is going to go on."

Scott, like tens of millions of other individuals whose sensitive data have turned up missing, remains at risk of becoming a victim of new-account fraud, arguably the most insidious variety of identity theft. Illegal immigrants have been doing new-account fraud for decades; they use someone else's Social Security number and exploit the credit bureaus' loose handling of data to amass loans, rental agreements, and utility bills. Typically, they'll even make payments and keep the accounts current, hoping the activity goes unnoticed, which it often does.

But data thieves and swindlers have begun exploiting the automated credit-issuing system and the anonymous Internet to dramatically accelerate new-account fraud purely for profit, leaving victims to battle often unsympathetic creditors and collections agencies. Scott Cummins, a forty-five-year-old insurance company manager from Columbus, Ohio, knows all too well what that's like. Cummins likes to bank and shop the old-fashioned way. He never used online banking services and only occasionally shopped on the Internet. So Cummins was perplexed when collection agencies began calling him, demanding payment for thousands of dollars worth of online purchases made on a Wal-Mart MasterCard and Gap store credit card issued over the Internet to one C. Scott Cummins.

It took Cummins weeks to convince creditors that he identifies himself as Scott Cummins—not any other variation of his legal name, Charles Scott Cummins—and that he was a victim of personal data theft and online fraud. "The biggest hassle I've ever been a part of in my life," Cummins says.

Most victims don't know their personal data has been stolen until about thirteen months later, often when collection agencies come calling, according to the Federal Trade Commission (FTC). Typically, it takes victims at that point 175 hours to clean up their credit records.

The most coveted Social Security numbers are those of individuals with no credit history, such as a child, since the credit bureaus pull credit reports based on logic that overlooks birth dates. "If you get one of those, you've hit the jackpot," says Betsy Broder, assistant director of the FTC's consumer protection bureau.

In 2002, Kevin Munro changed checking accounts after a thief tried to cash several checks using his checking account number. Yet Munro's name, Social Security number, date of birth, and home address have continued to surface in the hands of cyberthieves ever since. Crooks have used his good credit rating to order magazines, purchase three Dell computers, and attempt to take out a real estate loan.

In August 2006, Munro's personal data turned up for sale on an Internet relay chat channel, like the one Socrates haunted, where data thieves and money-laundering mules congregate. Four years after Munro had first caught thieves plundering his identity, his most sensitive personal data was still in play, being offered for sale to the next enterprising new-account scammer who wanted to give it a whirl. Meanwhile, that same month, Munro got a notice from MasterCard that it was canceling a credit card account he had had for twenty years and used only infrequently. "I'm pissed," says Munro. "I work for a living. I do everything on the up-and-up, and some lowlife comes by and takes it away from you."

Expediters
Marketing 101

The media glow emanating from the 2004 Shadowcrew raid arched well into the summer of the following year. The *New York Times*, the *Wall Street Journal*, *ComputerWorld*, CanWest News Service, and *Baseline* magazine all did extensive stories referring to Operation Firewall. None was more fawning of law enforcement's crowning achievement than *BusinessWeek* magazine's May 30, 2005, cover story, titled "Hacker Hunters: An Elite Force Battles the Web's Dark Side."

Dan Larkin, chief of the FBI's Internet Crime Complaint Center, graced the magazine's cover wearing an FBI baseball cap, his Windbreaker pulled back to reveal a holstered pistol at the ready. On magazine racks in airports and supermarkets across the land, Larkin loomed as a formidable Wyatt Earp of the digital age.

But the truth of the matter was that the cybercrime marketplace had hardly skipped a beat. First of all, Operation Firewall did nothing to hinder the freewheeling IRC chat channels readily accessible to any newbie hacker or wannabe cyberthief with a hankering to learn a few rudimentary tricks of the trade. The fraud chat channels were like wide-open flea markets. Communication took place in real time among whomever was logged on to a given chat channel. In effect these were group instant messaging sessions whose topics revolved exclusively around stealing, exchanging, and using stolen data.

These cybercrime chat channels shriveled away and sprouted back up like weeds: if one shut down for whatever reason, two might arise to take its place. "The IRC chat rooms kept going right along," says Dan Clements of CardCops. "The number of rooms increased, the number of hackers and ID thieves increased, and the volume of stolen data available on the channels increased, and that's continued to happen year after year after year."

Operation Firewall did have a measurable effect on the more sophisticated fraud Web sites, known as carding forums. The big-name English-language forums, CarderPlanet, Shadowcrew, Stealthdivision, and Darkprofits vanished from the Web. And for a few months, seasoned hackers and scammers scattered to smaller, foreign-language forums posted in Russian, Albanian, Spanish, Indonesian, and Vietnamese. "The little forums were always there; the little ones didn't get shut down; but if you didn't speak Russian or Vietnamese, your options were limited," says Clements.

But even as FBI chief Larkin posed for the cover of *BusinessWeek*, a phalanx of new English-language forums began to arise with names like CardersMarket, TalkCash, DarkProfits, TheVouched, UnixCrew, MazaFaka, and the aptly named International Association for the Advancement of Criminal Activity, or IAACA. Like CarderPlanet and Shadowcrew, these reconstituted forums were a throwback to the early days of the Web, when computer users gravitated to online communities formed to hash over topics ranging from aviation to zoology. In these forums communication took place not in real time, but by exchanging messages posted on bulletin boards arranged by topics and subtopics.

If the chat channels were the flea markets of cybercrime, then the carding forums functioned as well-run bazaars where buyers, sellers, middlemen, and service providers wheeled and dealed in a highly structured environment. The forums were organized and run by a hierarchy of system administrators, referred to as "admins," assisted by trusted moderators; the chain of command might have been taken straight off a standard corporate organizational chart. Each forum had security officers assigned to stay vigilant for conniving "rippers," double-crossing thieves who targeted other thieves. Rippers weaseled onto forums to prey on vendors and buyers of good standing. Security officers moved swiftly to ban rippers, but rippers could change nicknames as easily as changing socks, and slip back into action.

Then there was the specter of Wyatt Earp patrolling the cyberunderground to worry about. Cumbajohnny's escapades as a Secret Service informant would not soon be forgotten. The forum admins embraced the same security measures used by corporations: they began using encrypted Web pages and became much more selective about who they'd let participate on their message boards.

It went without saying that there was no way to keep federal agents, informants, and security analysts from assuming undercover personas to join the carding forums and monitor deals. The anonymity of the Internet cut both ways. Still, admins began insisting that initiates had to be "vouched" or "verified" by members in good standing, and a few imposed stiffer restrictions. IAACA, for instance, required anyone wishing to sell stolen credit card numbers to first provide ten examples confirmed by two trusted reviewers as being valid.

The admins also began banning the posting of any stolen data on public message boards, and explicitly discouraged any illegal transactions from actually being carried out on a public message board. You could openly discuss malware, stolen data, or scams on the public boards, but all nitty-gritty negotiations and transactions were to be consummated in one-to-one communiqués, via e-mail, cell phone, or a private chat channel.

The defunct CarderPlanet and Shadowcrew forums had set a high standard; CardersMarket, TalkCash, IAACA, and the rest built even more tightly run organizations. Competition heightened and specialties evolved. Highly efficient markets took shape for malicious software, stolen identity data, and the support services needed to convert stolen data to tangible goods and cash.

"The volume of trading in the various carding forums didn't slow down; quite the contrary, it accelerated," says Uriel Maimon, chief technology officer for RSA Security's consumer group.

Pricing structures solidified. A credit card number with expiration date and CVV or CVV2 code, good for a quick burst of online shopping, ran $7 to $200; a fake driver's license or birth certificate cost $150; a change of billing, or "cob,"—an online banking account log-in, complete with PIN or other data needed to change the billing address—would set you back $80 to $300, depending on the quality and extent of the data. Below is what a typical price list for stolen credit card numbers looked like. It was posted on the TalkCash forum on April 30, 2006:

```
We decided to offer a service for dumps selling on
this forum.
    Prices (per each, depends on order quantity):


USA
VISA/MC Classic/Standart/World <50pcs $15, >50pcs $13,
>100 pcs $11
VISA/MC Gold/Platinum/Business/Corporate/Signature
<50pcs $50, >50pcs $35, >100 pcs $30
AMEX $25
DISCOVER $30


CANADA
VISA/MC Classic/Standart/World <50pcs $20, >50pcs $17,
>100 pcs $15
VISA/MC Gold/Platinum/Business/Corporate/Signature
<50pcs $50, >50pcs $40, >100 pcs $35


EU, ASIA, OTHERS
VISA/MC Classic/Standart/ $100
VISA/MC Gold/Platinum/Business/Corporate/Signature $180
```

Unlike the wild-and-wooly IRC chat rooms, populated mostly by newbies, the carding forums fostered professional aplomb. Marketing 101 became de rigueur. Here's how one supplier of stolen credit card numbers with verification codes pitched his products:

~~ Cheapest CC/Cvv2 for you ~~, ᴧᴧ Give it a try ᴧᴧ

Hi everyone,

I'm just a newcomer here and I offer you a great service with cheapest prices. I sell mainly CC/Cvv2 US and UK. I also sell International Cvv2 if you want. I sold Cvv2 to some people in this forum. Check out their feedbacks for my service.

Payment:

I accept E-Gold and WebMoney

Terms of service:
-Payment must be done before CC/Cvv2 are sent.
-Order over 100 CC/Cvv2 get 10% discount.
-Order over 1000 CC/Cvv2 get 20% discount.
***I do replace new cards in case any died. ***

Contact details:
+PM (private message) me in the forum.
+E-mail me as cvvseller@gmail.com
+Yahoo ID: cvvseller
+ICQ (private chat): 311-099-344

Another vendor who specialized in supplying a high-end malicious code designed to hijack eGold accounts went so far as to prepare a video demo and include a link to a Web page for more information (eGold is an electronic currency backed by gold bullion, favored by cybercrooks because it converts funds into local currency and protects anonymity; the Web page probably ran on a zombie PC):

hi,

i sell the win32.grams trojan, a Trojan that steals
money and send to one of your accounts.

the price is $1000 for the EXE or $5000 for the SOURCE.

i can provide a video demo at demand.

for orders contact me at icq: 226-702-789

for more info visit

i would like to be reviewed for e-gold trojan

In the reconstituted carding forums, protocol prevailed. Vendors who specialized in related products and services congregated in assigned areas. Free research tools to do things like confirm the validity of a stolen credit card number or learn about security weaknesses at specific banks became widely available for community use. A few forums even began to offer escrow services, handling the details of large, complex deals for a fee, typically 4 percent to 8 percent of the value of the deal. Here's how TalkCash advertised its escrow service:

What(s) eScrow Service: As you know there are a lot of
rippers in world who don't believe in trading nicely
for this purpose we are introducing our own service
just like www.escrow.com but our commission is going
to be only 4%

How it'll WORK: Its easy you send us money which u've
to send to the seller we than ask seller to send you
the thing u want to buy from him and we've received
his money. Than we ask for proof of shipping and
finaly after doing all verifications and after

product's shipping we deduct our 4% processing fee from it and send the rest of the money to seller.

Benefits: Well you'll have a secure deal no chance of getting ripped. Other forums take from 5%-8% commission but we take only 4% commission. Your deals will be secure no fear of getting ripped or anything.

PLEASE DO NOT SEND US ILLEGAL MONEY

CHAPTER 11

Perception Challenge

Exploiters
March 27–29, 2005, Edmonton

Posing as Socrates, Biggie began setting up deals for which he would fail to carry out his end of the bargain. Jacques hustled to make side deals selling some of the cell's ID data to local drug dealers, though they had little clue how to cash in. Yolanda grew livid about the three-ring circus overrunning her apartment. When Jacques, who had had his driver's license suspended, left on an errand and failed to return with her Cavalier at the agreed-upon time, Yolanda went ballistic. She reached Jacques by cell phone.

"I'm, like, 'You fucking asshole, you're not supposed to be driving. I want my car! I want to go out!'" Yolanda recalls.

That touched off a tirade of threats from Jacques. Yolanda responded in kind: "He was driving my car and I didn't want him to. And he was angry at me because he can call me all these names on the phone but once I start doing it, then I'm the one in trouble. He'd call me whatever you can possibly imagine, make me feel really small. I couldn't handle it. I was feeding Biggie. I was feeding Socrates. I was cleaning up the bathroom constantly, cleaning up the kitchen if they tried to cook anything themselves. I was constantly cleaning up after this crap, right? And I was tired of that. It was, 'Jesus, get these people out of my house and give me car so I can leave!'"

A short time later, Jacques pulled into the apartment complex's parking lot, took a few moments to yank the fuses out of Yolanda's car, then stormed up the stairs. Before he could reach the apartment, Yolanda took an oversized screw and drove it into the faceplate of the dead-bolt lock on her front door, preventing the dead bolt from being turned to the unlocked position. Jacques pounded and kicked at the door. Yolanda refused to let him in. Each screamed obscenities at the other, drawing Socrates out of his lair. He advised Yolanda to let Jacques in. She refused. So Socrates got a screwdriver and began to remove the screw in the dead bolt.

Moist spring snow collected in drifts on the third-floor deck, just off the living room. Screaming hysterically, with no shoes on, Yolanda went out onto the deck, climbed over the wood railing, and swung herself onto the identical second-story deck below. Walter, a passive alcoholic, occupied the apartment below Yolanda's. He had become accustomed to the couple's boisterous battles.

"I had no shoes, no socks, and I just climbed down to the next balcony below," recalls Yolanda. "I woke Walter up. He was hungover or just drunk sleeping on the couch. He lets me in. Jacques came down, calling me a whore, a piece of shit, I'm going to kill you."

Walter managed to keep the couple apart as they argued at his door. Jacques threw a set of car keys at Yolanda, taunting her that she wasn't going anywhere, and went back up to her apartment. Yolanda made a phone call to Rodney, a drug dealer from her old Stadium neighborhood who had consoled her a couple of times after she and Jacques had fought. He was a hulking Native American who hung out with other drug dealers and petty thieves, none of whom had a car. Whenever Rodney was around, Yolanda felt safe. "I just said, 'I need to get out of here. I need my fuses back for my car. I guess I could drive you guys around a little, if you help me get my fuses back. He won't give them to me.' He's, like, 'OK. We'll be there in a couple of minutes. So they came over. I didn't know what their intentions were, actually. I didn't know how much they actually hated him."

About an hour after Yolanda placed the call for help, Rodney and three other denizens from her old Stadium neighborhood knocked on her apartment door. Socrates opened the door. Rodney said in a friendly tone that they were looking for Jacques, wanted to smoke a bowl with him. As the guests sauntered into the living room, one of them fell back and stepped into the kitchen. Socrates saw him grab a butcher knife from the kitchen counter.

Jacques was standing alert in the living room. He assented to smoking a bowl but said he needed to get a clean pipe. Just take him a second, he said; neighbor had it. Without waiting for an answer, Jacques slipped by the men out the front door and ran like hell. The four thugs took off after him, the one with the butcher knife leading the way. A foot chase in the dark ensued for several blocks. Jacques, who knew the neighborhood, got away.

Fifteen minutes later, the thugs again knocked on Yolanda's apartment door, but this time they were agitated and exuded menace. Assuming Jacques had circled back and was hiding inside, they threatened to kick the door in. So Socrates opened it.

"They rushed in. They're, like, 'Where the fuck is he. Where the fuck is he,'" recalls Socrates. "I'm, like, 'I dunno. He's not here.'"

The thugs gathered around Socrates's PC, the Golden Goose. They had heard stories about the cell's fraudulent activities and about Socrates's computer magic. They must have sensed that the twinkling hardware was far more valuable than it looked. Rodney improvised a line that he was confiscating the equipment until Jacques was man enough to face him.

"They're, like, 'Whose stuff is all this. We're taking it. You tell us where he is, and we'll give it back.'"

The thugs disconnected the computer gear and began hauling it out to the Cavalier. Socrates had a sinking feeling he would never see his prized machine ever again. His only solace: he was certain these clueless hoodlums would never crack his passwords or break the encryption protecting the zipped files holding the several thousand account profiles. Pulling a wad of bills from his sock, his last $120, Socrates asked Rodney if he would at least sell him an eight-ball. Rodney obliged. Sure, why not.

As the Cavalier sputtered out of the parking lot, its fuses inexpertly replaced, Socrates located a printout he knew lay amidst the litter. It was a list of his top twelve phished Royal Bank of Canada accounts. Just that afternoon, he had tested the accounts to confirm he could get in; he had tallied slightly over $2 million Canadian total in the accounts. Socrates figured if it came down to it, Jacques could get the drop accounts going again and together they could pull $40,000 to $50,000 out of the twelve accounts before the banks caught on and shut things down. They'd soon be back in business.

He folded the printout and tucked it into his sock, in the spot where he usually kept his cash. Then he loaded up a bowl of the crystals he had just purchased from Rodney. Still steaming over the turn of events, he fired up the bowl. He phoned Jacques and told him that the dealers had cleared out but were looking for him. The next morning Jacques showed up with an aluminum softball bat. Jacques's dad, Tony, had given him a ride. As Socrates and Tony hauled Jacques's possessions out to Tony's car, Jacques methodically slammed the bat into the apartment walls. He took particularly vicious whacks at anything that belonged to Yolanda, her framed photos and knickknacks, and for his coup de grâce, he obliterated the glass oven door.

Socrates rode out to Tony's place to help unload Jacques's possessions. Then he caught a ride back to Yolanda's apartment. He figured she would come back at some point to retrieve her beloved cat, Pringles, and might bring news about how he could get his hardware returned. Sitting on Yolanda's bed, Socrates wavered between hopelessness and optimism. Finally, he smoked the last of the eight-ball purchased from Rodney, and after the effects wore off, dropped into a semicomatose state, leaving the front door unlocked. Normally after a binge, he would sleep like a rock for two or three days. But Socrates would wake just a few hours later, heart racing, throat on fire, staring down the barrel of Detective Gauthier's .40-caliber Glock.

Enablers

Life Takes Visa

A crisply edited TV commercial appeared during breaks of the NFL playoff games leading up to the 2007 Super Bowl. A man in a drab sweater queues up in a fast-moving lunch line. Cooks shuffle deli meats like cards. Smoothies slide across a countertop like projectiles. Visa cards get swiped in rapid succession. The clueless man brings all this frenetic activity to a screeching halt, drawing dirty looks, by opening his wallet and reaching for crumpled bills to pay for his meal. "Life takes Visa," the narrator intonates. "Because money shouldn't slow you down."

The sales pitch echoes the one first articulated by the baton-wielding cartoon conductor in Bank of America's 1959 commercial: cash is passé; payment cards breed convenience and speed commerce. Visa's legendary first CEO, Dee Hock, and others who championed the notion of a cashless, checkless society would be pleased. Yet it has become clear that a card-based transactions system—a system conceived in the 1970s and security hardened in the 1980s and 1990s—may be wholly inadequate to stemming financial fraud as it is taking shape in the Internet-centric twenty-first century.

It turns out that the speed and automation infused into the global payments system—and now extending across the World Wide Web—is fueling a burgeoning cybercrime marketplace. In this dynamic arena, drug addicts and street crooks in affluent North American cities are able to form lucrative confederations with crime rings in Eastern Europe and other third world regions, where technical training is plentiful but jobs are scarce. In this vibrant new market, economic forces of supply and demand, convenience and customer service, specialization and reputation, are every bit as alive and at play as in the pork bellies market.

In the fast-emerging cybercrime industry, hackers and scam artists morph and advance magnitudes of order faster than the banking and tech industries have been willing to shore up basic security. From corporate America's point of view, convenience and speed are the drivers of the business models of the new millennium. Security is a perception challenge.

Nowhere is this philosophy more evident than in the debate over single-factor versus two-factor authentication. The former requires only a user ID and password to log on to an online banking account or payment service, such as PayPal or eGold; the latter requires physical confirmation that the user is who he or she claims to be. Thus two-factor authentication requires an added step: scanning of an access card or fingerprint impression; insertion of a USB security token; or use of a key fob that displays a changing pass code. It's not as convenient as single-factor authentication; like the drab man who insists on using crumpled bills, it slows down the economy. U.S. financial institutions spent the better part of 2004 and 2005 vigorously defending single-factor authentication and resisting the idea of widely moving to two-factor authentication. While U.S. banks balked, major banks in Europe and Asia began widely deploying two-factor authentication systems in 2005.

Two-factor authentication is not a cure-all, but it does make it less of a breeze for crooks to break into online accounts. Single-factor authentication has given rise to an array of online scams and has made account log-ins valuable commodities, harvested by keyloggers, phishing scams, or sophisticated man-in-the-middle attacks.

Keyloggers, those tiny programs that get implanted on a victim's hard drive by a virus or when a PC user clicks on a tainted Web page, increased by 250 percent between January 2004 and May 2006, according to antivirus software maker McAfee. Phishing expanded exponentially each year from 2003 through 2007, despite the concerted efforts of the Anti-Phishing Working Group, a consortium of big-name tech companies and financial institutions dedicated to its eradication. The pretenses used in phishing e-mails to lure even tech-savvy victims into clicking on links to counterfeit Web pages keep getting more clever and elaborate. The ruse often dupes the victim into typing in not just user IDs and passwords, but also Social Security numbers, credit card numbers, CVVs and CVV2s, and debit card PINs. The Anti-Phishing Working Group aggressively filters the Internet for phishing e-mail and continually hunts and shuts down phishing Web sites. Yet phishers have managed to stay several steps ahead. In 2006 phishing attacks doubled in volume as compared to 2004, and more people than ever were duped into clicking on dangerous links, according to Gartner Research. Phishing alerts posted by the Anti-Phishing Working Group multiplied 100-fold over that same two-year period. By the start of 2007, phishers had begun to focus on stealing larger sums from wealthier individuals, according to Gartner banking security analyst Avivah Litan.

While the war on phishing slogged on, lobbyists representing the financial services industry spent 2005 hammering on federal banking regulators to get them to back off a proposal to order U.S. banks to move to two-factor authentication. In the end, the Federal Financial Institutions Examination Council (FFIEC) ordered banks to adopt "stronger" authentication by the end of 2006. The FFIEC left it up to individual banks to consult with banking inspectors on how they complied with that guidance. More than two-thirds of U.S banks met the deadline, most by adding challenge-response questions to the log-in sequence, at least some of the time—such as when a user tries to log in from an unfamiliar PC. An example of a challenge-response question, beyond asking the user to type in a password, might be "What hometown was I born in?" or "What model car do I drive?"

Gartner's Litan observes that challenge-response programs "were already obsolete when the FFIEC deadline rolled around" and do nothing to block man-in-the-middle attacks, which, like keyloggers, are on the rise. In such attacks, the intruder waits for the victim to log on, then eavesdrops on the communication between the user and the bank. While the user does his or her online banking, the intruder quietly extracts funds.

Expediters
Plausible Deniability

When it comes to who gets to eat the losses from fraudulent activity, banks draw a marked distinction between individual consumers and small-business owners. Banks don't need the trust of its small-business customers in the same way they need consumers' trust. That's because small businesses must have access to banking services to survive. As the financial industry pushes Internet-based commerce to the fore, small businesses have had no choice but to go along for the ride under terms dictated by their banks.

Consider what happened to Joe Lopez, founder of Ahlo, a Miami-based ink and toner cartridge wholesaler. An irrepressible man with close-cropped dark hair, brown eyes, and a radiant smile, Lopez built Ahlo from scratch to annual sales of $20 million the old-fashioned way, one deal at a time. When it came time to pay his suppliers or receive payment from clients, Lopez made it a practice to drive down to his neighborhood Bank of America branch and execute wire transfers in person.

On each such trip to the bank, a teller never failed to urge Lopez to make the switch to an online business account, for convenience's sake. In October 2003, Lopez relented and opened an online business account. Not once during any of the relentless sales pitches, nor during the software installation, did any of the bank's representatives drill down on the security risks of online banking.

"They said it was safe," Lopez recalls from his office in a gritty industrial neighborhood.

On the morning of April 6, 2004, Lopez had a lot on his mind. His wife was nearing the end of a difficult pregnancy, and an important payment of $25,000 was due from a client in Venezuela. After accompanying his wife to a doctor's visit, Lopez hustled back to his office and logged on to his online business account. Noting an entry showing a large deposit from his Venezuelan client, he breathed a sigh of relief.

But then a wave of nausea struck. Lopez felt his left arm go numb. Below the deposit entry was a notation describing a fresh wire transfer of $90,348.65 to Deutsche Bank. "I thought I was going to vomit," he recalls, shaking his head. Ahlo had no business dealings in Europe.

Lopez immediately reported the robbery to a supervisor at Bank of America headquarters in North Carolina, who shut down online access and assigned a case number. The next day, Lopez and his assistant, Soraya Ahamed, worked the phones to retrieve Ahlo's cash. It became clear the bank was taking no steps to do so. "The bank didn't do anything," says Ahamed, Lopez's sister-in-law. "I thought Joe was going to have a heart attack."

Receiving no instructions from Bank of America, Deutsche, the intermediary bank, carried out instructions to forward the $90,348.65 to a personal account at Parex Bank in Riga, Latvia. The benefactor? A mysterious figure named Yanson Arnold, who showed up at Parex Bank the morning of April 7 and quietly withdrew $20,000 in cash.

Back in America, Joyce Munoz, a Bank of America customer-service manager, advised Lopez that a wire recall was under way and that Ahlo's account would soon be restored. Teresa Jones, a wire-room supervisor in North Carolina, subsequently told Lopez that the bank would issue a "provisional credit" to Ahlo in the amount of $90,348.65.

Relieved, Lopez resumed normal business dealings. After confirming the posting of the provisional credit, Lopez wired $25,908.74 to supplier Simon & Arrington in Fort Myers, Florida. A few hours later, Audrey Collins, from Bank of America corporate security, notified Lopez that the provisional credit for $90,348.65 had been frozen, pending further investigation of Arnold's claim of proper ownership of the money.

Two weeks later, Lopez's financial world came crashing down. He received a letter from Richard Heilbron, Jr., the bank's assistant general counsel. Heilbron took the position that since the theft could be traced to a security breach of Lopez's computer, the bank "was not in a position" to return Ahlo's cash.

The U.S. Secret Service, which is charged with investigating financial fraud, had gotten involved. Agents discovered a common data-stealing program, called Coreflood, embedded on Lopez's hard drive. A likely scenario: Lopez's teenaged son may have unwittingly surfed to a tainted Web page that implants Coreflood surreptitiously, bypassing the firewall and antivirus software Lopez assumed kept his home computer network safe. Coreflood carried a keylogger that took note when Lopez logged on to Ahlo's online business account and transmitted his user name and password back to the thief.

Armed with the Secret Service report, Heilbron invoked a provision of the Uniform Commercial Code, a collection of rules setting legal limitations and defining liability for commercial businesses. On the surface, the UCC has the imprimatur of independence because it is overseen by two private organizations: the National Conference of Commissioners on Uniform State Laws, and the American Law Institute.

In reality, attorneys representing financial institutions heavily influenced drafting of the rules, says Mark Budnitz, a professor at Georgia State University's College of Law. The banking industry interests saturate the UCC. For instance, Section 202 of Article 4A of the UCC provides that a customer order—authorized or not—is valid once the customer and bank agree on security and authentication procedures.

The rules make the bank responsible for "consequential damages" only if the bank explicitly agrees to be liable for such damages. Of course, most banks take pains to omit any such contract language. Thus the UCC has become a legal rampart for financial institutions to fend off a variety of lawsuits, says Budnitz. "The fingerprints of the lawyers representing financial institutions are all over this," says Budnitz. "That's not necessarily bad, because they understand the practicality of bank operations."

Practical daily operations are one thing. Yet banks can also use the UCC as a club to sweep aside claims from small-business customers like Lopez who are increasingly becoming victims of cybercrime. Budnitz has suggested adding provisions to various sections of the UCC so as to level the playing field somewhat for consumers and small businesses. But he says his ideas were shot down by attorneys representing financial institutions.

Indeed, in a letter to Lopez's attorney, Heilbron cited Article 4A of the UCC as rationale for assigning full responsibility for the robbery of Ahlo to Lopez.

The bank's internal investigation can "discount fraud or hacking at our end and . . . as a matter of law, the loss resulting from the payment order, even if unauthorized, is to be borne by your client and not the bank."

Bank of America canceled the $90,348.65 credit back to Lopez. Since normal business dealings had drawn Lopez's account down, at that point, to about $77,000, the bank claimed that Lopez was overdrawn $13,532.96. "Talk about adding salt to the wounds," Lopez says.

Arnold, the Latvian, would quietly slip into the shadows $20,000 richer, leaving $70,000 frozen at Parex Bank. Heilbron advised Lopez that Parex refused to return the money, and Bank of America had no legal recourse because it was a victim of fraud.

An exasperated Lopez was forced to sue the bank in February 2005, alleging breach of contract, negligence, breach of fiduciary duty, fraud and deceit, and intentional misrepresentation. He faced very long odds of prevailing. Corporate defense lawyers get paid handsomely by the hour to delay, distract, dissuade, and ultimately destroy individual plaintiffs. They maintain an unwavering focus on the endgame: making an example of the upstart plaintiff to discourage other individuals from filing similar lawsuits.

A time-honored corporate legal defense tactic is to engage in plausible deniability. It involves taking a position that can be defended by a very narrow interpretation of the facts, then daring the plaintiff to disprove the argument. To fend off Lopez, and discourage other small-business online account users from getting the same idea, Bank of America resorted to plausible deniability. After *USA Today* published a cover story about Lopez's plight in November 2005, Bank of America in mid-2006 agreed to a settlement.

Lopez's attorney, Ralph Patino, says his client was made whole but is constrained by the terms of the settlement from saying anything more. Patino says cybercrooks are preying on small merchants like never before, and an increasing number are left twisting in the wind. He says he's heard anecdotally about scores of small business that lose several thousands of dollars through theft from their online business accounts and are never able to recover any of it.

"I know it's happening on a wide scale. What's happening is you're getting individual merchants losing small amounts of money, $5,000, $10,000, $15,000 a crack, and they have no legal recourse because no one in the world is going to sue Bank of America over $15,000," Patino says.

Bank of America spokeswoman Betty Reiss said it was difficult for the bank to respond to Patino's assertion since she had "no idea where the attorney is getting his information or what it is based on." Reiss laid out the bank's final position: the Lopez case had nothing to do with online banking. "It is a wire transfer product used over a PC. But it was not online banking," says Reiss.

CHAPTER 12

Larger Rings

Exploiters

April–May 2005, Grass Valley, California

A few weeks after the Edmonton cell suffered a meltdown in Yolanda's Mill Woods apartment, Karl, a thirty-eight-year-old former cabdriver living in the rural Sierra Nevada foothills east of Sacramento, was about to embark on his brief career as a cybercriminal. In April 2005, Karl picked up a copy of his local newspaper, the *Grass Valley Union*, and, as was his habit, turned immediately to the help wanted ads in search of promising opportunities. An enticing pitch caught his eye:

> Look at this! WORK at Home! Corres-
> pondence manager vacancies. MAIL
> PACKAGES from home without
> Leaving your current job. Easy!
> Ship parcels from our clients. Get
> Paid $24 per parcel! Info:
> http://kflogistics.biz/vacancies.asp.htm.

To Karl, the prospect of getting paid to ship packages from home in his spare time seemed like a godsend. He had dabbled in online marketing and was studying to get his real estate license. Someday he hoped to start a small business with his father-in-law and a friend. Something like this could tide him over. Karl applied online and quickly landed the job. Soon digital cameras and laptop computers began arriving at his house. Karl dutifully transferred the goods to new packages and affixed new shipping labels, sent to him as an e-mail attachment, which he printed out on his home printer. Off the packages went to Moscow and other Eastern European postal addresses.

Karl had become an unwitting cybercriminal—a mule toiling for a reshipping ring. Reshippers specialize in credit card fraud and money-laundering rings. Mules serve two pivotal roles: they help keep goods and cash flowing through a tightly run distribution system, and they insulate their employers from detection. Should anyone try to track a suspicious order, the original tracking number indicates the mule as the sender.

"It's like a high-end fencing operation," says security consultant John Pironti, chief information risk strategist at Getronics. "The idea is to move this stuff overseas and to eliminate traceability."

Over a three-week period in April 2005, Karl reshipped half a dozen parcels for kflogistics.biz. He followed e-mail instructions from someone who identified himself as Michael Birman, the same name listed as the Web site's domain registrant. Occasionally, Karl spoke to Birman on the phone. In contrast to the polished text written in perfect English on the kflogistics.biz Web site, Birman wrote e-mail instructions in stilted English and spoke with a heavy Russian accent. Karl recalls Birman once bragging that he managed a network of 200 reshippers.

Karl began to get uneasy about what he was doing, although he hadn't fully formed his suspicions. So he began to keep a paper trail of his dealings with Birman. The authors investigated the paper trail and pieced together this chronology of a reshipment in motion:

April 18. Kflogistics.biz charges $1 on iWon.com, a prize-give-away Web page, using a Chase Bank One Visa credit card number stolen from Brian Spoutz, forty-eight, of San Jose, California. The nominal transaction serves as a test to confirm that the card is active.

April 20. Kflogistics.biz uses Spoutz's Visa card to place an online order at Newegg.com for a $2,607 digital camera and extra memory. Shipments in two separate parcels are directed for delivery to a home in Gilroy, California.

April 22. FedEx attempts to deliver the parcels. But the reshipper in Gilroy, for some reason, rejects the delivery. Using FedEx's online tracking service, Birman, the handler, notices the failed delivery. Birman then contacts FedEx and redirects delivery to Karl in Grass Valley. Next, Birman alerts Karl via e-mail to watch for the two parcels.

April 23. Birman surfs to USPS.com. Using a stolen credit card number, he purchases a $48 Global Express Mail shipping label addressed to Roman Radeckiy, Oktaybrski Ave., Moscow; he e-mails the new shipping label as a JPEG image file to Karl. Birman's e-mail includes instructions for Karl to combine the two parcels into one box, affix the label, and mail the box to Radeckiy.

April 24. FedEx delivers the two parcels to Karl in Grass Valley.

April 27. Karl prints out the JPEG label, repacks the camera and memory into one box, affixes the Global Express Mail label, and completes the reshipment.

"The operation was amazing," says Karl. "It was highly coordinated." Karl might have continued as a reshipper had Birman paid him $24 a parcel as promised. Instead, Birman tried to manipulate Karl into deeper money-laundering activities. Things began to unravel in early May once Karl began to press Birman for a paycheck.

Birman responded by asking Karl if he had an online account at Chase Bank One, Citibank, or Washington Mutual into which kflogistics.biz could deposit his pay. Birman probably already had fraudulent access to a portfolio of hijacked accounts in those banks, and was maneuvering to sweep Karl's account into that mix. Karl balked at first but discussed the matter with his bank manager, Paul Shelton, who promised to keep an eye out for any suspicious activity. Karl then gave the routing and account numbers for his checking account at the Nevada City branch of Bank of America.

A few days later, on May 5, an unusual deposit of $4,358 arrived in Karl's Bank of America checking account. The funds came from Chase Bank

One. "It caught my eye because it was an electronic credit card transfer," says Shelton. "That's not something you see every day."

That night Karl was contacted by e-mail by someone identifying himself as George Selembo, financial supervisor for kflogistics.biz. (The real George Selembo, fifty-five, was a quality-control inspector in Greensburg, Pennsylvania. In 2003, a cyberthief electronically transferred nearly $9,000 from Selembo's First Commonwealth bank account to an overseas account. No one was ever arrested. Selembo spent nine months resolving the matter, and got his money back, but his name and other personal data continued to circulate in the stolen data pool. His reaction when one of the authors contacted him to ask if he knew anything about kflogistics.biz: "You're saying that someone may be posing as me? Wow!")

Via e-mail, the supervisor calling himself George Selembo instructed Karl to "please withdraw the whole amount" and send $4,011 via Western Union to Andrey Jaremchuk, in St. Petersburg, Russia. Karl could then keep the remainder—$347—as his pay. "It set off an alarm; something was definitely wrong," Karl says. "I didn't take any of the money. I knew it was time to call the police."

Karl reported the matter to the Nevada County Sheriff. Shelton, his banker, froze the $4,358. That triggered an acrimonious e-mail Selembo sent to Karl on Friday night, May 6:

What?!!?? Give me the bank's [sic] manager phone. How
long do they plan to keep your money frozen???

On Monday afternoon, May 9, a male caller reached Shelton on the phone. The banker doesn't recall how the caller, who spoke with a heavy accent, identified himself. The caller claimed to have been cheated out of $4,300 by Karl, and asked Shelton to return the funds. Shelton advised the caller to file a police report. Shelton never heard from anyone about the money again. The next day, Karl received a final e-mail from Selembo:

I tried calling you a LOT of times. Reached only
voice-mail. When will you be home?

Karl turned the e-mail over to authorities. "They made it clear they wanted the money withdrawn," a nervous Karl recalls. "It began to freak me out. The tone of the messages were more threatening. I just wanted them to leave me alone."

But kflogistics.biz wasn't done with Karl yet. In late April, he began receiving regular mail intended for online banking customers from all around the nation. The letters—account statements, notices of credit limit increases, and discrepancy warnings—kept arriving in Karl's mailbox through June, long after he had broken off communications with Birman and Selembo. Without Karl's permission, his former employers were now using his mailing address as a drop point for account statements linked to hot accounts.

One of the first things fraudsters do is change the billing address on an account they've created or gained access to. Many online banking patrons, not receiving any bills or reports in the mail, don't notice for a month or two. Until the account holder reports a problem, the account stays active and online transactions get electronically approved.

One such letter Karl received shed light on how the $4,358 credit card transfer was executed. The letter, dated May 5, was a notice from Chase Bank One Visa to cardholder Ryan Sesker, twenty-eight, a banking loan officer in Des Moines, Iowa. Chase notified Sesker that his online request for a credit limit increase to $5,000, from $3,500, had been approved.

But Sesker never made such a request, and he never got the letter, which was mailed to Karl. Sesker didn't even know his account had been tampered with until one of the authors contacted him in late May. Sesker said he rarely used his Chase Bank One Visa. The last two transactions he recalled were made more than a year earlier, when he made online purchases of a computer printer and a Valentine's Day gift. By March 2005, Sesker had paid the balance down to zero, so the account wasn't on the top of his mind.

Upon notifying Chase of the break-in, Sesker learned someone had not only changed his billing address, but also the date of birth and mother's maiden name associated with the account. About a week after Chase approved the credit limit boost to $5,000, the bank next approved an electronic credit card transfer of $4,300 to a different account—the same kind of credit card transfer that put $4,358 into Karl's account. None of the speedy, sophisticated security systems in place set off any red flags, or, if they did, Chase ignored them.

Why less than $5,000? Just as the white plastic card scammers in the 1960s maneuvered around the $50-per-transaction floor limit, Birman and Selembo well knew federal regulators don't investigate or prosecute fraud unless the aggregate loss exceeds $5,000. Chase declined to tell Sesker who the funds were transferred to. The bank indicated that he would not be held responsible, then asked him if he would like a new Bank One Visa credit card number. Sesker declined. He says had he not noticed the breach for a couple more months, his credit might have become tainted and his career put at risk; a clean credit history is a condition of employment for loan officers.

"They probably would have been sending delinquency notices and collection letters to the wrong address," says Sesker. "I would have never have known until the collection agencies tried to track me down."

Enablers

Titanic Attack

While the financial services industry battled phishers and grappled with whether to toughen authentication and thus erode the convenience factor of online banking, cybercriminals stormed new fronts. A titanic coordinated attack that hit in February 2006 revealed a huge unaccounted-for gap in the global payments system.

Reports began to pour into at least eight major banks about a tidal wave of fraudulent cash withdrawals being made at ATMs in Canada, Great Britain, Eastern Europe, Russia, and South Korea. Counterfeit debit cards tapping the accounts of U.S. bank patrons were being used to make cash withdrawals of $1,000 to $2,500. The thieves somehow had obtained ready access to the PINs for each debit card.

As a rule, banks and big retailers will do everything possible to keep details about customer data breaches undisclosed for obvious reasons. But in this case at least 600,000 accounts were compromised. The eight banks—Citigroup, Bank of America, Wells Fargo, Washington Mutual, JPMorgan Chase, Wachovia, National City, and PNC Financial—would be forced to reissue debit cards to at least that many customers. Assuming each debit card holder got nicked for $1,000, that meant the banks would have to refund $600 million.

The scale of this attack was so massive, involving police, bank officials, and victims in several states, that reporters from the *San Francisco Chronicle*, CNET.com, the *New York Times*, and American Banker were able to piece together a fairly complete scenario of what must have happened. American Banker reported that data thieves were able to crack into databases holding debit card information stored at thirty of 945 OfficeMax stores, mainly on the West Coast and in the Southeast. OfficeMax spokesman William Bonner insisted to every reporter who asked that the company had "no knowledge of a security breach." Yet local police investigators, bank officials, and victims all pointed to the Itasca, Illinois–based office supply retail chain as the common denominator.

San Francisco Chronicle columnist David Lazarus flushed out what appeared to be a smoking gun. Lazarus interviewed Oakland resident Alicia Vagts, thirty-four, who patronized the OfficeMax in Sacramento while attending law school. Vagts discovered that someone in Estonia had used her Washington Mutual debit card—the same one she used regularly at OfficeMax—to go on a $2,500 spree. "I barely knew where Estonia was," Vagts told Lazarus.

Investigators began pursuing the theory that hackers somehow broke into Internet-connected computer servers that stored the data embedded on the magnetic stripe, or magstripe, of debit cards used in each store's daily sales. It's child's play to transfer magstripe data to blank magnetic striped cards, which are readily available for sale on the Internet. A popular tool for transferring the data is the MSR206 Manual Swipe Magnetic Card Reader/Writer. It sells for $425 on the Internet.

PIN data is another matter. PINs are typically keyed in separately by the consumer. According to the Payment Card Industry (PCI) Data Security Standard, merchants are prohibited from storing PINs, even in encrypted form. The PCI rules represent the latest iteration of data-handling security standards Visa and MasterCard have been separately trying to impose on merchants and credit card issuers for years with limited success.

The PCI rules set forth how merchants should store sensitive customer data and require regular testing of Web sites for security holes. Merchants or their acquiring banks who don't comply could face fines of up to $500,000 per incident or be denied the ability to process Visa or MasterCard transactions.

But PCI is controversial. Some merchants complain that it is too costly to implement, requiring additional staff or expensive consultants to install and test new systems. Whether OfficeMax routinely stored PINs has not been disclosed. However, it is a fact that many payment systems are programmed by default to store encrypted PIN data, which is a violation of the PCI standards. And many merchants may be unaware that they are routinely storing PINs.

However the crooks obtained the PINs, they still needed a way to unencrypt them. They could have done that by stealing the decoder, called the PIN blocks. Or they might have used brute-force hacking—testing every possible PIN combination for each card.

Whatever the case, it marked the first time criminals were able to purloin magstripe data with accompanying PINs for hundreds of thousands of debit cards and orchestrate withdrawals on a global scale. "This is the worst hack to date," Gartner analyst Litan told CNET.com at the time. "All the other hacks were trying to get to this hack. For criminals, this is the pot of gold."

It was also a sign of things to come. Phishers and keyloggers steal logins from one individual at a time. By contrast, hacking into the payment systems of big retailers, convenience store chains, and gas stations allows crime rings to abscond with magstripe data for tens of thousands of payment cards in one fell swoop.

Retail chains formerly transferred daily credit and debit card sales data gathered at cash registers, or point-of-sale (POS) terminals, back to a central computer server via dial-up phone connections. But today much of that data flows over the Internet. It's a safe bet that thieves at this very moment are trying to break the passwords to intercept data flowing from POS terminals across the Internet to computer server hubs. Gartner's Litan estimated that by 2008 more than 50 percent of attacks against retailers will be directed at their POS systems and by 2009 only 30 percent of POS systems will be compliant with PCI rules.

"The biggest weak point right now is [that] everywhere you shop and everywhere you do business electronically," says Litan.

On January 7, 2007, security cameras trained on an ATM machine in front of the Kon Thai Pub in bustling Patong Beach on Thailand's popular Phuket Island caught a couple of Sri Lankan tourists acting suspiciously. Police arrested Pathmathas Ganeshamoorthy, twenty-six, and Srikanthan

Veerasingam, twenty-nine, after the pair used a counterfeit payment card to withdraw money from the ATM.

According to local news reports, police turned down a bribe and confiscated a laptop computer, 2,703 fake white payment cards, and three USB thumb drives from a silver Honda used by the men. Police gathered another 2,533 fake cards, 483 of them plain green and the rest white, from the suspects' hotel room, along with an MSR206 card magnetic-stripe reader and encoder.

Police also arrested Sivagnanam Gnanakanthan, thirty-five. Detectives told local reporters that the men appeared to be part of a much larger ring operating in popular tourist areas throughout Thailand and other parts of the world, as the cards in their possession were similar to cards seized in Bangkok and Chon Buri encoded with magstripe data from active British bank accounts.

The drab man in the "Life takes Visa" commercial who insists on using cash may have it right after all. Bills and coins may not be as quick and convenient as plastic. But they're much harder to steal than digital currency.

Expediters
Clever Laundering

George Rodriguez counts himself among the well-informed and technically savvy. He's one of the hundreds of millions of consumers for whom Internet commerce has become second nature. By his early forties, Rodriguez had done well enough as an investment banking tech consultant to set himself up as a partner in a commercial real estate start-up, Waterstone Capital Partners, in Gastonia, North Carolina, a rural hamlet twenty miles south of Charlotte.

After diligent research, conducted mostly on the Internet, he socked away $60,000 in equities, purchasing shares in a dozen U.S. giants. He did this on his own, opening an account with online broker TD Ameritrade. He had no intention of ever becoming an active trader. The equities were strictly a long-term investment, the cornerstone of Rodriguez's retirement nest egg. To collect dividends and execute occasional trades, he had linked his TD Ameritrade account to a Wachovia Securities online banking account. Without question, the convenience of online transactions was compelling. It was also comforting. Rodriguez could check on his nest egg anytime the notion struck, from any Internet-connected computer, simply by typing in his TD Ameritrade user name and password.

The last thing Rodriguez expected when he logged in to his e-mail account the morning of May 5, 2005, were messages from TD Ameritrade confirming his requests to liquidate his holdings in Disney, American Express, and other blue-chip companies. Rodriguez quickly logged on to his TD Ameritrade account and watched, stunned, his heart racing, as an unseen stranger—obviously in possession of his account user name and password—liquidated positions in one company after another. Citibank. Sold. Cisco Systems. Sold. American Express. Sold.

"My entire portfolio was being sold out right before my eyes," recalls Rodriguez. "Minutes seemed like hours. My life was unraveling on a computer screen in front of me."

Horrified, Rodriguez picked up the phone and hurriedly called a TD Ameritrade customer rep. More transactions flashed across his monitor. Citigroup. Sold. Applied Materials. Sold. AstraZeneca International. Sold.

The day before, in preparation for the sell-off, someone had logged on to his TD Ameritrade account and discontinued the Wachovia link, instead designating proceeds from stock trades to be transferred to a Bank of America online account. Rodriguez acted in time to stop settlement of the trades, freeze his account, and preserve his holdings.

Had he not gone online when he did, proceeds from the sale of his nest egg would have vanished within three days, the time it takes to settle stock trades. "If I had been on vacation and had no access to e-mail, I would have been cleaned out," Rodriguez said.

More revelations were forthcoming. Bank of America confirmed that Rodriguez's TD Ameritrade account had been recently linked to an account in Austin, Texas, but refused to disclose the identity of the account holder, citing privacy regulations. Rodriguez took the matter to a local detective, Cody "J.C." Luke, who traced the Bank of America account to Kevin Maguire, fifty-three, of Austin, Texas. Contacted by one of the authors, Maguire said he was a manager of travel for a major corporation, and had "no idea" what happened to his account. He said Bank of America informed him of the incident but told him little else. "They just told me this stuff happens," Maguire says.

TD Ameritrade, likewise, did not seem too excited about what had happened to Rodriguez. Kurt McDonald, a fraud-ID theft analyst at TD Ameritrade, sent Rodriguez a one-page letter asserting that "there was no indication at the time these orders were placed that they were unauthorized. As a one-time courtesy to you, TD Ameritrade cancelled the unauthorized transactions. Going forward, you are responsible for any transactions placed in your account."

"They treated me as if I screwed up," Rodriguez says.

Police and cybersecurity experts say what happened to Rodriguez had all the earmarks of an increasingly common rip-off perpetrated by individuals or small groups of cyberthieves who use e-mail and instant messaging to communicate and spontaneously form and dissolve alliances.

"It's a very interesting crowd," says retired Edmonton economic crimes detective Al Vonkeman. "They're very networked, which is quite a bit different than any other drug or organized crime group we see. It's quite social, and they share their ideas and they share their crimes and information about the scams that they find work. But they only know the people they deal with by first name or by a nickname. And most are known by nicknames."

It is probable that two or more groups of specialists, communicating over the Internet, collaborated to tap into Rodriguez's account. A drop-account specialist—an individual or a cell much like the one in Edmonton—probably breached Maguire's account in Texas and made it available to the crooks who tapped into Rodriguez's TD Ameritrade account.

Once proceeds from the stock sale landed safely in the Texas account, the funds probably would have been transferred a few more times until they landed in an account controlled by an accomplice in cahoots with the drop specialists. The accomplice tasked to make the withdrawal would send part of the loot back to the TD Ameritrade hackers via a Western Union wire, closing the loop. Bouncing illicitly obtained funds among several accounts is called "laundering," a time-honored criminal specialty made much, much easier by the Internet and by an automated, built-for-speed payments system. Laundering makes tracing back to the original source of the money difficult, thus lowering the risk of arrest for all the coconspirators.

In the months after Rodriguez's discovery, cybercrooks stampeded online brokerages. By October 2006, E-Trade Financial Corporation, the nation's fourth-largest online broker, was forced to disclose $18 million in fraud losses in its third fiscal quarter alone. TD Ameritrade, the third-largest online broker, along with top online broker Charles Schwab, declined to disclose fraud losses, but nonetheless said they too would reimburse clients for any losses from online theft, though they were not required by any legal obligations to do so.

During a conference call to discuss earnings, E-Trade CEO Mitchell H. Caplan blamed "concerted rings" in Eastern Europe and Thailand and noted that the Securities and Exchange Commission, Secret Service, and FBI were actively investigating online brokerage scams.

"I think that this thing is so widespread and it's such a significant impact on the industry at large, and you have so many players involved in this, not only from Wall Street, but also . . . the SEC and the Secret Service and the FBI and everybody else that I think you're going to end up seeing structural changes in the industry," Caplan predicted.

Aleksey Kamardin, a twenty-one-year-old Russian student, allegedly got his piece of the action. According to an SEC complaint, Kamardin was living with a fellow Russian-born roommate in a Tampa Bay, Florida, apartment on July 13, 2006, when he opened an E-Trade online trading account.

Over the next six weeks, Kamardin acquired positions in seventeen small, thinly held public companies, referred to as "penny stocks." Meanwhile, others acting in concert broke into online trading accounts at E-Trade, Scottrade, TD Ameritrade, JP Morgan Chase, and Charles Schwab, the SEC says. Much like what happened to Rodriguez, the intruders sold off holdings. But instead of trying to extract the cash, they orchestrated what's known as a "pump-and-dump" scam. They used the proceeds to buy stock in Kamardin's seventeen penny stocks, driving up the share price.

At the moment the share price jumped, Kamardin sold off positions, making a profit, totaling $82,960.18, in fourteen trades. In late August, Kamardin transferred the funds to his roommate's bank account; the roommate then wired the loot to a bank in Riga, Latvia. The SEC believes Kamardin fled the United States to Russia to conceal his whereabouts.

Kamardin was by no means the only practitioner of pump-and-dump scams. In a more elaborate caper busted up by the SEC, twenty individuals, listing residences in Russia, Latvia, Lithuania, and the British Virgin Islands, set up multiple brokerage accounts at www.parex.lv, an online brokerage run by Riga, Latvia–based Parex Bank—the same bank that took receipt of $90,000 transferred from Joe Lopez's small-business account. The gang then began acquiring an array of penny-stock companies.

Using stolen user names and passwords, intruders broke into online trading accounts at E-Trade, Charles Schwab, TD Ameritrade, Scottrade, Vanguard Brokerage Services, Fidelity Investments, and Merrill Lynch, the SEC says. At an appointed time, the intruders would sell off the entire portfolio in a hijacked account and use the proceeds to buy shares in penny stocks held by the gang of twenty in the Parex Bank accounts.

For instance, on February 9, 2006, someone sold off the portfolios in breached accounts at TD Ameritrade, Scottrade, and E-Trade and used the proceeds to buy enough shares in Remote Dynamics, a Richardson, Texas, tech firm, to drive the share price from 29 cents to $1.10. That same day, the Parex account holders sold 512,200 shares of Remote Dynamics, clearing a $75,720 profit. The ring pulled off fourteen other similar scams, costing the brokerages more than $2 million to make the account holders whole, says John Reed Stark, chief of the SEC's Office of Internet Enforcement.

In March 2007, the SEC moved in and froze $732,941 allegedly accumulated by the gang of twenty in the Parex Bank online trading account, on grounds that the proceeds came from manipulating trades in hijacked accounts to drive up the share price of penny stocks owned by the gang.

"The victims woke up in the morning, and all their blue-chip stocks were gone," says Stark. "All they were left with was a bunch of worthless stock."

CHAPTER 13

Public Acceptance

Exploiters

Summer 2005, Global

In the summer of 2005, recruitment ads seeking U.S-based reshippers like Karl could be found all over popular employment Web sites such as Monster.com, JobFinder.com, and CareerBuilder.com. The authors identified twenty-one reshipping operations, similar to kflogistics.biz, running such recruitment ads linked to polished Web sites set up to disseminate professional-looking online job applications to prospective mules.

The recruitment ads and Web site hosting services were most likely paid for with stolen credit card numbers. Criminals know that investigations of suspect online payments only go so far, especially if nominal amounts are involved. The *Grass Valley Union*'s records, for instance, showed that kflogistics.biz paid for the classified ad that attracted Karl with a credit card number linked to a Milford, Michigan, billing address. No one from the Union actually spoke to the ad buyer, who used the credit card to pay $427.97. No one ever stepped forward to challenge the transaction, according to a spokeswoman for the newspaper.

Similarly, a reshipping group going by the name of U.S. Mail Service used a credit card to pay $97 for a three-month ad on JobFinder.com. JobFinder CEO David Lizmi could not confirm that a stolen card number was used to pay for the online ad. But Lizmi says he pulled the ad after receiving a complaint. No one from U.S. Mail Service ever contacted Lizmi for a prorated refund.

"Nothing can be done to prevent this type of ad," contends Lizmi. "I would have to hire twenty people to contact every company individually and vouch for their ID. It's like someone posing as something they aren't on an online dating service. Buyer beware."

Monster.com and CareerBuilder.com officials say they deploy teams to screen advertisement orders, investigate complaints, and educate customers about scams. But fraudsters easily skirt such defenses by changing names and Web sites every few months, a trivial matter. Web site domain names can be purchased for $6 a month; space on computer servers to collect job applicant data, $15 a month. As long as the credit card payment gets approved, no questions are asked. "Registering a domain name and putting up a Web site to perpetrate these schemes is easy and cheap," says Joe Stewart, senior security researcher at SecureWorks.

If anyone should complain or begin investigating, the reshippers simply move on and set up shop under another domain name on a different server. "Just fill in the information, use a credit card to pay, and you're up and running in less than half an hour," says Stewart.

Kflogistics.biz, for instance, registered its domain name and launched its Web site in April 2005, just prior to the *Grass Valley Union* publishing the help wanted ad that enticed Karl. It almost certainly had been operating under other names prior to that time. A similar reshipper, westernforce.biz, for a time used the same Internet protocol address as Kflogistics.biz. "So they've moved on to a different name, but I bet it's the same people," says Stewart.

The name, kflogistics.biz, in fact, imitated an existing Web site, kflogistics.com, registered by a legitimate El Paso, Texas, freight-forwarding company. The copycat Web site listed Michael Birman as its registrant, along with a New York mailing address and phone number. However the e-mail address associated with Birman in the Web site registration, tyler052@yandex.ru, routed his e-mail to Russia.

The authors' attempts to contact Birman and kflogistics.biz were unsuccessful. Most Web site registration data is "almost certainly bogus," says Stewart. "It would be stupid for them to use real information; there's no need to."

Reshippers continue to dupe and recruit U.S.-based mules because America is teeming with unemployed and underemployed able-bodied citizens hungry to earn extra income, law enforcement officials say. "It's very frustrating to track something to a house in Texas—only to find a retired seventy-four-year-old housewife," says a veteran U.S. postal inspector, who asked to go unnamed. "As long as they are paid, they don't ask questions."

Irene Rodriguez, thirty-eight, a bulk-mail handler from San Jose, California, regularly surfed employment Web sites, like Monster.com and CareerBuilder.com, looking for opportunities to earn extra income. Hoping to pay for her daughter's senior ball gown, Rodriguez responded to a U.S.

Mail Service pitch she spotted on JobFinder.com. U.S. Mail Service offered $30 to $50 per reshipped package.

"When you see a job listed on a respected Web site, you think it's legitimate," says Rodriguez. "I thought this was a legal company."

About the same time, Lynn Malito, forty-six, single mother of two, got laid off from her job as a dispatcher for a food and drugs distributor in Memphis, Tennessee. Malito responded to an ad on CareerBuilder.com to handle reshipping chores for Estonian FF. She also considered similar job offers from CNETEXPRESS and TSR Corp. she found on Monster.com

Like Karl, Rodriguez and Malito toiled as reshipping mules but cut off their activities and reported their experiences to authorities after becoming suspicious about the work and nervous about their involvement. "It petrified me," says Malito. "I thought I was going down, getting arrested, for my role in this."

However, only the most egregious mules—those who reship products over several months, for example—run the risk of getting prosecuted. Most are viewed as unwitting victims dealing in goods of incidental value not worth pursuing, law enforcement officials say.

Enablers

Fluid Numbers

As the most populous and productive of the fifty United States, California boasts what is arguably the nation's richest, most diverse economy. It produces great wine, cutting-edge technology, and A-list celebrities. And in the digital age, the Golden State has earned one other distinction: it has emerged as a privacy champion. With hackers and scammers finding endless ways to steal and make use of sensitive data, California in 2005 became the first state in the nation to enact a data-breach disclosure law. Any company, government agency, institution, or organization in control of sensitive data, and doing business in California, is required to notify any individual whose information becomes lost or stolen. One of the first companies to run into California's pioneering disclosure law was ChoicePoint, the giant data broker duped by Olatunji Oluwatusin, Mr. O.

To meet the California law, ChoicePoint in early February 2005 quietly sent letters to 35,000 Californians notifying them that their data had turned up missing. The letters divulged no details about how a scammer sitting in a North Hollywood condo was so easily able to acquire the data. Word soon reached MSNBC reporter Bob Sullivan, who broke the news story about ChoicePoint's California disclosures on Valentine's Day. Not long after MSNBC posted Sullivan's story on the Internet, the heretofore obscure data-handling giant tucked away in a nondescript business park twenty miles north of Atlanta burst into the global spotlight.

Major daily newspapers in Los Angeles, San Jose, Atlanta, Miami, New York, Washington, D.C., and London jumped on the story. It was widely reported that the Alpharetta, Georgia–based company possessed 10 billion records on individuals and businesses, sold data to 40 percent of the nation's top 1,000 companies, as well as supplied thirty-five government agencies, including several law enforcement agencies, with data on individuals.

Launched as a spin-off of Equifax in 1997, ChoicePoint had emerged, along with Lexis-Nexis and Acxiom, to form the big three data brokers. While the big three credit bureaus—Equifax, Experian, and TransUnion—fulfilled the narrow mission of assembling credit reports based on histories of loans and loan payments, the big three data brokers covered everything else. Using advanced data-mining technologies, the data brokers assembled names, addresses, property records, and other public records into individual data dossiers. The contents of such dossiers—Social Security numbers, birth dates, maiden names, criminal records, civil judgments, and real estate records—proved to be in high demand from diverse parties. Lenders, landlords, and employers wanted as much data as they could get their hands on to size up applicants; law enforcement officials wanted it to track down criminals and terrorists.

But the revelation that two-bit Nigerian scam artists could so blithely pass themselves off as legitimate businesses and so easily purchase thousands of dossiers touched a raw nerve with privacy advocates. California state senator Jackie Speier blasted ChoicePoint for not disclosing the breach sooner and for being fooled by unsophisticated criminals. ChoicePoint officials countered that they had needed time to set up a complaints center, and that only a handful of people, at most, were ever shown to be victims of actual fraud stemming from use of the stolen data.

New York state representative James Brennan nonetheless called for the suspension of existing contracts with the data giant unless ChoicePoint agreed to notify any New York residents whose data had been stolen; New York at the time had no data-breach disclosure law. It does now. Within days of Sullivan's scoop, ChoicePoint announced that it would send out 110,000 more disclosure letters nationwide. And thus began the game of fluid numbers. In the George Clooney movie *Good Night, and Good Luck*, newsreel footage of Senator Joseph McCarthy repeatedly shows him adjusting the number of communists he asserts work inside the federal government, continually testing what the public will accept. Similarly, ChoicePoint adjusted its public references to the number of people whose data were stolen—and the subset of those who also had fraud committed with their data. It gave police investigators one set of estimates and news reporters another set.

Asked by the authors how many people whose data were stolen actually became fraud victims, ChoicePoint spokesman Matt Furman made this assertion in May 2007: "It is very hard for us to tell from afar. Some of the indictments list names of victims; some just assert a number. The range, as far as we can divine, is between five and forty-five and we really don't know anything more than that."

That estimate flatly contradicts intelligence the company provided to the L.A. County Sheriff in February 2005. The *Los Angeles Times* reported at the time that investigators were examining reports of some 750 people whose personal data had been used to buy jewelry, consumer electronics, and computers. Similarly, ChoicePoint for months insisted 145,000 was the maximum number of profiles stolen. But that figure quietly rose in public references to 163,000. Then in a February 2007 *New York Times* story, for which ChoicePoint senior executives were extensively interviewed, the number morphed to 166,000. Asked about the 166,000 figure, Furman would say only that the company does not dispute it.

By maintaining the public perception that the total number of profiles stolen from ChoicePoint was in the low six figures, the company artfully diverted attention from a much higher estimate given to Detective Decker. Shortly after Mr. O's arrest, ChoicePoint advised Decker that the number of stolen profiles ran well into the seven figures, 4 million to be precise. Decker believes that estimate is closer to the truth. He even gave sworn testimony about it at Mr. O's preliminary hearing presided over by L.A. County

Commission judge Kristi Lousteau. During the December 14, 2004, hearing, Mr. O sat implacably at the defense table wearing a blue L.A. County prisoner's jumpsuit as Detective Decker took the witness stand. In response to questioning by Deputy District Attorney Patrick Frey, Decker testified that ChoicePoint's attorneys and investigators told him that they knew of twenty-two other suspected fraudulent accounts similar to the MBS Financial and Gallo Financial accounts Mr. O had tried to open.

Frey: You said something about the size of the case, detective. What were you referring to?

Decker: It would have been the ChoicePoint accounts. There was something like 17,000 searches between those accounts saying something like 4 million people have been exposed.

Frey: When you say "between those accounts," what do you mean?

Decker: The ChoicePoint accounts that access people's personal information.

Frey: So you're saying that they've told you that there have been 17,000 searches of accounts that were done without the proper people's permission?

Decker: That's correct.

The court: Based on these two applications?

Decker: They are connected to twenty-two other accounts that were opened within the past two years.

Frey: And you're still working to see if there is a connection between the applications in this case and what you just described, the other accounts and searches.

Decker: Yes, sir.

Frey: Have you seen any connection so far?

Decker: Yes. Through cell phone numbers, merchant mail accounts at C.M.R.A [commercial mail receiving agencies], postal drops, those match up; post office boxes to the applications themselves, as well as the searches.

Frey: Okay. You haven't been able to obtain the necessary documentation to file charges based on those counts?

Decker: That's correct. ChoicePoint's overwhelmed with the amount of searches and how it connected with each victim.

As news reports of his thievery spread, Oluwatusin pleaded no contest to a single charge of identity theft and received a sixteen-month prison term. He declined requests from the authors to be interviewed at the Correctional Training Facility South in Soledad, California. During the course of the investigation, Detective Decker came to know the tall man with a limp as inquisitive, but secretive, as if absorbing lessons to be learned. "He asked us a lot of questions about what we knew and when," Decker says. "He was not forthcoming."

Expediters
Iceman Cometh

Consolidation is a fact of life for any maturing industry. Swallowing a competitor translates into instant growth. Most often big fish eat little fish. But sometimes ambition and daring count for more than size.

In December 2005, a hungry newbie, calling himself Iceman, surfaced in the IRC chat room #ccpower looking to horse-trade:

```
log:21:03 * iceman i need CVV2 trade with shells msg
me
log:21:03 * iceman i need CVV2 trade with shells msg
me
log:21:03 * iceman i need CVV2 trade with shells msg
me
log:21:03 -!- iceman was kicked from #ccpower by Root
[Text repeating detected. (3 repeats in 1.38 secs) ::
[Wed Dec 28 18:48:25 2005]
```

Iceman had "shells" to trade. These were access to free shell accounts hacked from a hosting site. In exchange, he sought stolen bank card numbers with CVV2 verification codes, presumably so he could make fraudulent online purchases. But he had committed the classic newbie faux pas, repeating his query so often—three times in under two seconds—that he got booted from the chat room.

Iceman learned quickly. Within a short time he outgrew the chat rooms and graduated to the up-and-coming forum CardersMarket. Clearly enterprising, and given to posting rambling messages explaining his strategic thinking, Iceman rose quickly and by the summer of 2006 he was CardersMarket's top admin.

Two-and-a-half years had gone by since Operation Firewall, and the carding forums that re-formed like amoebas in Shadowcrew's wake had splintered into fifteen to twenty smaller-scale co-ops. These message boards ran so smoothly, save for the constant presence of rippers, that they had become collegial, even predictable. TalkCash was one of the biggest, with 2,600 members, and CardersMarket was in the top ten, with about 1,500 members.

But Iceman was restless; he began to fancy himself the architect of a new paradigm. He had taken note that the admins of rival forums cavalierly left vulnerabilities unpatched on the PCs they used to serve up their message boards. So he crafted a bot to slip in through one such security hole.

On August 16, 2006, exuding the cool competence of a seasoned corporate raider, Iceman made his move. He sent his bot snaking into the message boards of four top-tier forums: TalkCash, DarkMarket, TheVouched, and ScandinavianCarding. The bot hijacked the entire archive of messages posted by the four forums' combined 4,500 members. In one stroke, Iceman quadrupled CardersMarket's membership to 6,000.

Next, with the braggadocio of an obsessed marketing executive, Iceman immediately began touting his business rationale and hyping the benefits sure to accrue. He wrote this in a forum message posted shortly after completing the hostile takeovers:

> the old forums were negligent in their security, using shared hosting, failing to use encryption of the data, logging ip addresses, using "1234" as administrative passwords (yes really people this is true!), and general administrative nazism.
> you ask what is the meaning of "all this"? basically this was overdue. why have five different forums each with the same content, splitting users and vendors, and a mish mash of poor security and sometimes poor administration and poor moderation.
>
> what is the point? security. convenience. increase quality and decrease the noise. bringing order to a mess, means CM is temporarily bulky and rough edges but this will be fixed and smooth within 24hrs.

To "bullet proof" CardersMarket—that is, to put its message-board activities as far out of the reach of U.S. law enforcement as possible—Iceman had moved CardersMarket's message boards to a host computer server registered to "Mohammad Hassan Rahimi Nasab" at "Abarkouh Azad Univercity" in "West Azarbaijan," Iran. In an upbeat welcoming e-mail dispatched to all of his new, albeit involuntary, members, Iceman heralded CardersMarket's superior security safeguards:

> the new and improved CardersMarket is hosted in IRAN,
> which is possibly the most politically distant country
> to the united states in the world today. we also have
> strict policy of encrypted https connections ONLY.

In the spy-versus-spy world of cybercrime, where trust is ephemeral and credibility hard-won, Iceman's masterstroke rattled his rivals and raised suspicions among his peers. Glib reassurances aside, the irony of his coup was not lost on a forum member nicknamed Silo, who posted this comment:

> despite our community doing what it does, all of our
> online communications with each other has to be built
> on "trust". (i say "trust" on some small level)
>
> if i DO NOT TRUST Mr. xxx who has contacted me about
> one of the products i vend, i'm not going to risk
> doing the transaction.
>
> iceman, by hijacking db's (databases), merging them
> into this board . . . how can we TRUST you and this
> boards admin?
>
> you breached our community's security. stole the
> Databases of other forums.
>
> what's the difference of myself hacking your e-mails
> and reading up on your business and posting your
> communications on my board?
>
> you've breached what little trust exists in the commu-
> nity.

The deposed forum leaders may have been caught off guard, but they weren't about to just sit back and let Iceman revel in victory for very long.

One tried-and-true competitive tactic used in business and politics is to denigrate a rival by spreading FUD—fear, uncertainty, and doubt. Shortly after Iceman swept up TalkCash's 2,600 members onto CardersMarket's boards, TalkCash's top admin, nicknamed Unknown Killer, ignited a FUD campaign to cast Iceman as another Cumbajohnny, the informant who helped federal agents knock down Shadowcrew. Unknown Killer e-mailed this shrill warning to TalkCash members:

> a board just popped up claiming to be a merger of a
> number of boards. well they are liars. they are the
> people who tried to scam TC in the past.
>
> i've talked to a number of guys and all say that they
> didn't merge a fuck with that site, so please beware
> as they can be feds because cm was owned by Feds in
> past and now they claim its back

Unknown Killer may have lit the fuse, but David Renshaw Thomas, aka El Mariachi, supplied the dynamite. A onetime member of Shadowcrew and a self-styled carding-forum expert, Thomas pitched himself to the media as a hacker-and-con-artist-turned-white-hat. Canadian reporter Sarah Staples, of CanWest News Service, and Kim Zetter, a correspondent for Wired News, both produced long stories recounting Thomas's supposed escapades as an undercover FBI informant. The FBI and Secret Service declined to confirm working with Thomas.

On forum message boards and blogs covering security topics, Thomas began to bombard Iceman with accusations that federal agents helped him set up CardersMarket in Iran and pull off the hostile takeovers. As painted by Thomas, Iceman was a mere pawn, assigned at the behest of law enforcement to establish a seemingly impregnable megaforum as a trap to ensnare kingpin cybercrooks, much as Cumbajohnny had lured Shadowcrew's leaders into the virtual private network set up by the Secret Service.

Iceman vehemently repudiated Thomas. Iceman and El Mariachi engaged in a raging back-and-forth tirade posted on the blogging site after-life.wordpress.com. Iceman fired back that Thomas, who is in his early fifties, was a nonfactor as an FBI informant who contributed little to the

Shadowcrew takedown, and who failed to start a new life, as Cumbajohnny presumably did:

> The fact of the matter is I have never been affiliated
> with LE in any way. This entire smear campaign by this
> punk David is nothing more than a jealousy fit. He has
> been completely wrong on almost every single technical
> argument, and there is no degree of evidence that can
> possibly dissuade him in his irrational conquest. He
> is a small person with delusions of grandeur.
> Any rational person who reads everything David El
> Mariachi had to say would see the mountain of contra-
> dictions and obvious lies and misdirection. He contra-
> dicts himself in almost every post.
> Which is it punk, I'm a criminal, or I'm a fed? MAKE
> UP YOUR MIND YOU PATHETIC MEDIA WHORE

Iceman openly ridiculed El Mariachi's limited technical expertise, and to add insult to injury, knocked out a Web site operated by Thomas with a DDoS attack. El Mariachi responded with this macho challenge:

> tell ya what Iceman, if you are so bold, come on over
> and we can talk about it in person, but since your a
> chicken shit wannabe piece of gutter trash that sticks
> on the bottom of my shoes you will weasel out of that
> offer every day of the week.
> Come on big man, come on over and lets talk man to
> man you slime bag piece of shit.

Out of clever technical counter arguments, Thomas was reduced to trying physical intimidation; yet he may have gotten the last laugh. El Mariachi got under Iceman's skin to such an extent that the CardersMarket admin was unable to pay full attention to the new, highly motivated enemies he had created. Ten days after the forced mergers, the deposed leaders of DarkMarket and ScandinavianCarding managed to reconstitute forums under those names. Thereafter CardersMarket repeatedly came under heavy DDoS attacks, with some of the features on its Web site functioning sporadically.

The infighting would run its course, and CardersMarket would shrink back down to its original size of about 1,500 members. Sometime in late 2006 or early 2007, Iceman made a quiet exit, supposedly retiring from forum management and turning over the admin reins to a colleague, nicknamed Aphex, an experienced hacker with extensive knowledge of malicious software, says Uriel Maimon, chief technology officer for RSA Security's consumer group.

As for Iceman, Maimon says: "Some fraudsters claim that Iceman never really left the board."

CHAPTER 14

Gaps in the System

Exploiters
April–June 2005, Edmonton

Within a week of the meltdown at Yolanda's Mill Woods apartment, Jacques apologized. Yolanda said she was sorry, too, and the couple set up their household in Clearview, a subsidized housing project on the city's north side. They moved into a two-bedroom condo rented by Carole, a crack cocaine addict who had recently had her children taken away after failing her third drug test. Carole had become intimate with Jacques's dad, Tony, and had moved in with him. Since Carole was spending very little time in her subsidized condo, Biggie volunteered to pay Carole's monthly rent. By nature, Biggie was a generous soul. The second of three children from a working-class family, he began taking Ecstasy and frequented the rave scene as a teenager, and moved from there to the speeder crowd. Social by nature, Biggie, like Socrates, loved video games, and he was always ready to party.

Biggie's close acquaintances were other addicts and thieves he jokingly referred to as his "co-accused." They would rip him off in a heartbeat, yet they knew they could count on him to come through in tight spots. Biggie had taken to bouncing between sketch pads and his parents' home. His mother tended to be protective of him. Though he had been arrested multiple times, Biggie never spent more than a day or two in jail. The cops never caught him in the act of, or in possession of, anything that could make serious criminal charges stick. Socrates, for instance, took all of the criminal charges stemming from the Beverly Motel bust because it was his laptop the detectives found linked to the Telus dial-up account and e-mail folder containing 500 PayPal log-ons.

Somewhere along his slide into drug addiction and financial fraud, Biggie was diagnosed as a schizophrenic. He would see things flying at him and was prone to destructive outbreaks if not on his medication. Biggie held a string of jobs but could never keep one longer than a few weeks. He qualified for benefits under Canada's Assured Income for the

Severely Handicapped (AISH) program. At the end of each month, depending on how much or how little he worked, he received an AISH supplemental income check, as much as $1,000. In that sense, Biggie had a base level of financial security his co-accuseds lacked. It was from his monthly AISH check that Biggie planned to cover Carole's subsidized rent of $200.

With Socrates in jail, Jacques and Biggie began to set up fraud deals working out of hotel rooms whenever they could. Hula Girl often showed up to help out. At the conclusion of a scam, they would check out of the hotel and meet up at Carole's condo to party. In Edmonton, certain hotels, including the moderately priced Travel Lodge South, offered in-room broadband Internet connections for no charge, even supplying the necessary T1 cable on loan from the front desk. Should law enforcement ever attempt to trace the cell's online fraud activity, the trail would end at the hotel's switchboard, not at Carole's condo.

Jacques soon was able to establish regular contact with a fraudster in Quebec who appeared to control an endless portfolio of hijacked online bank accounts but needed drop accounts to extract cash. Jacques preferred setting up transactions via untraceable cell phone calls—both he and the contact used phone accounts set up with stolen credit card numbers. As soon as Jacques could recruit an addict to open a drop account, he would call his Quebec contact and supply the account routing number. You got the stuffing. I got the turkey. Let's stuff the turkey.

Biggie focused on trying to rebuild the cell's contacts in the cybercrime chat channels, although he had done much by now to ruin Socrates's reputation on the Internet; in the frenzy at Mill Woods he had impersonated Socrates too often, and ripped off one too many accomplices. But a breakthrough came when Biggie was able to establish contact and begin to build a working relationship with the Blackwell twins, Darrell and Derrick, of Abbottsford, British Columbia, a suburb of Vancouver.

Darrell, a broker of stolen credit card numbers, also specialized in producing counterfeit credit cards and fake drivers' licenses. He had built his reputation on Internet chat channels and carding forums. Darrell's twin brother, Derrick, lived back east in Ontario, where he was supposed to be serving time in jail on weekends. But at the time Biggie made contact with the Blackwells, Derrick had just skipped out on his jail sentence and was hiding out at Darrell's place under an assumed identity. Soon Biggie and Derrick were chatting regularly online and via cell phone. For whatever reasons—whether his brother got tired of him or Biggie cajoled him— Derrick in early June 2005 rented a car at the Vancouver airport and drove east to Edmonton. He used a counterfeit credit card and fake driver's license supplied by Darrell.

While Biggie and Jacques did what they could to return the cell to its glory days of making mad cash, Socrates was detoxifying himself the hard way, cold turkey in a jail cell. Vonkeman and Gauthier went to bat for him, pulling strings to get his case assigned to a prosecutor they knew would work to get Socrates released to his parents. Gauthier's gut told him that Socrates wasn't a truly bad kid; Vonkeman, ever the pragmatist, boiled it down to saving taxpayers' money: getting Socrates out of the speeder life and on track to becoming a productive citizen would burn fewer public resources over the long haul.

In early June, about the time Darrell Blackwell was thinking about heading east to Edmonton to hook up with Biggie, Socrates was getting processed for conditional release to his parents' home. The judge attached more than three dozen conditions. Socrates had to attend Sunday church services, spend quality time with his family, stay away from computers and drugs, and adhere to a strict 8 p.m. daily curfew. Socrates was grateful. He knew the speeder life had nearly killed him. "Basically I was at the point where I didn't care anymore. I thought, 'I'm going to die anyway, so I'll keep smoking.' It makes you feel hopeless. All you live for is the drug. And you'll do anything to get it. Anything."

Although Socrates sincerely wanted to put the speeder life behind him, Biggie and Yolanda had other ideas.

Enablers

In the Know

A display advertisement showing a young woman loading a curly-haired toddler into the back seat of a van filled a quarter page in the features section of the December 6, 2006, *Seattle Times*. Emblazoned on the woman's blouse: "nanny for hire. 3 drunk driving convictions." The tag line: "Background checks at Intelius.com. Live in the know."

A similar quarter-page newspaper ad, this one depicting a young couple moving in together, ran in the technology section of the April 30, 2007, *New York Times*. The woman is shown laughing—blind to the man's "2 domestic violence convictions" and "1 bankruptcy" notated on the box of fragile household goods he is packing. The tag line: "Get the whole story on him, before it's too late. Our background checks are instant, accurate and reassuring. —Intelius."

The ad campaign bespoke a portentous advancement in self-directed Internet research. Google users habituated to researching which movie to watch, what car to buy, or where to spend their next vacation could now conveniently probe deep into the background of people they chose to associate with. Data dossiers had become as easily accessible to consumers as they long had been to lenders, employers, and law enforcement.

Intelius, founded by Microsoft and InfoSpace alumni, uses the same type of data-mining technology as ChoicePoint to assemble much the same sensitive information culled from public records: addresses, phone numbers, driving records, criminal histories, civil judgments, and real estate documents. But instead of competing against the big three data brokers to supply data dossiers to businesses, agencies, and institutions, Intelius focuses on making them available to the general public via the Internet. Anyone who plunks down $50 can get a full data dossier.

"Intelius doesn't just display public records," says company spokeswoman Katie McFadzean. "We actually analyze and integrate an array of different pieces of information intelligently."

So do rival data suppliers such as Zabasearch.com, PrivateEye.com, USA-People-Search.com, and Voompeople.com. These online services typically require payment by credit card for background checks of varying thoroughness. Intelius is a representative example. It supplies basic data for free, through its retail Web site, Zumende.com. On that site you, or anyone else, can access your home address and age, along with similar data on relatives who share your surname, as well as strangers with similar names. Pay $10 or $50 and you can get correspondingly more information.

This new breed of consumer-centric data miners has made it possible for anyone with an active debit or credit card account number to access a rich trove of sensitive data. They empower consumers to do background and criminal checks on their nannies, blind dates, plumbers, pastors, or new neighbors. You might even want to look at your own information to see how accurate it is. There is no longer any need to slog down to the county clerk's office or state vital statistics office and copy data off public documents.

Yet more widely dispersed public data also means more criminal opportunity. Carol Ybarra, a hospital clerk from Houston, had never heard of Intelius until the company debited $64.94 from her bank account in August 2007. Ybarra phoned Intelius and got the runaround. So she contacted one of the authors through USA Today's watchdog mailbox, an online service set up to field tips from readers. Subsequent interviews with Intelius illustrated how dot-com companies are struggling to come to grips with the many ways cybercrooks are harvesting sensitive data and converting it into cash.

Intelius cofounder Ed Peterson insisted that whoever completed the transaction typed in Ybarra's correct account number and CVV code. This, he contended, proved the thief had actual possession of Ybarra's debit card. Intelius communications manager Liz Murray added that Intelius's automated systems conducted 147 other security checks—all within one second—and no red flags went up. Intelius had no choice but to deliver an advanced background check and a federal criminal check for a Texas woman—not Ybarra.

"This wasn't fraud; it was a case of friendly misuse," insisted Peterson. "Someone in her circle of trust used the card."

But Ybarra, who keeps her purse in a locker at work, said she's certain the card never left her possession on the day Intelius approved the online transaction in question. Later that same day, the thief also used Ybarra's account number to purchase a $15 membership from 24ProtectPlus, an online auto and household assistance service, earning a cash rebate. What Intelius failed to grasp was that with data harvesting running rampant, Ybarra's account number and CVV could have landed in the pool of stolen identity data any number of ways.

"It's infuriating," she says. "I'm the innocent one here, and they're guessing that I did it?"

Using stolen account numbers to purchase data dossiers, which contain very rich data, makes obvious sense to an identity thief; having a consumer-oriented data broker, like Intelius, supply access to data dossiers, via a few taps at a keyboard, makes it all the more convenient. A crook could start with any list of names and addresses, say, from a phone book, and order data dossiers online to round out profiles useful for scams. No need to rummage through garbage cans for bank statements or 7-Eleven receipts, as Marilyn and Frankie had; or to trick a big-three data broker into believing you are a business with a legitimate interest in personal data, as Mr. O did. One has only to spend a few hours cruising the back alleys of the carding forums and IRC chat rooms to observe the cyberunderground revolving around a thriving commodities market for what's known as personally identifiable information, or PII. Any scrap of information, anything useful for constructing a bogus identity—mother's maiden name, a PIN, former residences, former employers' names, homes owned, a divorced spouse's name—has value and can be found for sale.

"Since a fake ID is an integral part of most fraud operations, there are entire sections within the underground that are dedicated to forging IDs," says Idan Aharoni, senior fraud analyst at RSA, security division of EMC Corp.

Just as pork bellies undergird the sausage industry, the market for stolen personal information provides the grist for meticulously orchestrated identity theft scams. San Diego–based security firm ID Analytics has uncovered evidence of dozens of fraud rings operating across the United States. One ring submitted 100 new loan applications for fifty stolen Social Security numbers, two per identity, so as not to draw suspicion. In each instance, the victim's name was submitted along with a new billing address, a cell phone number as a home number, and the main line to a Los Angeles–area hospital as a work number.

By listing the hospital's phone number, the crook was playing it safe. Should a real person review the loan application and actually follow up with a phone call to verify place of employment, the phone would ring at the hospital, says ID Analytics' Mike Cook.

IDology, an Atlanta-based identity theft prevention firm, supplies technology that analyzes data submitted for online loan applications and big-ticket purchases, such as electronics and jewelry. Cofounder Raye Croghan estimates that 18 percent of such data gets flagged as highly suspicious or clearly fraudulent. In one caper, a would-be thief used the name, home address, and Social Security number of a twenty-two-year-old woman from Lilburn, Georgia, to fill out an online credit card application. But a red flag went up when the applicant requested that the card be mailed to Overland

Park, Kansas. Then, minutes later, the same scammer filled out a similar application at another Web site, this time using the data belonging to a woman from East Liverpool, Ohio, and again requested a credit card mailed to Overland Park, Kansas.

"We frequently see people using multiple identities attempting to ship to an unrelated address," says Croghan.

The credit card issuer declined both applications. However, it was able to do so only because it bore the extra expense of using IDology's theft-monitoring service, which spotted the suspicious patterns. As of late 2007, the vast majority of online merchants did not yet use such defenses.

Expediters

Zero Day Attack

As the accountant for a boutique Atlanta law firm, Shaillie Gattis was naturally expected to be the resident techie. Gattis actually was well qualified. Her father, Roger Thompson, made his living as a virus guru, and as a teenager, she had worked for Thompson's antivirus start-up, Leprechaun Software, back in Brisbane, Australia, before the family moved to America. So Gattis knew her way around computers.

But one day in early 2005, Gattis found herself stumped. The desktop PC of a coworker was hopelessly bogged down. She took the machine to her father, who confidently broke out the best set of diagnostic tools money could buy and went to work. Four hours later, Thompson was stumped.

"I couldn't get file access to delete files, so I rebooted the system to safe mode and still couldn't manage it," said Thompson, cofounder and CTO of Exploit Prevention Labs. "I ran other diagnostics, trying to unpick this and unpick that. I eventually rendered the system unbootable."

Gattis told her father that the last thing her coworker remembered doing was an Internet search for lyrics to "Pictures," a duet sung by Kid Rock and Sheryl Crow. So Thompson fired up a test machine he used for analyzing malicious code and did a Google search for "lyrics Pictures Kid Rock Sheryl Crow."

Clicking through a few music Web sites, he eventually came to one that displayed a prominent dialogue box, dense with text, and a "close" button at the bottom. Most PC users in a hurry would click the close button to make the box disappear. But clicking the close button also began a down-loading sequence.

Thompson clicked the close button and watched his test computer get loaded up with a swarm of malicious code, including an adware installer for embedding pop-up ads, and a back door through which the attacker could turn his test PC into an obedient bot. Thompson's test machine then began displaying a particularly intrusive ad for SpySheriff—a sales pitch kept popping up every two minutes badgering him to pay $49.95 for a fake anti-spyware program that purportedly would clean up his computer.

Thompson also spotted something relatively rare at the time: a cloaking mechanism, called a root kit, that rendered the malicious code inaccessible. It was the root kit that prevented Thompson from cleaning up the law firm's PC. With a little sleuthing, Thompson learned that SpySheriff was distrib-uted by a Russian Web site called iframeCASH.biz, one of the pioneers of a quick, surefire way to compromise PCs: Web exploits.

In a Web exploit, the attacker embeds malicious code on a Web site, then sits back and waits. The victim activates the code simply by visiting a tainted Web page. The malicious code probes the visitor's Web browser, looking for security holes. When it finds one, it installs code through the visitor's browser that gives the intruder complete control over the now-compromised PC.

The iframers, and other Russian groups like them, showed boundless inventiveness deploying Web exploits. First they commissioned purveyors of porn and gambling Web sites to taint their pages with malicious code. Then they began openly recruiting "affiliates" to plant malicious code on other kinds of innocuous-looking Web sites run by the affiliates, or, even better yet, to hack into popular travel, social-networking, and retail Web sites run by others to taint their Web pages and turn them into moneymakers.

Displaying a sleek, black automobile as an example of an attainable status symbol, the iframeCASH.biz home page brazenly offered to pay affil-iates $61 per 1,000 infections, no questions asked. The sedan was similar to a $124,000 Mercedes S600 known in underground circles to be the personal ride of a St. Petersburg resident in his early twenties named Andrej Sporaw, believed to be the group's leader.

Web exploits took off in 2005 for a couple of reasons. First, the anti-spamming community had gotten highly proficient at filtering spam, thus slowing down old-style e-mail viruses, while PC users, in turn, became more wary about opening viral e-mail attachments. Second, Microsoft in August 2004 delivered Service Pack 2 for its Windows XP operating system. Service Pack 2, or SP2, represented the first fruits from the Trustworthy Computing initiative Bill Gates launched so dramatically in early 2002.

SP2 turned on a personal firewall to block the ports most commonly used by botnet controllers, and it activated Windows Auto Update, a free online service set up by Microsoft to send PC users the latest security patches automatically. SP2 had a profound effect on the overall security of the Internet. All new Windows PCs sold after August 2004 came with SP2, and Microsoft launched an aggressive marketing campaign to distribute SP2 to 260 million current Windows XP users.

Thus SP2 put in place a basic level of security for hundreds of millions of Windows PCs, though it remained up to individual PC users to keep paid subscriptions for antivirus and antispyware protection up to date. Cybercrime gangs, like the iframers, responded by turning their full attention to Web exploits—a huge tunnel through firewalls. Thompson explained why: "When you start a browser, you punch a hole right through the firewall. Your browser immediately trusts the Web site you're visiting and authorizes it to operate inside your firewall, so the intruder can go straight to your hard drive and install whatever he likes."

By the close of 2005, Sporaw and the Russian iframers were ready to open the floodgates on Web exploits, says Mikko Hyppönen, virus hunter at F-Secure. They did so by retaining the services of a top-notch black hat virus researcher who went off in search of the next great, gaping vulnerability. In the cat-and-mouse world of criminal hacking, a security hole discovered and exploited before a patch can be developed is known as a zero day attack. The flaw is known only by the discoverer, not the public or the software vendor; day one would be the first day the vendor makes a patch available.

Andrej Sporaw's iframe gang reportedly paid $5,000 to the researcher who discovered the Windows metafile, or WMF, zero day flaw, and designed an exploit to take advantage of it. Though consummately profit motivated, Sporaw took the trouble to also grab credit for what would emerge as a watershed attack. F-Secure was among the first to discover and decrypt the original WMF exploit. The Finnish security company noticed a superfluous string of numbers deep inside the code. The string turned out to be the license number of Sporaw's Mercedes S600.

"We think he just couldn't resist leaving his mark in the code," says Hyppönen.

WMF was ripe for exploitation; it was a clunky old image format that became supplanted by the GIF and JPEG formats familiar to anyone who has ever worked with photos on a computer. It was one of those carelessly written features Microsoft developers churned out by the truckload in the early days of personal computing.

The mercenary programmer earned his $5,000 by concocting a way to take advantage of the fact that WMF files can execute programs, including, of course, malicious programs. He crafted a corrupted WMF file that could open a back door through which the iframers could install adware and cover it all up with a root kit. That would happen anytime someone simply viewed the doctored image. In mid-December, a wave of pop-up ads carrying corrupted WMF images began appearing on Web sites across the Internet. Anyone who saw such an ad was infected.

By December 28, the security firm Websense identified more than 1,000 Web sites carrying tainted WMF files distributed by iframeCASH.biz and its affiliates. Other hacking groups jumped on the bandwagon. A tool called WMFMaker began circulating that made it a snap for anyone, even script-kiddie hackers, to spread corrupted WMF images and create their own zero day attacks, says Johannes Ulrich, CTO of the SANS Internet Storm Center.

By January 3, Ulrich counted 200 unique variants of WMF zero day exploits. F-Secure discovered one that sent waves of corrupted WMF images into the Google Desktop indexing service, infecting countless users of that service. Websense found one circulating on instant messaging services. Another type inserted a tiny, imperceptible tainted WMF image on banner advertisements on hundreds of Web sites. Yet another went out as an attachment in an e-mail virus.

"Any application that automatically displays a WMF image can be a vector for infection," warned Alex Eckelberry, president of Sunbelt Software, in his blog. "This is a zero day exploit, the kind that gives security researchers cold chills. You can get infected simply by viewing an infected WMF image."

The inaugural WMF zero day attack had been launched on Wednesday, December 14, a day after Microsoft's Patch Tuesday for that month. The next Patch Tuesday was scheduled for January 10. That gave the iframers a full month of zero days to compromise PCs before Microsoft was scheduled to issue more patches. Releasing a new zero day exploit on the day after Microsoft's Patch Tuesday would become a common practice. In a highly unusual move, Microsoft broke from its monthly pattern and issued a patch for the WMF zero day vulnerability on January 5, five days early. The two-week turnaround was blazingly fast compared to the weeks and often months Microsoft usually took to develop and test patches for newly discovered security holes.

Debby Fry Wilson, a director of Microsoft's Security Response Center, downplayed the significance of the forces at work compelling the software giant to move so quickly.

"Normally we do an out-of-band release when things change or a problem is more severe than we first anticipated," Wilson told eWeek reporter Paul F. Roberts. "In this case, the data continues to show that attacks are limited."

CHAPTER 15

Keys to the Puzzle

Exploiters

May–July 2005, Edmonton

Hula Girl wasn't the answer. As gutsy as she was, fearlessly donning disguises and using fake drivers' licenses to open drop accounts and make withdrawals, what Hula Girl added to the cell did not nearly make up for the loss of Socrates. The cell could no longer tap Socrates's networking ability in the chat rooms. Socrates had spent countless hours chatting up key partners and establishing a level of trust, prerequisites for any enduring business relationship. It's likely that without Socrates, the Edmonton cell never would have branched beyond petty local scams and advanced to supplying drop accounts for far-flung cybercoconspirators.

On April 13, 2005, Detectives Vonkeman and Gauthier, moving quickly on a tip, obtained a search warrant for the north-end condo. The detectives arrested Hula Girl as she was about to get into a taxi in front of the residence. From inside the condo they confiscated a desktop PC belonging to Hula Girl on which she had stored thousands of online account profiles, including customer data for more than 3,000 clients of a Michigan company that sold uniforms online. Socrates admitted that it was he who had hacked into the Michigan company's Web site and that he had given the 3,000 profiles to Hula Girl as a gift.

The detectives also found on Hula Girl's PC digital templates to make counterfeit drivers' licenses from more than twenty different Canadian provinces and U.S. states. They confiscated hard copies of an array of licenses, using various aliases, each with Hula Girl's photo, and took from Hula Girl a cell phone whose call log showed several calls made to Quebec, Bulgaria, and Romania. Hula Girl would go to jail for a long stretch.

In May 2005, Vonkeman and Gauthier, acting on another tip, arrested Jacques shortly after he departed the north-end condo riding a car with the vehicle's female owner (not Yolanda). In the trunk the detectives found two laptop computers belonging to Jacques, which contained large caches of stolen identification and online account data. Jacques, too, would go to jail for a long stretch.

With Jacques back in the Edmonton Remand Center and Socrates under house arrest, Biggie and Yolanda could manage only sporadic success committing financial scams. "You never, ever have all the keys to the puzzle, and when you think you do, you really don't," says Yolanda.

It was about this time that Biggie connected with the Blackwell twins and began his campaign to get Derrick Blackwell to make a trip to Edmonton. Then one day, in a moment of clarity, Biggie recalled that one of Socrates's chat channel passwords happened to also be his parents' home phone number. Biggie dialed the number and got Socrates to come to the phone.

After inquiring how his old friend was doing, Biggie said he wanted to drop by for a friendly visit. Socrates asked him not to. Biggie would hear none of it. In a gently insistent tone, he replied that he didn't care what Socrates said—he was coming out; he'd obtained Socrates's parents' phone number and it would be just that easy for him to get their home address, as well.

Knowing Biggie would follow through, Socrates asked him to please come alone. A short while later, Yolanda's white Cavalier pulled up in front of Socrates's parents' home. Yolanda was behind the wheel, Biggie in the front passenger seat. Socrates climbed into the backseat and Yolanda drove off.

Biggie and Yolanda got a good laugh when Socrates told them about the laundry list of court conditions governing his house arrest. Yolanda rambled on about Jacques's arrest, and what a travesty it was that the woman who owned the car containing the damning evidence—Jacques's co-accused—got off scot-free. She railed about the injustice of Jacques's bail getting set at $15,000 and about how they all owed it to Jacques to raise the money to get him out of jail.

Neither Yolanda nor Biggie said much when Socrates mentioned that he was looking for a job and really wanted to clean up his life. Biggie was uncharacteristically pensive. Before pulling up to Socrates's home, he had placed a bowl of crystal meth in the Cavalier's center console, leaving the hatch lid open. As Yolanda drove on aimlessly and the banter continued, Socrates could not take his eyes off the glass pipe.

"I seen it sitting there for a good hour," he recalls. "Then I grabbed it and started smoking it."

A few days later, Biggie, using part of his AISH disability check, rented the corner suite on the top floor of the fourteen-story Tower in the Park long-term-stay hotel. All the pieces of the puzzle appeared to be falling into place. Derrick Blackwell had just rolled into Edmonton, preceded by the Blackwells' reputation as big-time fraudsters. Socrates was back in the game. First some partying was in order. Word got out. Dealers and addicts drifted in and out of the fourteenth-floor suite.

On June 12, 2005, the third day of partying and plotting at the Tower in the Park, Biggie dispatched Yolanda to pick up Socrates and bring him over to meet Derrick.

She was heading back to the suite, with Socrates in tow, when the hotel manager called the police to report that someone on the fourteenth floor had smashed a window. As Yolanda's Cavalier turned the corner approaching the hotel parking lot, she and Socrates spotted Detective Vonkeman's unmarked police sedan pulling up behind marked police vehicles already parked at the curb in front of the hotel.

Yolanda phoned Biggie to warn him that the cops were on their way up. Everyone in the corner suite scrambled to get out except Biggie. Derrick was among the last to leave, taking with him a laptop PC, but he was arrested in the hall by uniformed constables who had just arrived on the floor. Biggie was alone in the suite. He began chucking cell phones, counterfeit credit cards, and drug paraphernalia off the balcony. The building's maintenance manager notified police that debris was raining down on the asphalt parking lot from the fourteenth floor. The suite clear of incriminating evidence, Biggie sat down to wait for Vonkeman and Gauthier.

The Edmonton cell never again came close to the high-flying days in Yolanda's Mill Woods walk-up, pushing $10,000 a day through drop accounts and burning through the cash on drug binges as fast as it came in. Following his arrest at the Tower in the Park, Biggie, who had managed to avoid extended jail time despite multiple arrests, would spend several months in lockup. Yolanda and Socrates moved into a condominium rented by one of Jacques's get-high acquaintances, Barney, a forty-something speeder with an affinity for video games.

Yolanda turned her attention to the matter of raising funds to pay Jacques's $15,000 bail. But focusing on such a complex task long enough to bring it to fruition proved daunting. Jacques could no longer contribute his flair for recruiting speeders to open new drop accounts. Biggie's frenetic networking, not to mention his monthly AISH disability check as a source of start-up capital, was gone. Left on their own, Yolanda and Socrates were reduced to mooching off Barney and cajoling acquaintances to get them high.

Out of a job and short of cash, Yolanda sold her white Cavalier for $700; the money didn't go very far. One day, out of groceries and desperate for some spending cash, Yolanda strolled down to a nearby Wal-Mart superstore. She had with her a friend's driver's license. After leisurely filling a shopping cart full of groceries, Yolanda meandered to the linen department and stuffed a $200 duvet into a bag. She then circled around to the return desk and tried to get a refund for the duvet, using her friend's identification.

"I was stupid enough to stay there while they took the ID to see if it really belonged to me. I was just hungry," she says. Yolanda was arrested for shoplifting and got fined $400.

Socrates, meanwhile, fell back on his first love. He would lose himself for days at a time in Counter-Strike combat missions, intermittently dabbling in manufacturing and trying to sell fake Canadian drivers' licenses. He set up a Web site and advertised samples for sale for $20, using a photo of himself on the prototype. It was a halfhearted enterprise.

Acting on a tip, Detective Gauthier in July 2005 hustled to Barney's north Edmonton apartment and obtained a passkey from the manager. Upon bursting into the apartment, he found Socrates sitting in an easy chair, computer on his lap, tapping away at a program for doctoring drivers' licenses. Barney was sitting across the way on a couch, watching a movie on another laptop PC.

Gauthier gathered up meth paraphernalia, a container of turpentine, an SOS pad, and transparent sticky sheets—supplies to alter stolen province of Alberta drivers' licenses—and several fake IDs in various stages of production. Socrates reacted calmly to his third arrest at the hands of Gauthier. He knew he would be spending a long time in jail. In a sense, Socrates felt relief, along with an obligation to protect Barney. "I looked up," recalls Socrates, "and I said, 'Hi Bob, I figured you guys would be coming here pretty soon. All this shit's mine.'"

Enablers

Mortgage Triggers

Daniel and Mary Braden have three children and run a small business distributing tortillas to local grocers in Fort Collins, Colorado. In February 2006, the middle-aged couple sought to refinance their home. So they turned to a trusted mortgage broker, Douglas Braden (no relation), to get them a good deal. The Bradens had dealt with Doug over the years and had always been satisfied. They expected the process to go smoothly.

They couldn't have been more wrong, though through no fault of Doug. Within a few hours after Doug pulled their tri-merged credit reports from the big three credit bureaus, the Bradens appeared on "mortgage triggers"—lists of recent mortgage applicants compiled by the big three and offered for sale to hotly competitive mortgage lenders and brokers.

A basic "trigger lead" included their name, contact information, and the fact that they were shopping for a mortgage. The big three openly advertised such mortgage triggers on their Web sites. Effective marketing, of course, always includes an element of choice. The big three also offered to deliver up even richer data, such as the Bradens' credit scores, a summary of their credit card debt, even an estimate of the available equity in their home, to anyone willing to pay a premium.

By the next day the Bradens began to receive a flood of too-good-to-be-true offers from subprime mortgage companies—the burgeoning group of lenders that cropped up in the early 2000s to specialize in risky, expensive loans. The Bradens say they were persuaded to agree to a high-risk, adjustable-rate mortgage, offered by Columbus, Ohio–based Oxford Lending Group. But the loan closed under less-favorable terms than those explained to them, and a second loan didn't go through despite promises from Oxford. As this classic bait-and-switch ruse played out, the Bradens' once-pristine credit score went into the tank and their household budget imploded.

"We went from seeking a loan to facing bankruptcy a year later," Dan says. "It boggles the mind."

Mortgage triggers epitomized how the big three credit bureaus continually make it easy to commit fraud. Triggers accelerated the placement of sensitive data into the tornado of credit-fueled consumerism. In this fast-spinning commercial world, hucksters aren't always easy to tell apart from legitimate merchants. And in yet another demonstration of the big three's adroitness at wielding political clout, triggers also eviscerated consumer protection laws.

The Fair Credit Reporting Act requires mortgage lenders to make a "firm offer of credit." Consumer advocates and FCRA attorneys construe this to mean that the lender ought to have an appraisal in hand and know how much cash the borrower has available for a down payment; in short, have a relationship with the borrower and do enough due diligence to actually extend the loan if the offer is accepted.

But mortgage triggers lend themselves more to superficial pitches, and, in fact, result in a storm of unsolicited calls, e-mails, and pitch letters heralding "prescreened" or "preapproved" mortgages. Once Experian began marketing mortgage triggers in early 2005, they were snapped up by the hungry pool of subprime lenders. Soon Equifax and TransUnion offered competing products.

By the end of 2006, dozens of consumers like the Bradens had complained to the Federal Trade Commission, the agency charged with enforcing the FCRA, about unscrupulous lenders using trigger leads to lure them with deceptive bait-and-switch offers. The credit bureaus defended the lucrative service, arguing that triggers gave consumers more choice. "Mortgage triggers are like going to the mall, where you can shop for the best possible deal, easily and efficiently," says Consumer Data Industry Association president Stuart Pratt.

In February 2007 the FTC finally weighed in. But instead of restraining triggers, it gave the big three its blessing to carry on. The agency posted on its Web site a "consumer alert" describing how mortgage triggers work and noting that "federal law allows this practice if the offer of credit meets certain legal requirements."

The FTC's statement went further: "Clearly, some mortgage companies benefit from this practice. But the FTC says consumers can benefit too: prescreened offers can highlight other available products and make it easier to compare costs while you carefully check out the terms and conditions of any offers you might consider."

The FTC's paternalistic guidance was roundly lambasted by privacy advocates, credit-industry experts, and the National Association of Mortgage Brokers (NAMB). Madison Ayer, cofounder of Denver-based Veracity Credit

Consultants, for one, observed, "While in theory more competition is better, in reality, it is overwhelming the consumer. You apply for a mortgage, and within twenty-four hours, you start getting bombarded with calls. Your mailbox fills up. And pretty soon you've been told so many different things by so many different people that you have no idea what you're getting into.

"Consumers get confused. How is that good for the consumer? It's not. With consumer confusion comes vulnerability. And one of the big problems with these trigger lists is that it's an easy setup for bait-and-switch schemes. Once you confuse the consumer, then that consumer is vulnerable. It becomes so time-consuming just to try to make sense of it all, that the next time they hear, 'Oh, we'll get you the best rate and close it tomorrow!' they jump at it, and it turns out that's not really what they're getting."

The Bradens filed a complaint about Oxford Lending Group with Ohio's Consumer Complaint Department. They also are considering suing Oxford, who they say offered them a token $1,000 settlement. "The tone of the conversation went from, 'We can work this out' to 'We can wait you out and do nothing,'" says Mary Braden.

Meanwhile, Harry Dinham, president of NAMB, worried about another side effect of mortgages: they caused a swirl of personal data to be mass distributed across the Internet. Moving such sensitive data seemed a surefire way to accelerate identity theft. Trigger leads, Dinham noted, instantly attracted the patronage of a group of middlemen, referred to in the credit industry as "lead generators," who operate unfettered by the FCRA or any regulations. Lead generators make money by steering prospective borrowers to lenders for a finder's fee; they snap up mortgage triggers like candy, typically following up with telephone solicitations.

"They ask you a few questions, like, 'We need to confirm your Social Security number,' and in a matter of moments they have all the information they need to steal your identity," says Dinham. "This information being sold without the consumer's permission is a wide-open hole the consumer doesn't need to be faced with."

Dinham blasted the FTC's hands-off policy. "They're not willing to take sides on it," he says. "And if you can't get the oversight agency to take action, then you need Congress to step in."

Privacy Times editor and publisher Evan Hendricks concurs that the FTC "should be aggressively protecting consumers from this." But the Washington, D.C.–based Hendricks is a realist. His incisive book, *Credit Scores & Credit Reports: How the System Really Works and What You Can Do*, includes a historical account of the decades of backroom influence that shaped the decidedly probusiness Fair Credit Reporting Act. Hendricks believes that ever since CDIA outmaneuvered Senator William Proxmire, the people's privacy champion, back in 1970, credit bureaus have become untouchable.

The credit bureaus' clout in the nation's capitol is embodied by Deborah Platt Majoras, whom President George W. Bush appointed chairman of the FTC. Majoras arrived directly from a partner's seat at mega–law firm Jones Day, and was sworn in as head of the FTC on August 16, 2004. Her clients at Jones Day included Chevron's Texaco and Halliburton subsidiary Kellogg Brown and Root. Another of her law firm's billion-dollar corporate clients: Experian, the originator of mortgage triggers.

Majoras declined comment about her appointment. "Like other commissioners and staff, the chairman is recused in matters that would present a conflict of interest, or the appearance of a conflict of interest," says FTC spokeswoman Claudia Bourne Farrell.

Longtime political observer and privacy advocate Hendricks, however, pointed to the bottom line: "The big three are insulated. They don't have to change their practices and can rebuff any effort to enter the modern age of data handling."

Expediters
Silly Samy

Taking the word "limited" in a comparative sense, Microsoft's characterization of the iframers' zero day attack as being narrow in scope was accurate. In the three weeks before the software giant could get a patch out for the Windows metafile vulnerability, Andrej Sporaw's crew tainted an estimated 3,000 Web sites with pop-up and banner ads carrying corrupted WMF images.

Assuming each tainted Web site infected, on average, 100 computers before Microsoft could deploy patches through its Windows Auto Update service, that would have put 300,000 new zombie PCs in Sporaw's control.

Compared to the self-propagating MSBlast worm, which opened back doors on 25 million PCs, the WMF zero day attack, indeed, could well be described as limited.

However, Microsoft was using a 2004 paradigm to describe a 2006 threat. Much had changed on the cybercrime landscape in the two years since MSBlast's creator chided "billy gates" to "stop making money and fix your software!!" Profits, not bragging rights, had become the main driver of malicious attacks. Quick-strike, self-healing botnets had become the tool of choice to spread spam and spyware, carry out extortionist DDoS attacks, and implant data-harvesting programs.

And now the biggest genie of all was out of the bottle. The iframers set a new benchmark for how to execute a well-planned zero day attack that made large quantities of quick cash while also replenishing their botnets for an array of future attacks. What's more, they appeared to be perfecting the use of root-kit cloaking devices to keep their botted PCs permanently under control.

"These are all threats facing consumers today; increasingly sophisticated, organized, and profitable for organized professionals," says Ken Dunham, then director of iDefense VeriSign's rapid-response team.

Back in Atlanta, Roger Thompson's encounter with the iframers' early attacks had sparked inspiration. Thompson took a honeypot PC—a computer he left connected to the Internet to receive malicious attacks, so he could analyze them—and converted it into what he called a "hunting pot." He programmed the PC to systematically click on Web sites likely to be serving up tainted pages: sites serving up free lyrics, pirated movies, pornography, and the like. Thompson's hunting pot quickly became infested with malicious programs.

Thompson discovered the World Wide Web to be saturated with tainted pages poised to infect visitors; his hunting pot revealed a wellspring of Web exploits so vast that he was able to cofound Exploit Prevention Labs, a security start-up selling a firewall extension tool, called LinkScanner, that checked data moving across a Web browser for malicious code. With LinkScanner, Thompson began to catalog Web exploits on the Internet.

Thompson and other virus hunters watched as profit-minded intruders intensified probes for vulnerabilities in Web page servers and Web browsers that they could take advantage of. In the wake of the WMF zero day attack, a distinctive pattern emerged: well-funded criminal groups would move aggressively to find and exploit the next zero day hole, hitting it hard with coordinated campaigns to compromise as many machines as they could with spyware, back doors, and root kits. Mimicking the iframers, they often launched a new zero day attack on the day after Microsoft's monthly Patch Tuesday.

If Microsoft was able to get a patch readied by the next Patch Tuesday, the pioneering gangs would move on to the next zero day exploit, leaving tech-security companies to defend against an onslaught of script-kiddie hackers and newbie fraudsters sure to swarm in with copycat attacks.

"These guys were a thinking enemy, but not too inventive," says Thompson. "They'd take the attacks that other folks worked out, and then try to obfuscate the attacks to make them hard to detect; then they'd prey on the people who hadn't bothered to patch."

A textbook example came to light on the Friday before the 2007 Super Bowl, held at Dolphin Stadium in Miami. San Diego–based security firm Websense took a call from a customer inquiring as to why Websense's ThreatSeeker scanner was blocking access to the Dolphin Stadium Web site.

A quick test revealed the Web site to be tainted. On the eve of the most widely viewed sporting event on the planet, anyone using a Microsoft Internet Explorer browser lacking the latest security patches who happened to click on the Dolphin Stadium Web site would be turning over his computer to hackers. A malicious program would direct the visitor's PC to a Web site hosted in China, which would then install a back door and a keylogger assigned to capture certain keystrokes.

What made this particular keylogger distinctive was what it did not do. It was programmed to collect user names and passwords for two popular online video games featuring medieval themes: World of Warcraft, a megahit in North America, and Lineage, a favorite in Korea and elsewhere in Asia. The thieves, it seemed, assumed that a certain percentage of visitors to the stadium Web site would be gamers from whom they could loot "gold" used to purchase better weapons and spells.

"They planted data stealers, but only for these games; there was no banking aspect to this particular one," says Dan Hubbard, Websense's vice president of security research.

The gamer hackers, had, in fact, simply mimicked a zero day attack that took place the previous fall. A cybercrime ring, linked to several Russian porn sites, in September 2006 became the first to crack into a component of the Internet Explorer browser called Vector Markup Language, or VML, a tool for rendering graphics. The group tainted Web sites all across the Internet with an exploit that wormed its way into the VML browser flaw to spread spyware and to replenish the attackers' botnets. To slow the rapid advance of VML exploits, Microsoft was forced once more to rush out a patch, this time eight days early. Even so, four months after the VML patch was made available, as the world's most widely viewed sporting spectacle approached, there were still plenty of Internet Explorer browsers with the VML flaw unpatched.

On the Friday and Saturday before the big game, security companies and law enforcement agencies worked together to shut down the Chinese Web site and get the Dolphin Stadium Web site cleaned up and inoculated. As the Super Bowl got under way, virus hunters continued working, cleaning up fifty other high-profile Web sites that were similarly compromised by the gamer hackers, including the home pages of Massachusetts General Hospital, Olympus America Inc., the *American Journalism Review*, the National Multiple Sclerosis Society, and the city of Boston.

Gadi Evron, formerly the Israeli government's Internet security manager, and now the head researcher for Israeli-based Beyond Security, renowned as a vocal advocate for wider collaboration among white hats, noted the good news about the Dolphin Stadium hack: it showed how hypercompetitive tech security companies can set aside rivalries to stop a high-profile attack before it gets out of hand.

Then there was the bad news. Known for expressing his views rather frankly, in rapid-fire bursts, Evron observed that "every single day there are hundreds, thousands, even millions of attacks taking place on the Internet, and each and every single one of them is problematic," he says. "The truth is we can't respond to all of that. We think we can, but we can't. It's become background noise. It's important. We want to respond. We're doing our best to mitigate whatever we can, and respond to whatever we can. But what it comes down to is the Dolphin Stadium attack was the big incident we could devote our goodwill resources to."

The rumble of cybercrime's steady advance, indeed, was becoming a dull, all-too-tolerable roar. It wouldn't take long for the next major move by a well-funded cybercrime group to underscore Evron's observation. It took place a couple of weeks after the Super Bowl and would draw comparatively little notice. The attackers combined a tried-and-true e-mail virus ruse with a cutting-edge Web exploit, and mixed in some next-generation techie magic for good measure.

First, the attackers used a botnet to send out millions of e-mails purporting to carry news about Australian prime minister John Howard, sixty-seven, suffering a heart attack. Howard was in good health at the time; the ruse was a throwback to old-style e-mail viruses that drew attention to naked tennis stars and politicians in compromising positions. Instead of trying to get the recipient to open an attachment, the e-mail suggested clicking on a Web page link to a news story about the heart attack in an Australian newspaper.

By clicking on the link, the victim connected his or her browser to a tainted Web site that silently and swiftly installed a back door and a keylogger—a serious one designed to recognize the log-on pages of sixty different banks, and to capture all keystrokes typed into those pages.

As a final bit of flourish, the attackers engineered something called a Google Maps "mashup." They took the Internet address of the compromised PC and cross-correlated it with a detailed street location drawn from interactive maps supplied as a free online service by Google. "That way they would know from the Google map which bank credentials might be the best ones to use," said Hubbard. "If the victim was in Germany, they'd take the Deutsche Bank data first, instead of the Citibank one."

In the scramble to inoculate PCs against the latest back doors and keyloggers, it was generally taken for granted that corporate PC users, with access to the latest security products and tech staff, were generally better protected than home computer users. But that turned out not to be the case, at least for home PC users who activated their Windows Auto Update service, since they received security patches as soon as Microsoft put them out. That turned out to be much faster than corporate PC users typically got the latest security fixes.

Why so? Most large organizations had become wary of the propensity for patches to crash other software programs, so office workers often did not get their PCs patched until after their company's tech staff could test the patch. The bigger the corporation, the more time-consuming the testing.

"Most large enterprises will spend sometimes as long as a week testing a patch before they roll it out companywide," said Steve Manzuik,

Juniper Networks' senior manager of research and security engineering. That meant criminals' window of opportunity for infecting PCs with zero day attacks was actually open longer in the corporate world than in home settings.

In another sort of counterintuitive development, a vast new sector opened up where cybercriminals could roam, but it did not derive from the work of a brilliant, handsomely paid mercenary programmer. It blossomed thanks to a popularity-starved script kiddie from Los Angeles, nicknamed Samy, who at age nineteen had too much free time on his hands.

Samy was one of the 32 million denizens—including a good many teenagers and adolescents—who populated the MySpace social networking site. MySpace used a hot new technology called AJAX, which stands for asynchronous JavaScript and XML. AJAX has been widely hailed as the enabling technology for "Web 2.0," the coming generation of Web sites that are more feature rich and interactive.

Samy would underscore a lesson tech companies should have learned by now—hastily adding convenience-driven features to the Internet was akin to adding flimsy new doors and windows for criminals to test. Miffed by the brevity of his "friends" list, Samy scratched around for a way to hack into the Microsoft Internet Explorer browser and the Apple Safari browser of anybody who happened to click on his MySpace profile.

He began spending a couple of hours a day tweaking the AJAX component that allowed visitors to view his profile. After about a week, he discovered how to manipulate the code moving through AJAX, and contrived a way to install a self-propagating worm on the Internet Explorer or Safari browser of anyone who clicked on his profile. He included Apple's browser because his girlfriend used a Mac.

Samy's MySpace worm did three silly things: it added Samy to the visitor's friends list; it printed ". . . and Samy is my hero" on the bottom of the visitor's own profile; and it replicated itself to everyone on the visitor's friends list. In an interview on German blogger Phillip Lenssen's popular Google Blogoscoped Web site, Samy noted that "it didn't take a rocket or computer scientist" to guess that his worm had the potential to spread exponentially. In a blog interview, Samy advised Lenssen:

I just had no idea it would proliferate so quickly.
When I saw 200 friend requests after the first 8
hours, I was surprised. After 2,000 a few hours later,
I was worried. Once it hit 200,000 in another few
hours, I wasn't sure what to do but to enjoy whatever
freedom I had left, so I went to Chipotle and ordered
myself a burrito. I went home and it had hit
1,000,000.

Samy was never arrested. He received hundreds of messages from angry MySpace users who didn't consider him a hero for worming his way onto their friends list. It took Los Angeles–based MySpace, purchased in July 2006 by Rupert Murdoch's News Corp. for $580 million, a day to clean out the worm. MySpace deleted Samy's account.

Not long afterward, a copycat hacker launched the Yamanner worm against Yahoo's free e-mail service to spread spam across Europe, and another hacker released the Spaceflash worm, which installed adware on the hard drives of more than a million MySpace users. Both hacked in through AJAX.

That drew the attention of some of the well-funded crime groups. At least six progressively more sophisticated MySpace worms appeared in the second half of 2006. Serious hackers began gathering up MySpace user names and passwords and systematically testing them to see if they might work as log-ons to other popular online services, said SPI Dynamics lead engineer Billy Hoffman.

"These criminals have programs to automatically check all the other big bank and e-commerce sites to see if you use that same user name and password," said Hoffman, "which, chances are, if you're lazy, that's exactly what you do."

AJAX is an enabling technology. It allows users of Google Maps to zoom in on a satellite photo of just about any address. It makes Yahoo Calendar, Yahoo Sports, Yahoo Photos, Yahoo Flickr, and Yahoo Mail come alive. It is the technology behind Windows Live, the slate of cutting-edge online services Microsoft continues to roll out. It is a fountainhead of thousands of ethereal data exchanges between the Web page program and the

Web browser. And as Samy demonstrated, each such exchange is susceptible to being corrupted.

"AJAX introduced a huge attack surface," said Hoffman. "AJAX works under the covers to make Web sites really responsive, but criminals can just as easily use it under the covers to do some really bad stuff."

CHAPTER 16

Self-Contained Units

Exploiters

November 2006, Gainesville, Florida

Anthony Ray works as an undercover house detective. Because he is employed by the giant discount retail chain Wal-Mart, where cashiers are referred to as "associates," Ray's official title is "loss prevention officer." On November 1, 2006, Ray's suspicions were raised by two Hispanic males who entered Wal-Mart 538 in the north end of Gainesville, Florida, and purchased $18,000 worth of gift cards. The men—one who looked to be in his thirties, medium build and clean shaven; the other, much younger, solidly built, with a shaved head and thin mustache—went through several different checkout lines purchasing batches of gift cards in $400 denominations.

Using immaculately produced counterfeit Bank of America Visa credit cards to make the purchases, they amassed a cache of forty-five gift cards. VisaNet's Advanced Authorization fraud-detection technology cleared each transaction in 1.4 seconds. The men made friendly small talk with the Wal-Mart associates, then melted into the sea of shoppers leaving the store. By the time Ray ascertained that the Visa cards were counterfeits, the pair was long gone. Ray pulled the surveillance tapes of the transactions and called Detective Randal Roberts of the Gainesville police.

A short while later, the same two men, joined by a third Hispanic male, entered Wal-Mart 1081 in the south end of Gainesville, fanned out, and this time purchased $24,000 worth of gift cards. Again they used counterfeit Bank of America Visa cards. Again VisaNet cleared each swipe of a counterfeit card in a flash. Before you could say "Life takes Visa," the men were strolling out the door with a stack of some sixty $400 gift cards.

Brent Chewning and Alex Dias, store 1081's loss prevention officers, could do nothing except follow the trio into the parking lot, watch them climb into a white late-model Jeep Commander, and zoom away. The loss prevention officers did, however, jot down the vehicle's license plate number. They, too, pulled the surveillance tapes and began working with Detective Roberts.

A few days later, Marsha Carney, a sixty-five-year-old retiree in Oceanside, California, received a phone call from Bank of America, advising her that her Visa account number had been used to purchase gift cards in sixty-six separate transactions, totaling $24,000, at Wal-Mart store 1081 in Gainesville, Florida. There was one other charge: a $290 meal tab at Stonewood Grill & Tavern, also in Gainesville, on the same day. The gift card scammers evidently treated themselves to a celebratory meal.

"I was shocked," says Carney. "I never would have believed that they could amass such an amount. I hardly used the account, and I never shop at Wal-Mart."

Back in Florida, it didn't take Detective Roberts long to establish that the white Jeep was a rental paid for by the young man with the shaved head and thin mustache. Roberts identified the renter as Irving Jose Escobar, eighteen, of Miami. Escobar's elder partner in the two Gainesville scams was identified as Erick Fernandez Rodriguez, thirty, and the third man was identified as Alexis Arcia, thirty-four, both also from Miami.

The fake Visa cards the men had used had embossed names on the front of the cards that matched fake drivers' licenses the men carried—but did not match the true account holder's data embedded on the magnetic stripe on the back of the card. The account data on the magstripes traced back to purchase records for some 45 million individuals, which retail giant TJX, parent of the TJ Maxx and Marshall's chain of stores, reported as having been hacked from its central databases. That data heist—the biggest ever reported—had unfolded over an eighteen-month period dating back to July 2005. TJX had disclosed the theft on January 17, 2007. By that time, scams using TJX data had turned up in at least six states and eight countries.

Several banks and banking associations would later file a lawsuit against TJX and its transactions bank, Fifth Third Bancorp, seeking to recover losses stemming from fraud committed with data heisted from TJX. The banks estimated their fraud losses from stolen Visa data alone could range as high as $83 million. In an October 2007 court filing, the banks would assert that TJX had drastically underreported the number of records lost. Citing testimony from security officials at Visa and MasterCard, the banks pegged the number of TJX transaction records plucked by hackers at 94 million, not 45 million.

One of those pilfered records belonged to Marsha Carney, who only sporadically used her Bank of America Visa credit card. The retiree recalled using her Visa card at a Marshall's outlet near her Southern California home about a year prior to receiving a phone call from Bank of America informing her about the flurry of gift card purchases approved on the opposite corner of the country. In Florida, Wal-Mart's loss prevention officers had stumbled into what would turn out to be the biggest caper yet converting data stolen from TJX into tangible loot. "I never realized it was going to be this big until I read about it in the newspapers," says Detective Roberts, in a thick Southern drawl. "I was shocked, this happening in a town as small as Gainesville."

Detective Roberts and the Wal-Mart officers began poring over surveillance tapes, credit card receipts, and witness accounts to piece together the crooks' movements. They documented that between October 25 and October 31, Escobar by himself or accompanied by Rodriguez had crisscrossed north Florida making gift-card purchase runs for $35,251, $41,200, $34,000, and $18,000 at different Wal-Mart stores, always in increments of no more than $400—a figure that did not require a manager's approval.

The crooks would pick times of the day when each cavernous store was swarming with shoppers and divide their gift card purchases among the dozens of jammed checkout lines. With each swipe of a counterfeit credit card, VisaNet's brain contacted all the banks involved, set the requisite accounting transactions speeding along, ran Advanced Authorization security checks, and spit back intelligence that Bank of America could use to decide whether to approve the transaction. This all happened in the blink of an eye.

Even though the active account numbers embedded on the magstripes of the counterfeit cards had been stolen from TJX, and even though the true account holders lived in places such as Victorville, California; Warrington, Pennsylvania; Amherst, Massachusetts; and Silver Spring, Maryland, any red flags raised by VisaNet's Advanced Authorization security review went ignored. Escobar and Rodriguez made small talk with the Wal-Mart associates as the built-for-speed payments system kept humming along. Each stack of $400 gift cards issued by Wal-Mart represented a seamless conversion of stolen TJX data into near cash.

On November 2, the day after the two Gainesville heists, Escobar and Rodriguez turned up at a Wal-Mart in Starke, Florida, and used four counterfeit credit cards to purchase $32,800 worth of gift cards. Again VisaNet processed the transactions without a hitch, allowing Escobar and Rodriguez to add to their carload of $400 gift cards. Escobar then drove south to Miami for some serious shopping.

Though only eighteen, Escobar appeared to be the ringleader of nine other coconspirators, including his mother, Nair Zuleima Alvarez, and his wife, Zenia Mercedes Llorente, police say. Between November 2006 and January 2007, Escobar personally went on several outlandish buying sprees at the Miami Sam's Club warehouse store, a Wal-Mart subsidiary, located a short drive from his home near the Miami International Airport. As himself, or sometimes going by the alias Anthony Lostaglio, he spent at least $225,000 on plasma TVs, computers, jewelry, and other goods, paying with fistfuls of $400 Wal-Mart gift cards.

To allay suspicion, the smooth-talking Escobar posed as the owner of an import-export business and chatted up female employees. Escobar stashed some of the booty at his mother's home. He returned some merchandise for cash refunds, and he probably sold some of the gift cards, according to Florida law enforcement officials. Wal-Mart spokesman John Simley pointed out that Sam's Club patrons include many small-business owners who routinely purchase big-ticket items such as computers, furniture, and office supplies. It wasn't unusual, Smiley says, for customers to plunk down gift cards worth thousands of dollars on any given visit.

Escobar, Alvarez, Llorente, Dianelly Hernandez, Reinier Alvarez, and Julio Alberti were arrested on March 8, 2007; Alexis Arcia was arrested shortly thereafter. Erick Rodriguez, Hector Rodriguez, and Armando Ochoa remained at large as of fall 2007. The Escobar gift-card ring was believed responsible for using counterfeit credit cards to buy gift cards at stores in fifty of Florida's sixty-seven counties, which they then used to acquire more than $1 million worth of electronic gear, jewelry, and other goods, police and prosecutors say.

Escobar would plead guilty to an organized scheme to defraud and would receive a prison sentence. Four others—including his mother, Nair Alvarez, and wife, Zenia Llorente—also pled guilty and got probation. Alvarez would be deported to Venezuela, and Arcia was let go.

The bust up of the Florida crime group provided law enforcement with a snapshot of how easily the full cycle of financial fraud in the digital age can be spun into a big-time operation. The Edmonton meth addicts had relied on Socrates to keep them connected to a ragtag collection of maverick data harvesters and account hijackers via IRC chat channels. Then to carry out the last, riskiest step—turning stolen data into cash at the street level— the Edmonton cell organized enough for cell members to gorge themselves on $10,000-a-day drug binges.

Escobar's crew operated at the same street level except that the stakes were magnitudes of order higher, and the organized crime component much more professional, so much so that the takedown of the Miami gift-carding cell raised more questions for law enforcement than it answered.

Organized crime groups have much in common with terrorist cells. Both are organized to resist penetration. Information is passed along on a need-to-know basis. Cells operate as much as possible as self-contained units. That way, if anyone gets arrested or any cell gets knocked out of commission, the damage to the overall organization is limited.

Escobar told U.S. Secret Service agents that his introduction to gift-card scamming came by way of a high school acquaintance he knew only as Miguel, whom he ran into one day at a BP gas station on Flagler Street in Miami. Escobar supplied Miguel with a passport photo, and, later that day, Miguel produced a counterfeit driver's license for one Anthony Lostaglio bearing Escobar's photo.

Using counterfeited credit cards in the name of Anthony Lostaglio, Escobar purchased his first gift cards in Orlando, many of which he turned over to Miguel. Miguel, in turn, sold the gift cards for 50 percent of face value and split the profits with Escobar. Since most merchants consider gift cards as good as cash, and since anyone can confirm the value of a gift card simply by calling the toll-free number conveniently posted on the back of most gift cards, selling discounted cards was a snap.

Escobar started traveling north on I-95, ranging as far as Savannah, Georgia, and stopping at towns along the interstate to haul in gift cards using the fake IDs and credit cards supplied by Miguel. To prove himself worthy to graduate to a higher-level role, Escobar had to supply a new contact—known only as "El Flaco," the Skinny One—with proceeds of a major haul.

Escobar, who became known as "the Venezuelan," a reference to the country of his birth, satisfied El Flaco by delivering twenty-six $400 gift cards with a face value of $10,400. After that, El Flaco directed the Venezuelan to work with a handler named Alian, who lived near Miami's Dolphin Mall. Alian would typically supply Escobar with two counterfeit drivers' licenses, one in the name of Anthony Lostaglio and the other in the name of Michael Juares, each bearing a copy of the passport photo Escobar originally handed over to Miguel.

Alian would also usually supply Escobar with at least twenty-five counterfeit credit cards with the name Anthony Lostaglio and twenty more with the name Michael Juares. The magnetic stripe on the back of each card would already be encoded with data from a stolen credit card account.

After completing a successful road trip, Escobar dutifully obeyed instructions to hand over the ill-gotten gift cards to Alian, along with the counterfeit drivers' licenses and the bogus credit cards. That way Alian could control use of the aliases Anthony Lostaglio and Michael Juares. He could also reload fresh stolen account data onto the magstripes of the fake credit cards.

Sometimes Alian would accompany Escobar on a road trip, bringing along a laptop and a device called a magstripe reader/writer, which can delete and insert data onto any wallet-sized plastic card bearing a magnetic stripe on the back. Possession and use of magstripe reader/writers are completely legal; they are widely used to reset hotel room keys, create grocery store discount cards, enable phone calling cards, and the like. And crooks use them to embed stolen account data on payment cards.

Escobar gained enough trust so that he was allowed to take the laptop on a couple of trips and learned how to encode stolen account data onto the counterfeit cards. On Alian's laptop, the software program that worked in conjunction with the magstripe reader/writer to encode cards was accessed by clicking on an icon labeled "Christmas Cards."

Under the cell structure of the Florida gift-card ring, Escobar had no need to know anything about the skilled counterfeiters adept at using commercial embossers and printers and graphics software to turn the blank front sides of magnetic striped cards into works of art: counterfeit credit cards slick enough to fool most sales clerks. Those master forgers, in turn, had no need to know anything about the cells controlling the ebb and flow of the stolen account data. Neither the street scammers, nor the forgers, nor the hackers who broke into TJX's database had any reason to be knowledgeable about the deep-pocketed crime lords who likely funded the TJX hack and skimmed the cream off the profits.

In August 2007 Turkish police picked off what they believed to be a key cell leader with the arrest of Maksym Yastremskiy, a Ukrainian, at a nightclub in the resort city of Kemer. A police official described Yastremskiy as "one of the world's important and well-known computer pirates," according to Turkish news agency Anatolia.

Greg Crabb, an investigator for the U.S. Postal Inspection Service, told *Boston Globe* reporter Ross Kerber that Yastremskiy was likely the largest seller of stolen TJX account numbers. Crabb said Yastremskiy allegedly sold stolen TJX data through online carding forums hosted overseas. Prices ranged from $20 to $100 per stolen account number, depending on credit limits and other variables, and buys were made in batches of up to 10,000 numbers.

Irving Escobar had no reason to know, or care, where the account numbers on the magstripes of the faked Visa cards he used came from. Whether Yastremskiy supplied El Flaco was meaningless. All that mattered to the Venezuelan was that by focusing on his cell's tasks, he was able to earn enough cash in a matter of months to tool around Miami in a black 2006 Dodge Charger. The Florida attorney general's office and the Florida Department of Law Enforcement concurred that Escobar's role was limited to risky grunt work that nevertheless represented an essential final step in a well-funded, tightly run organized crime operation.

Following his arrest, Escobar agreed to assist in a U.S. Secret Service sting to take down Miguel Bruguera, twenty, of Miami, a recruiter and distributor on the level of Alian. Cooperating with Special Agent Shannon Jayroe, Escobar arranged to meet Bruguera on April 17, 2007, in room 709 of the Orlando Embassy Suites to load up on fresh counterfeit credit cards.

Just prior to the meeting, Agent Jayroe frisked Escobar to confirm that he was not in possession of any counterfeiting equipment or fake cards, fastened a hidden recording device on his torso, then sent him up to the room. After a few minutes inside the room with Bruguera, Escobar stepped outside and called Jayroe by cell phone. Bruguera had come bearing forty fake credit cards, Escobar reported, some embossed with the name Anthony Lostaglio, one of Escobar's aliases. Bruguera was at that moment receiving credit card magstripe data over the phone from someone named Frank, Escobar told the agent.

Bruguera's main task was to embed the data on the empty magstripes on the back of the forty counterfeit cards. Frank, who was now relaying the magstripe data over the phone, was the next level up in the hierarchy.

After relaying this intelligence to Jayroe, Escobar went back into the room. A short while later, he and Bruguera climbed into Bruguera's white Cadillac Escalade and, tailed by Secret Service agents, drove to a nearby Wal-Mart superstore. There they purchased several gift cards with the freshly minted counterfeit credit cards supplied by Bruguera, then drove back to the Embassy Suites. Jayroe and other agents moved in to arrest Bruguera in the parking lot.

From inside Bruguera's Escalade the agents confiscated eight counterfeit credit cards encoded with account numbers on the magstripes that were different from those showing on the embossed front of the cards. And they grabbed one Wachovia debit card in the name of Miguel Bruguera. The number embossed on the front of Bruguera's personal card—4828-5357-4511-3016—was different from the number on the magstripe—4388-5491-5349-4563, which belonged to a breached account.

The agents also took into evidence two portable skimmers—small plastic devices, black in color, about half the size of a pack of cigarettes. These Mini-Mag Portable Magstripe Readers, model number PMR202, sold on the Internet for about $550 and were described on a Web site as "ideal for applications that require the capture and storage of magnetic stripe data without the presence of a computer or an external power supply." Each skimmer had enough internal memory to store magstripe data for 1,000 payment cards.

"Based on my training and experience," agent Jayroe wrote in an affidavit, "a skimmer, or skimming device, is used to store credit card information including but not limited to credit card numbers, credit card account information, and account holder information. A skimmer is a common device used by an individual to secretly obtain and store fraudulently obtained credit card information."

After helping authorities take down Bruguera, Escobar, at age nineteen, received a five-year prison sentence. He was also fined $50,000 and ordered to pay $509,770 in restitution. Escobar remained stoic, saying little, at his September 2007 sentencing hearing in state court in Jacksonville. Earlier, however, the ambitious young man had complained in a series of letters to prosecutors that he was "the smallest fish" in a vast criminal enterprise.

"I was just a regular kid until I met those people that put me into this," Escobar wrote in a June 2007 letter. "What's really bothering me the most is that the real ringleaders of all this are still in the streets committing other crimes."

Enablers

Credit Freeze

Let's say you have reason to believe your personal information is in play for criminals. Perhaps you've received a letter of notification from your college, your bank, a government agency, or a major retailer, like TJ Maxx, that your data has been lost or stolen. Maybe, like Melinda Scott, you've actually experienced bogus transactions and endured the hassle of producing affidavits and switching account numbers. Or maybe you've got a nagging feeling that you may have fallen for a phishing scam or clicked on a link to a tainted Web site that planted a data-stealing keylogger on your PC.

If your Social Security number, in particular, is circulating in the vast pool of stolen identity data, you're at risk of becoming a new-account fraud victim, like David Hernandez. New-account fraud is by far the most invasive type of identity theft. It is difficult to detect, tough to resolve, and problematic to prosecute. Scammers use your Social Security number to open and control new financial accounts by piggybacking on your good credit. They typically pile up outstanding balances and destroy your credit rating. You can end up paying thousands of dollars in excess interest fees, and full recovery often takes years.

According to the Federal Trade Commission, the best thing you can do to protect yourself against new-account fraud is go to Experian, Equifax, or TransUnion and subscribe for a ninety-day fraud alert. It will cost you $6 to $12 a month, and you'll have to remember to renew it every three months. The good news, the FTC says, is that you have to buy the fraud alert from only one of the credit bureaus, since federal rules require the other two to be notified and activate fraud alerts as well.

What the FTC won't tell you is that even with a fraud alert, the credit bureau will still issue your credit report to lenders, albeit flagged, as part of the automated credit-issuing system. Neither will the FTC give you any guidance on how diligent you can expect the first bureau to be about following the rules and alerting the other two bureaus. Nor will the FTC advise you that some lenders routinely disregard fraud alerts.

"There are companies in such a hurry to issue credit that they will open an account with a fraud alert on there," says Mari Frank, an attorney and privacy consultant. "You're only protected to the degree that creditors choose to follow the law."

Banks that issue credit cards, in particular, have a disincentive to heed fraud alerts, which tend to slow down the automated credit-issuing and payments system. And, after all, fraud losses most of the time are borne by merchants, through charge-backs. So the credit card–issuing bank really risks very little by issuing a card to a crook. Meanwhile, that $6 to $12 monthly fee you pay to "alert" you that someone has requested your credit report is almost pure profit for the credit bureaus. By the spring of 2007, fraud alerts had become a major generator of revenue and profits, with Javelin Strategy and Research estimating that 11 million Americans subscribed to credit-monitoring services.

"These so-called credit-monitoring services are really just a marketing gimmick because they don't actually block thieves from opening credit accounts," wrote Eric Bourassa, a consumer advocate with Massachusetts PIRG, in a July 2006 report to the Massachusetts legislature.

If you really want protection against new-account fraud, the absolute best thing you can do, say credit consultants and security experts, is to do a credit freeze. A credit freeze bars the credit bureaus from issuing your credit report to anyone. Because few lenders will issue credit without first seeing a credit report, identity thieves won't be able to use your data to open new accounts.

"We believe a credit freeze is not only the strongest tool; it is the only tool consumers can use to prevent identity theft before it happens," says Lauren Moughon, associate state director of advocacy for AARP Washington.

And yet, credit freezes didn't exist until 2003, and by the end of 2007 they were still impossible to do in a few states. Why? Credit freezes are anathema to credit bureaus. Since Equifax's hoop-skirted spies first gathered intelligence on Atlanta newcomers, the credit-issuing system has gotten faster and faster at pulling histories and issuing reports.

Credit freezes represented a completely foreign mechanism, and credit bureaus refused to acknowledge they were even possible until California's first-of-its-kind credit freeze law took effect in January 2003. The credit bureaus dispatched the Consumer Data Industry Association—the organization that came to power by derailing Senator William Proxmire, back in 1970—to try to block passage of the California law.

CDIA argued that a credit freeze wouldn't stop someone using a stolen credit card number to purchase items or steal cash advances, conveniently declining to mention that the credit card issuer generally made consumers whole in such cases. Joined by lobbyists representing major retailers, auto lenders, and mortgage brokers, CDIA made the case that consumers might not be able to get a new credit card, buy a home, or get a mortgage without first lifting the freeze, which could take several days.

CDIA couldn't stop the California law, but it got California lawmakers to insert a $10-per-bureau fee—which was really a $30 fee since a freeze was useless without all three bureaus participating. It also won placement of a provision requiring credit freeze requests to be made by certified mail, requiring the consumer to shell out another $10 in postage. Unable to block credit freezes in California, CDIA at least made them an expensive hassle.

The credit bureaus reinforced that strategy by requiring additional fees to unlock, or thaw, a freeze, and requiring that consumers include copies of a driver's license and other documentation in the certified letter. None of the credit bureaus made mention of the availability of freezes on the main pages of their Web sites.

For the next two and a half years, credit bureaus were able to rest easy as far as credit freezes were concerned. Only four other states followed California's lead. The CDIA got Louisiana to also require a $30 fee along with a cumbersome application process involving certified mail. And its persistent lobbyists actually won back ground in Texas, Vermont, and Washington, where CDIA convinced lawmakers to limit credit freezes to those who could prove they were victims of identity theft and produce a police report to that effect.

Washington state attorney general Rob McKenna, who would later push to rescind that limitation in his state, says, "It was like telling someone you can't put a dead bolt on your front door until after you've been burglarized."

The obstacles planted in California, Louisiana, Texas, Vermont, and Washington ensured that relatively few consumers would opt for credit freezes. That, in turn, allowed the credit bureaus to argue in states where freeze proposals subsequently cropped up that there really was no demand for such things. And so credit freezes remained a minor irritant—until the escapades of Mr. O and compatriots hit the national headlines in early spring 2005.

The controversy over ChoicePoint's fluid numbers game—and ChoicePoint's cavalier sale of records for upward of 4 million individuals to

Nigerian con artists—was followed by a nonstop series of disclosures of other high-visibility data heists. Privacy advocates began demanding credit freezes and questioning why the process had to be so expensive and difficult to implement. Almost overnight nearly two dozen states proposed credit freeze bills; by the end of 2007 close to forty states would enact credit freeze laws.

As credit freeze fervor spread through the states, CDIA retrenched on its home turf and the setting of its greatest successes: Washington, D.C. It lent behind-the-scenes support to Representative Steven LaTourette (R-OH), who coauthored the Financial Data Protection Act of 2006. LaTourette's proposal sought to preempt all state credit freeze laws, superseding them with a federal law modeled after the Vermont law, which limited credit freezes only to those who could produce a police report proving they were the victims of identity theft.

In a June 2006 interview with one of the authors, LaTourette argued that the patchwork of state-by-state credit freezes needed to be kept in check to keep the nation's financial system from unraveling.

"Even the simplest process of buying groceries with your credit or debit card will break down if we allow a patchwork of competing and conflicting state laws," he asserted.

LaTourette's bill died in committee in the summer of 2006. The credit bureaus' hope to undermine troublesome state laws and retrench around a probusiness federal law—a tactic that worked so well in shaping the Federal Credit Reporting Act in 1970—this time would fall short. A national news event came along to cripple the credit industry's campaign. In May 2006, the Veterans Administration disclosed the theft of sensitive data, including Social Security numbers, for 26.5 million veterans and active-duty military personnel—everyone alive with a military service record.

Privacy advocates argued, effectively, that if the LaTourette bill became law, and limited credit freezes became the national standard, then vets and military personnel who lived in states permitting unrestricted credit freezes would lose that option. With their Social Security numbers in play, they would have to wait to be burglarized before they could install a dead bolt on the front door.

Expediters

Gozi

While studying computer science at the University of Alabama in Huntsville in the early 1990s, Don Jackson volunteered to serve as a reserve deputy for the Jefferson County (Alabama) Sheriff's office. That got him into a Rolling Stones concert for free to work security. He also got to help dismantle and analyze video poker machines used by nightclubs to distribute promotional prizes. His task was to verify that the programming incorporated the element of chance. His brief taste of security and digital sleuthing foreshadowed Jackson's ensuing career as a virus hunter.

In January 2007, Jackson, a security researcher at Atlanta-based SecureWorks with fifteen years of experience, began tracking a Web-based data-stealing program that had the look of a milestone. He christened it Gozi, after a little chameleon-like cartoon character he and a friend in grade school had invented.

Gozi, the malicious program, was cutting-edge, to be sure. It lurked on several thousand Web pages, mainly specialist-interest Web sites, the online gathering spots for hobbyists of every stripe and discussion forums on every imaginable topic. Such Web sites typically ran on Web page servers that used bare-bones security. Anyone using Internet Explorer who clicked on a Gozi-tainted page would get infected with a keylogger designed to steal typed-in data. Gozi then transmitted the stolen data to a server in St. Petersburg, Russia.

Gozi was choosy. It captured only the data moving across the Secure Socket Layer, the mechanism that encrypts data typed into online forms; such forms included anything with a submit button—account log-in pages, online banking pages, shopping cart pages, job applications, medical benefits pages, opinion surveys. Gozi was smart and quick. It grabbed the data just before it hit the Security Socket Layer encryption sequence. And Gozi was elusive. Jackson tested thirty of the top antivirus programs and found that none detected Gozi.

Going largely undetected for fifty days, Gozi hauled in more than 10,000 records containing sensitive data from about 5,200 PC users. Jackson traced back to where Gozi was sending all this data and discovered a stunning repository—a server located on a Russian-owned business network that was notoriously slow to respond to complaints, and known to be a haven for purveyors of viruses and phishing kits with names like Snatch, Grab, Pinch, Haxdoor, and Rockphish. Stored on this server Jackson found employee log-in sequences from more than 300 companies and government organizations, including several law enforcement agencies at the federal and state level; medical records of health-care employees and patients; payment system and online banking user names and passwords; credit card numbers with CVV2 codes and PINs; and some 3,000 Social Security numbers.

Yet for all of its capabilities, there was nothing in the technical pedigree of Gozi that Jackson hadn't seen before. The coding it used to corrupt Web pages derived from other Web page exploits like the Dolphin Stadium Super Bowl 2007 hack and the Windows metafile zero day attack in December 2005. The way it grabbed data from the Security Socket Layer, while a highly sophisticated technique, had been accomplished by others, as well. In fact, Gozi appeared to be assembled from off-the-shelf components, like a garage-built hot rod. Anyone with determination and the right connections could have shopped for its main parts on the Internet and assembled it modularly with a modicum of technical expertise.

What set Gozi apart, however, was the way it packaged its storehouse of stolen data for sale so as to extract maximum profits. The server storing the stolen data hosted a slick, customer-friendly Web site. Patrons were required to log on to individual accounts. Once logged on, they could use a search function to find precisely the data that suited their particular scamming needs, along with associated prices, including discounts for bulk orders. The reference currency: WMZ, a Web money unit roughly equivalent to the U.S. dollar. Cumulative listed value of all the data for sale: $2 million.

"They put in a customer-friendly front end and priced everything according to what might be considered valuable in the data," says Jackson. "Having configurable price points and customer log-ins in server applications that manage stolen data was novel. The database and interface customization features were indicative of the growing trend of malicious software being sold as a service."

Gozi's creators were by no means the only thieves experimenting with clever ways to turn ordinary Web pages into snares. By spring 2007, profit-minded intruders were corrupting Web pages by the tens of thousands, implanting an array of malicious programs that connected the PC of anyone who simply clicked on the tainted page to a "mother ship" server, often in Russia or China. Silently, these mother ships sucked up any data typed into online forms—especially banking, stock trading, and payment system log-ins and shopping cart pages. Some mother ships also sent out bot programs, thus slotting the captured PC into a bot network useful for spreading spam, phishing attacks, and DDoS attacks.

Cyveillance, an Arlington, Virginia–based security firm that monitors e-mail traffic and Web pages, identified 2 million tainted Web pages between October 2006 and March 2007. The corrupted pages either distributed spyware and adware without the recipients' consent, or embedded data-harvesting programs on the hard drives of unwitting visitors. Whenever possible, Cyveillance traced back to the mother ships. It routinely found repositories holding sensitive data for 10,000 to 200,000 individuals. By early 2007, the security firm had retrieved from such mother ships data stolen from 3.2 million individuals, including more than 1 million Social Security numbers.

"We're seeing a huge increase in Web sites doing this," says James Brooks, Cyveillance director of product management.

Data harvesters who specialized in Web page exploits proved to be endlessly enterprising. In April 2007, Roger Thompson at Exploit Prevention Labs discovered that anyone who Googled "betterbusinessbureau" saw a sponsored link to www.bbb.org among the paid-for search results on the right edge of Google's results pages. A crook had purchased the ad slot from Google and posted the Better Business Bureau's true Web site address. However, by clicking on the sponsored link, the user's PC was actually linked to a mother ship in Russia. The mother ship installed a standard keylogger.

It also inserted a series of questions that appeared if and when the PC user happened to click on the links to the Web sites of 100 major banks. The questions sought to gather more details from the banking client—mother's maiden name, PINs, and the like. Google deleted the corrupted ad soon after Thompson alerted them. The search giant declined to say how many other similar ads it had taken down. Thompson observed, "It speaks to the level of cunning and sophistication of the bad guys."

Even as insidious Web site hacks like Gozi and tainted Google ads rose to the fore, cybercriminals continued to refine and improve good old-fashioned e-mail viruses. The notorious Storm e-mail virus first began spreading in Europe and the United States in January 2007 enticing recipients to click on a tainted Web link purporting to be a news story about a deadly weather catastrophe. As the antivirus companies updated filters to block such e-mail, Storm's controllers switched tactics and began sending out tainted links to online greeting cards.

"It's the perfect example of the cat-and-mouse game where the author modifies the threat to stay ahead," says Ben Greenbaum, senior researcher at antivirus supplier Symantec.

Clicking on a corrupted e-card link caused the victim's PC to be turned into a spam-spreading bot. Storm's controllers emulated Netsky's creator, Sven Jaschan, by tweaking versions of their virus faster than antivirus companies could update filters to block new infections. By the summer of 2007 Storm e-mail inundated the Internet. In one two-week period, e-mail management company Postini blocked 415 million Storm e-mails, as many as 49 million in a twenty-four-hour period. Prior to Storm, Postini blocked about 1 million viral e-mails on an average day.

Storm-infected bots were distinctive: they spread spam hyping certain penny stocks in support of a variation of the pump-and-dump scam. Storm's controllers infected PCs for the express purpose of creating a massive bot network they could use to broadcast spam urging investors to buy penny stocks they owned. When the share price spiked, they would sell at a profit. In March 2007, the Securities and Exchange Commission suspended trading for thirty-five companies that allegedly benefited from such spam e-mail campaigns hyping their thinly traded shares.

In late summer 2007, SecureWorks' researcher Don Jackson discovered that Storm's controllers had adopted an additional method to infect PCs: they began planting invisible infections on hobby Web sites and community forums, including a forum for Apple Macintosh users. Merely browsing to one of these low-traffic, seemingly innocuous Web sites infected the visitor's computer.

None of the techniques Storm used, taken alone, were particularly innovative. But combining them toward a single goal had never been done on this scale. "It's a vivid illustration of how run-of-the-mill crooks are taking yesterday's scams and leveraging them forward using e-mail and sophisticated malicious hacking tools," says Patrick Peterson, vice president of technology for security firm IronPort Systems.

Elaborate stock-manipulation scams represented just one way cyber-crooks had begun to turn stolen data and hacked PCs into cash generators. In early 2007, Chicago-based security firm Authentify caught a cybercriminal using bots and stolen data to fill out online loan applications by the thousands. Authentify supplies technology that helps merchants and banks verify that the PC user instigating an online transaction is who he or she claims to be. One of its security systems flushed out a bot network programmed to search for Web pages where consumers can apply online for credit cards, cell phone accounts, and auto loans. Upon finding such Web pages, the botnet filled out the applications with stolen data; on each application the mailing address and phone number routed new credit cards and billing statements to the thieves.

John Zurawski, Authentify's vice president of sales and marketing at the time, estimated that fraudulent online credit applications had increased 50 percent since early 2006. "They'll hit the same store, the same bank, the same payment gateway," says Zurawski, "anything where you can apply for instant credit or a line of credit online."

In the thriving world of cybercrime, the scammers using stolen personal information to fill out new-account applications or manufacture counterfeit credit cards were at the top of the food chain. They depended on data harvesters—hackers, insider thieves, phishers, and virus writers—to continually replenish the pool of stolen identity data. IRC chat channels and carding forums, like CardersMarket, provided a venue for wholesalers and brokers. And some independent-minded harvesters, like the Gozi crew, sought to bypass the middlemen and sell directly to the scammers.

Reacting to Jackson's findings, antivirus companies began to detect and block the original version of Gozi. But improved derivatives soon cropped up. It quickly became harder for virus hunters and law enforcement to trace back to the mother ship.

"It all points to the evolution of this kind of software," Jackson said. "Gozi was relatively simple. But they made a lot of money using these techniques. So they made changes to avoid takedowns. The next variants of something like Gozi will extend even further."

CHAPTER 17

Under Siege

Exploiters

April–June 2007, Edmonton

Detective Bob Gauthier returned from a Hilton Head, South Carolina, vacation in April 2007 raving about long walks on gorgeous beaches bordered by fields of vibrant wildflowers. Then it was back to the gritty work of stopping cybercrooks. With his longtime partner, Al Vonkeman, having taken early retirement the previous summer, Gauthier had become the city's de facto top cop on the cybercrime beat. Yet the more fraudsters and scammers Gauthier arrested, the more they seemed to multiply. Meth and crack cocaine invariably added to the mix. The drugs seemed to fuel the crooks' uncanny ability to find and exploit endless weaknesses in a card-based payments system built for speed—and now extended fully to the Internet.

A tip came in from the Holiday Inn Express in downtown Edmonton. The hotel's manager suspected a guest of trying to use a fraudulent payment card. Gauthier recognized the name of the guest—Contreras, a twenty-six-year-old Filipino-Canadian he had been hunting for months. Word on the street was that Contreras, a native of Manitoba and an old associate of Frankie, was the leader of a new cell of Edmonton hotshot scammers. Gauthier also heard that Socrates had fallen back into a criminal life. After his third arrest by Gauthier and a long stint in jail, Socrates had stayed clean through the fall of 2006. He successfully completed a work-release program and had been clean and sober, toiling as a short-order cook, and finding a girlfriend. But word on the street was that Socrates was back on meth, back on the Internet, and was conspiring with Contreras.

Informants told Gauthier that Contreras's cell was being fed large blocks of magstripe data phished and keylogged from credit card customers of U.S. and Canadian banks. Contreras was reportedly doing something novel with the stolen data. Instead of embedding the data on the magstripes of counterfeit credit cards, like the Florida gift-card scammers had done, Contreras had perfected a much simpler ruse: embed stolen magstripe data

214   ZERO DAY THREAT

onto prepaid MasterCard and Visa gift cards, especially prepaid Mytreat Visa gift cards issued by Vancity, Canada's largest credit union.

When Visa, MasterCard, and American Express jumped into the marketing of prepaid gift cards a few years ago, it was to compete against the rising popularity of gift cards issued by just about every major retailer from Blockbuster and Starbucks to Target and Wal-Mart. The credit card companies began pitching bank-issued gift cards as more universally useful than individual store gift cards, which limit usage to the namesake store.

To get their gift cards to work everywhere, Visa, MasterCard, and American Express simply integrated gift cards into the same automated payments system used for credit and debit card transactions. Thus, bank-issued gift cards can be purchased from thousands of banks, credit unions, supermarkets, drugstores, and convenience stores. They can be acquired in person at a checkout line, online at banking and credit union Web sites, or at Web sites like icardgiftcard.com. Acquiring a bank-issued gift card is now as easy as buying a pack of gum at the grocery store or ordering movie tickets online.

Like store-issued gift cards, the bank-issued gift cards are flat, with no embossed lettering or numerals and no individual's name imprinted anywhere on the card; like credit and debit cards, they have a magnetic stripe on the back. At millions of restaurants and retail outlets, bank-issued gift cards are as good as cash—no proof of identity is required to use them.

Consumers pay a steep premium for all of this convenience. Bank-issued gift cards cost $3 to $6 to activate. Some charge transaction usage fees: 45 cents to pump gas, 50 cents to check your balance by phone, $9.95 to process a refund should you lose the card. Most also charge an "aging fee"— after the sixth month of ownership, $5 is docked from the card like clockwork each month until the value of the gift card reaches zero. So if you were to stick a $100 bank-issued gift card in a drawer and forget about it, its value would shrink to zero after twenty-six months. Pure profit for the bank.

Scammers like Contreras recognized fresh criminal opportunities in bank-issued gift cards. They soon figured out how easy it was to convert an authentic, bank-issued gift card into a stolen credit card, simply by altering the magstripe data. To the automated, card-based payments system, the altered bank-issued gift card would be recognized as the credit card whose account data was embedded on the magstripe.

Since merchants long ago stopped imprinting credit card account numbers on sales receipts, there would be no way for a cashier to visually confirm that the sixteen-digit account number approved by the system matched the sixteen-digit number imprinted on the face of the nameless gift card.

"This is a way to convert small-value cards into big-value plastic," says John Pironti, information risk strategist at Getronics. "It's not very easy to create a counterfeit Visa card from scratch. But if I whip out a generic Visa gift card, with an altered magstripe, with no name on it, and no way to trace it, as long as I exude confidence while making the purchase, no sales clerk in the world is going to stop me."

Gauthier got on Contreras's tail after fielding a tip about a mailbox account Contreras opened at a private mail center that was receiving a flood of bank-issued gift cards, fraudulently ordered credit cards, bank statements, and the like. Contreras appeared to have no permanent residence. He moved from hotel room to hotel room accompanied by a twenty-two-year-old woman from Sherwood Park, an upper-middle-class suburb east of the city.

Upon returning from his spring holiday, Gauthier hustled over to the Holiday Inn Express. But Contreras and his girlfriend, apparently spooked over the delay in trying to check out of their room, had hightailed it without paying their bill. They left behind six pieces of luggage and a cache of evidence of criminal activity. From the trash can, Gauthier plucked a torn-up piece of paper on which was scribbled magnetic stripe data for a half dozen credit card accounts.

Gauthier rummaged through the luggage and recovered lists of stolen magstripe data, how-to manuals on phishing, skimming, and using magstripe reader/writers, and dozens of gift cards and counterfeit credit cards. But that wasn't all.

"In his luggage he had a magstripe reader/writer, thumb drives, a load of phished data from U.S. banks and credit unions, like Wachovia and Citibank," says Gauthier. "There was a ton of stuff there.

"Let's say your credit card data gets stolen. The information gets wired over the Internet. They have this magstripe reader/writer, and now they're downloading this information onto prepaid MasterCards and Visas. So they're loading all this money onto these prepaid cards using information skimmed from the States."

Three days after Contreras gave him the slip at the Holiday Inn Express, Gauthier received another tip. Contreras has set up temporary shop in a restaurant-bar called Peppers, at the Westmount shopping mall, a couple of miles northwest of city hall. He was there now. Gauthier mobilized a team of plainclothes cops to surround Peppers and begin tracking the suspect's movements.

Contreras, accompanied by another male who turned out to be uninvolved, was typing away on his laptop, while his girlfriend fed cash into a video lottery gaming machine. As Gauthier entered the restaurant to make the arrest, the suspect had just stood up and was stepping away from his laptop. Contreras tried to lie about his name, but Gauthier would have none of it.

On the table next to the laptop was a sheet of paper listing the full personal and financial profile of a male ID theft victim. "He was obviously doing something on his computer with this stuff," says Gauthier.

From the suspect's pockets Gauthier recovered an expandable baton, a switchblade knife, a canister of pepper spray, and a couple of thumb drives, the small data-storage devices that plug into computers' USB ports. In a briefcase sitting nearby, the detective found more thumb drives, CDs filled with identity theft scam how-to manuals, and a ream of computer printouts—about 500 pages containing account data phished from customers of U.S. banks, many in southeastern states.

"From source information we think all of the stuff we got from him in the bar ties back to the hard-copy papers we pulled from one of the suitcases, and that all of this will be loaded with international stuff," says Gauthier.

As Contreras sat in jail awaiting trial, word on the street was that another magstripe reader/writer had surfaced and someone had replaced him churning out altered bank-issued gift cards. Working with the Royal Canadian Mounted Police, Gauthier began reviewing surveillance tapes of suspects using altered bank-issued gift cards to make purchases at major retail outlets all around Edmonton. Socrates turned up on one of the surveillance tapes.

In early June 2007, Gauthier got a tip that Socrates had set up shop with a new girlfriend in a tiny apartment in an ancient building called the Devonshire. Gauthier secured a search warrant and took a team of eager young cops, letting them lead the way down the hall to Socrates's ground-floor pad. When no one obeyed the order to open the door, the young cops tried to kick it open. But the door was rock solid. It took a couple of minutes and multiple heavy kicks to break the door free from its hinges.

Socrates and his girlfriend were inside. The cops face-planted Socrates to the floor and handcuffed him. In the bedroom Gauthier found two laptops, one of them hooked up to a giant HDTV, turned on and showing a green screen gently raining numerals, much like the computer screens in the movie *The Matrix*. A third laptop in the living room was connected to a wireless router, with the reception unit dangling out of the window to search out and tap into a neighbor's unsecured Internet connection. This was a variation of the trick Socrates and Marilyn had used back in 2004 when they operated out of a camper van parked in an alley and tapped into the Internet by stringing a phone cord into the telephone conjunction box of a nearby apartment building. Strewn around the apartment were meth pipes, empty baggies, and other drug paraphernalia.

This time—the fourth time in three years he was arrested by Gauthier—Socrates had nothing to say.

"I said, 'Buddy, what are you doing?'" recalls Gauthier. "He wouldn't even look at me."

Gauthier found no magstripe reader/writer in Socrates's apartment. He did, however, take into evidence several prepaid Mytreat Visa gift cards, with Socrates's signature on the back, and later confirmed that a Mytreat Visa card had been used to purchase the flat-screen TV raining digits in Socrates's bedroom.

Enablers
Bow-Tied Warrior

When the Consumer Data Industry Association deployed Eric J. Ellman to Montana in the spring of 2006, things weren't going terribly well in the credit industry's war of attrition to eradicate, or at least defuse, credit freezes. The credit bureaus' plan to push through a limited federal credit freeze that would preempt the sudden onrush of unrestricted state freeze laws was beginning to bog down. More and more state-level politicos had begun to jump on the privacy-protection bandwagon. State by state, credit freeze proposals were becoming increasingly proconsumer.

Ellman, forty, with a fleshy face and boyish countenance, and given to wearing bow ties, enthusiastically embraced his orders to turn the tide. A seasoned lobby warrior, Ellman had served as political affairs director for the National Coalition to Ban Handguns in the early 1990s, and moved on to become a lobbyist for the Direct Selling Association, promoting the interests of Amway and Tupperware before joining CDIA. Always well prepared for battle, he delivered his arguments in bursts of speech, glossing over tenuous assumptions and hammering home simplistic position statements.

He had been a reliable combatant in the trenches for CDIA from the time the heavy salvos began exploding over credit freezes. Testifying before a Louisiana legislative committee in 2004, he vilified credit freezes as "the most dramatic and draconian alteration" ever to hit the credit-reporting system.

He trekked to Washington, Nevada, and Massachusetts in 2005 to assert that CDIA did not support credit freezes in any form. "It has not been proven to be a viable identity-theft tool," he testified in Massachusetts. "Ultimately, it's our hope that legislatures will see that file freezing isn't the silver bullet that people think it is."

Heading into Montana, Ellman well knew that the efficacy of Washington D.C.–style power brokering faded rapidly in the hinterlands. What's more, the opposition had momentum going for them. Privacy advocates, many of whom Ellman had come to know on a first-name basis, had obliterated any notion that Montana would go for a Vermont-style restrictive freeze.

So Ellman's mission was to establish the credit bureaus' second fallback position: the California standard, a $30 freeze fee coupled with a cumbersome application process, requiring certified mail. Over the course of nearly a year he would commute several times from CDIA's Washington, D.C., offices to Big Sky Country and become as comfortable roaming the halls of the Montana legislature as he was in his ubiquitous bow tie.

"He was here so often, I jokingly told him he should start paying state income tax," says Claudia Clifford, associate state director of advocacy for AARP Montana.

Testifying before the Montana Senate's Committee on Business, Labor and Economic Affairs on January 19, 2007, Ellman characterized credit freezing as "an expensive burden to bear" for credit bureaus.

"We're being asked to build a system that so far nobody is using," he said in a fast, clipped, confident cadence. "We think $10 is not a barrier to entry. It is merely an administrative fee to recoup the costs of an investment that no one is using."

Stetson-wearing Montana lawmakers didn't buy what the bow-tied Easterner had to sell. They recognized that the $10-per-bureau fee translated into a cost of $30 for an individual to do a complete freeze—and $60 for a couple. Montana lawmakers approved a credit freeze, setting a $3-per-bureau fee and a much-streamlined application process. They went a step further by adopting a provision that made Montana the first state to require credit bureaus to freeze on a consumer's credit report within twenty-four hours, if the request came from a consumer who could prove he or she was the victim of identity theft. Otherwise, the bureaus had up to five days to honor freeze requests.

A twenty-four-hour freeze for identity theft victims was a galling precedent the credit bureaus did not want to see established. With the pressure on, Ellman resorted to power tactics. He could have tried cajoling Governor Brian Schweitzer into exercising an "amendatory veto," under which the governor could send the bill back to the legislature with a promise to sign it into law once they deleted Section 3(2), the twenty-four-hour freeze. Montana might set a new benchmark for cheap credit freezes, but at least it wouldn't give other states ideas about following its lead on requiring twenty-four-hour freezes for identity theft victims. Instead, Ellman went for the jugular, asking Schweitzer to veto the entire law. In a March 29, 2007, letter to the governor, Ellman wrote,

> CDIA does not oppose the enactment of a security freeze law and, in fact, has worked in good faith over the past eighteen months . . . to develop a bill with which consumer reporting agencies can comply. However, the Section 3(2) of the bill represents a substantial compliance problem for the consumer reporting agencies and may have a negative impact on consumers who desperately need assistance.

Ellman argued that protections in federal laws for identity theft victims were more than adequate, and warned that a twenty-four-hour freeze would create undue hardships for the credit bureaus, possibly even disrupt the national economy:

> Section 3(2) unnecessarily could undermine the accuracy of consumer reporting agency files. Federal law requires consumer reporting agencies to maintain reasonable procedures to assure maximum possible accuracy. The mandate of placement of a freeze within twenty-four hours may compromise the accuracy and integrity of consumer reporting files, the very files banks, credit unions and other businesses rely upon to ensure safe and sound lending decisions. In short, the foundation of the credit economy is the credit bureaus. Rattle the foundation of the credit bureaus and you rattle the foundation of the credit economy.

Schweitzer would have none of it. He signed the bill into law, as delivered to him by the legislature, including the twenty-four-hour freeze. "We were told he [Ellman] was going to send this letter and ask for an amendatory veto, meaning the governor would send it back to the legislature with instructions to amend out this one provision," says Clifford. "Instead, he asked for the whole bill to be vetoed, and that wasn't going to happen. His whole tone was so patronizing. He was just arrogant. Either that or the guy didn't realize we had an amendatory veto."

Ellman had little time to lick his wounds in Montana. Intensifying battle fronts in Massachusetts and Maryland beckoned, and so he moved on. In Maryland, Ellman's home state, the potent forces that lined up to argue on behalf of credit bureaus included Bruce Bereano, one of the state's highest-paid lobbyists, who was retained by First Advantage SafeRent, a niche player in credit reporting. Bereano's former clients included tobacco and liquor interests, and he had championed Experian's interests for a time in the late 1990s. Convicted of eight counts of mail fraud in 1994 for overbilling his clients, Bereano liked to say that he represented "subculture industries."

Despite the best efforts of Ellman and others championing the California standard, Maryland passed a freeze bill in spring 2007 allowing the bureaus to charge a $5-per-bureau fee, or a total of $15 for a full freeze, half of California's fee. What's more, Maryland joined a pack of states, including New Jersey, Utah, Delaware, and Washington, ordering the bureaus to allow consumers to unfreeze, or thaw, their credit files within fifteen minutes by supplying a four-digit personal identification number.

Ironically, the fifteen-minute thaw arose at the behest of auto dealers and retailers, at one time the credit bureaus' strongest antifreeze allies. Seeing the groundswell of support for freezes, the auto dealers and retailers suddenly realized that backing the California standard also meant advocating an onerous provision. California's freeze law required consumers to wait three days after unfreezing their credit before they were able to apply for a new line of credit.

The auto dealers and retailers panicked over what for them was a nightmare scenario: millions of consumers alarmed about identity theft begin to enact freezes; the freezes prove to be so cumbersome to thaw that most just leave them in place; impulse buying of big-ticket items, driven by quick access to easy credit, begins to sharply decline.

"Instead of just two sides arguing, it became a triangle," says Lauren Moughon, AARP's Washington state lobbyist.

Given rising populist support for credit freezes, a fifteen-minute thaw resolved the auto dealers' and retailers' concerns. They backed off opposing freeze proposals that contained a "fast thaw" provision. With two pivotal allies suddenly gone neutral, Ellman and other credit industry lobbyists retrenched. CDIA argued that the technology and protocols to do a fast thaw required study and could not possibly be readied before July 2009.

As various states hashed out how much credit freezes should cost and whether fifteen-minute thaws should be implemented, Senator Mark Pryor (D-AR) in April 2007 introduced a national credit-freeze bill, based on the California standard—a $10-per-bureau fee and certified mail application, but with no preemption provision. With a newly elected Democratic Party majority in Congress and news of large data thefts continuing in a steady flow, there appeared to be little appetite for probusiness legislation that would knock down any of the state credit-freeze laws.

Undeterred, Ellman continued launching salvos. He wrote an editorial page opinion piece published by the *Nashville Tennessean* on April 3, 2007. Citing a suspect survey, he claimed that "for the first time since ID theft records have been kept, the crime numbers are going down."

In his essay, Ellman reconstituted the credit bureaus' most fundamental position that "security freezes may not work" and optimistically pointed out that "consumers are more careful about protecting their personal information, fraud detection products are stopping the crime before it happens . . . and law enforcement has been devoting more resources to the prevention and prosecution of identity theft."

The warrior in a bow tie concluded, "We believe consumers should be encouraged by the data that show identity theft rates are starting to fall."

Expediters

Superior Weaponry

Bill Gates seemed weary and disengaged. He had just codelivered a keynote address to about 3,000 tech-security executives, analysts, and researchers at San Francisco's Moscone Center and was sitting in a vast room behind the stage waiting to do a requisite one-on-one interview with one of the authors.

The February 6, 2007, speech was billed as Gates's final command performance at the giant RSA Conference, the tech-security industry's premier convention held early each year. At his first RSA keynote, delivered in 2004, Gates had a good story to tell. It had been two years since he had issued his Trustworthy Computing edict, ordering his troops to alter their features-first worldview and make security their new religion. Microsoft developers at the time were in the home stretch of hammering together Windows XP Service Pack 2, which would make the use of personal firewalls and automatic patching standard practice for most home computer users.

Now here he was, five years into Trustworthy Computing, with Windows Vista, the first Microsoft desktop operating system with security accounted for in every major component, freshly delivered to store shelves. Yet Vista's gala rollout, held just a week before in New York City, had been anything but a sweeping triumph. Gates originally projected that Vista would begin replacing XP in 2005. But the need to staunch headline-grabbing worms, like MSBlast and Sasser, had forced him to slam the brakes on Vista's development and pull out all the stops to shore up basic security in XP. Service Pack 2 was the result.

Gates, in fact, had no choice but to heed the snide advice from MSBlast's creator who had chided him to stop making money and fix his software. He would endure ridicule from the tech community as he was forced to strip Vista of many of the advanced features he had hyped before ordering his developers to get religious about security. Gates's commitment to security-harden Vista would trigger one delay after another, costing Microsoft and its partner PC hardware makers billions of dollars in anticipated sales.

But with Vista, Microsoft now had a more well-rounded security story to tell. And tell the story it did. Beginning in the summer of 2006, a crack team of Vista "evangelists"—the product managers and marketing specialists assigned to wine and dine researchers, analysts, and reporters at conferences and other events—began spreading the SDL gospel. SDL stood for Security Development Lifecycle, a process for meticulously rooting out coding errors and security holes throughout the development of a new software product.

A typical sermon went something like this: Vista, Office 2007, and Internet Explorer 7 were the initial beneficiaries of SDL; these products are so far advanced from Microsoft's past products that they should dramatically boost security. The SDL evangelists stopped short of stating the conclusion they presumably hoped listeners would draw for themselves: the faster computer users replaced their XP systems with Vista, the quicker overall security would improve.

Given the timing of his swan song appearance at RSA, Gates had the perfect pulpit to drive home the message his SDL disciples had delivered to many of the people seated in Moscone Center's main hall. But Gates's focus appeared to be elsewhere. Several months earlier, he had announced his intent to retire in mid-2008 to turn his attention to eradicating disease in third world nations.

Before he could reinvent himself as a full-time philanthropist, he was obligated to sign off on Trustworthy Computing as a success—at least on his watch—and formally turn over the security reins to Craig Mundie, Microsoft's chief research and strategy officer. For his final RSA keynote, Gates chose to share the stage with Mundie, crediting him as "the one who motivated me to send that memo around."

Gates told the audience of security experts he thought it would "be fun" for him and Mundie to "talk about some of the needs that are out there, particularly the evolving needs, and some of the advances that are going to fulfill those needs." The two executives then engaged in a dry, jargon-laden dialogue covering a laundry list of security technologies and standards whose limitations were well-known to most in the audience.

Sitting on a couch backstage after the keynote, Gates looked haggard. The reporter gave him another chance to hype Vista by opening the interview with this question: "Bill, the rate of threat mutation has never been higher and cyberintruders are more organized than ever, using ever-more stealthy, targeted attacks. That said, how far can Microsoft's SDL products go toward stemming the wider security problem?"

Gates looked up, glared angrily at the reporter, and said he didn't understand the question. The interview looked like a bust. After a few more awkward exchanges, Gates took a swig from the can of Diet Coke his handlers invariably kept within his reach. The jolt of caffeine appeared to fire his synapses and perk him up.

During the forty-five-minute interview that ensued, Gates pointed out breakthrough security features in Vista and expressed disdain for whoever was responsible for shaping the automated payments and credit-issuing system built for speed—but ill equipped to handle digital transactions securely.

"It's a stupid system," Gates said, waving his hands dismissively. "It's a weak system when someone with your Social Security number or mother's maiden name can apply for credit without you knowing it."

Warming to the interview, Gates opined that "computer security is one hundred times better today than in 2002. But there has been an evolution in spam and phishing, and you can't apply Band-Aids to the problem."

SDL, Microsoft's blueprint for developing more secure software, was a lot more than a Band-Aid, of course. Chief SDL architect and evangelist, Michael Howard, took a stab at quantifying SDL's anticipated benefit in an article for MSDN magazine in which he wrote,

> So the big question is "does SDL work?" Does the employment of Security Development Lifecycle techniques result in software that is more secure? The answer is a resounding "Yes!" We have seen the number of security defects be reduced by approximately 50 to 60 percent when we follow SDL. The simple fact is that every product touched by SDL

has fewer security defects. Period. And that certainly makes it worth pursuing.

SDL forced Microsoft's designers and developers to address the reality that any software program touching the Internet can be attacked through the Internet. Still, SDL was no panacea. By mid-2006 white hat vulnerability researchers had swarmed all over the beta, or test, versions of Vista and uncovered scores of vulnerabilities.

"We are still seeing a substantial number of vulnerabilities in code developed under the SDL, a significant number discovered by external people," says Michael Cherry, security analyst at the independent research firm Directions on Microsoft. "Why weren't these caught by the process? Yes, things are getting better, but there are still bad design and bad coding practices that slip through."

John Pescatore, longtime tech-security analyst at Gartner, singled out another major shortcoming: Howard designed SDL to strengthen old-style software programs sold in shrink-wrapped boxes, programs that typically spent years in the development lab. It did very little to improve security of Web 2.0 software typically developed on the fly and deployed quickly as a service over the Internet.

Yet Microsoft—like most other major tech suppliers—believed interactive, Web 2.0 services represented the future of computing, not software sold in shrink-wrapped boxes. Microsoft had invested billions of dollars to launch Xbox Live and the Xune as platforms for selling digital entertainment online. And it was pushing aggressively into advertising-supported Web services under its Windows Live collection of free search, e-mail, and instant messaging offerings. What's more, a beta service, called Office Live, tested a model for how Microsoft hoped to someday get Office users to pay a monthly fee for access to Web-based word-processing, spreadsheet, and slide-presentation programs.

"SDL is aimed at traditional two-year- to five-year-type software development cycles," says Pescatore. "When you think about all this Web 2.0 stuff that might get done in two days and pushed out to a billion browsers, tell me how SDL applies to that?"

Ben Fathi, Microsoft's corporate vice president of security technology, contends, "SDL does include requirements that are specific to Web services and the common code flaws and vulnerabilities found in online services," and notes that Microsoft continually tests new programs it puts out "to identify these application-layer vulnerabilities prior to the applications moving into production."

While Fathi scrambled to shore up security of Microsoft's newest products, a fresh threat cropped up in early 2006 for which SDL offered no protection: white hat, black hat, and gray hat researchers began probing for—and readily discovering—zero day security holes in existing versions of Office programs used as the de facto clerical tools throughout the working world. Security researchers began to flush out zero day flaws—vulnerabilities for which no patch existed—in Word, Excel, PowerPoint, and Outlook.

Having been designed at a time when the Internet was an obscure experiment between military and college researchers, and software developers thought about cool features first, second, and last, Office was rife with security weaknesses. By mid-2006, as Microsoft hustled to issue patches for the deluge of Office zero day flaws being discovered almost weekly by white hat researchers, black hat hackers began to glom onto this newest attack vector.

They began using tools called "fuzzers" to throw random data at Office programs until they found a combination that crashed the program in a way that allowed them to take control of the host PC. "The bad guys said, 'Cool, I have all day, I'll let this fuzzer run for months, so I can try billions of variations, and if I find one that causes unexpected things to happen, I'll drill down,'" says Pescatore.

By the close of 2006 and the start of 2007, a select group of cybercriminals had begun sending out e-mail messages to workers at certain government agencies and large corporations. The e-mails contained corrupted Word, Excel, PowerPoint, and Outlook files as attachments. These were zero day attacks. No patches were on Microsoft's radar.

The e-mail messages were carefully crafted to look like they came from a coworker or an acquaintance. Once the recipient clicked on the corrupted Office file, a back door loaded onto the machine. The intruder now had access to install a root-kit cloaking mechanism, along with tools to monitor traffic for clues on the best ways to drill deeper and stealthily infect other PCs inside the organization's intranet. The ultimate goal: harvest sensitive data.

In blog entries on Microsoft's Security Response Center Web site, operations manager Mike Reavy downplayed the deluge of Office zero day attacks as "super, super targeted," while a colleague, Scott Deacon, called them "very, very limited and targeted." Yet another Microsoft security manager, Christopher Budd, blogged,

> Unlike these broad, random attacks, these very
> limited, targeted attacks are carried out against a
> very small number of customers (sometimes only one
> or two even) and are carried out in a very delib-
> erate fashion against a specific organization or
> organizations.

But, once again, Microsoft was using an outdated paradigm to characterize what was important about a cutting-edge threat. The bad guys were purposely trying to keep the lowest profile possible, while looking to establish a single beachhead from which they could roam far and wide inside an organization's systems.

"Super, super targeted? That's crap," says SPI Dynamics lead engineer Billy Hoffman. "Office is Microsoft's biggest revenue generator behind Windows. Worldwide business runs on Office. Almost everyone is vulnerable. E-mail filters will block zip files or other 'executable' content but will allow these evil documents through."

Hoffman also noted that workers increasingly transfer work-related files onto portable storage devices to carry from home to work. "Office documents are commonly moved in and out of an organization through USB thumb drives and plugged directly into a machine, completely bypassing more security," he says.

Five years into Trustworthy Computing, with Office zero day attacks on the rise, Microsoft was compelled to issue Security Advisory 933052 notifying its customers that even documents appearing to arrive from trusted contacts may not be entirely trustworthy: "As a best practice, users should always exercise extreme caution when opening unsolicited attachments from both known and unknown sources."

If all of that weren't bad enough, a singularly chilling aspect of the Office zero day attacks was the fact that the slickest exploits traced back to elusive Chinese hacking groups. One tainted Word file discovered by security firm Symantec, for instance, loaded a back door, then immediately created a clean Word document named "Summary on China's 2006 Defense White paper.doc."

Chinese hackers, led by a team of virus writers in Guangdong Province, had been systematically breaking into U.S. systems since at least 2003, as part of an operation U.S. intelligence agents dubbed Titan Rain. Citing sources at the Naval Network Warfare Command in Norfolk, Virginia, *Federal Computer Week* (*FCW*) reported in a February 13, 2007, story that cyberattacks coming from China continued to far outstrip attempted intrusions on U.S. government systems from any other nation in terms of volume, proficiency, and sophistication.

"They will exploit anything and everything," a senior military official told *FCW* reporter Josh Rogin. Although impossible to definitively implicate the Chinese government, the attacks are so deliberate, "it's hard to believe it's not government-driven," the official told Rogin.

It was difficult to tell whether the Guangdong Province–based hacking group linked to the Titan Rain attacks was behind the Office zero day attacks, says Alan Paller, research director at the SANS Institute, a Washington, D.C.–based tech-security think tank and training center.

But Paller says a consensus among tech-security experts and Defense Department officials held that China's military leaders remain obsessed with gaining a position of strength vis-à-vis the United States by using the Internet to spy on government agencies and their contractors.

"China's military has been very outspoken in saying the next war with the U.S. will be fought asymmetrically and that the Internet is going to be one of the primary battlefields," says Paller. "This I know for sure: China would spend any amount of money to put itself in the position of holding absolute control over our government's computer systems."

With attack vectors multiplying, Russian cybercrime lords enriching themselves, and Chinese cyberspies roaming wild, Bill Gates unburdened himself of a heavy load at RSA 2007. Compared to trying to put the cybercrime genie back into the bottle, stamping out major diseases in third world nations might seem a snap. The fight to keep cyberthieves and cyberspies from rendering Microsoft's products untrustworthy now fell to Craig Mundie, the executive who goaded Gates into launching Trustworthy Computing.

In his onstage chat with Gates, Mundie acknowledged that "the threat landscape has evolved in fairly dramatic ways. . . . Today, it's a lot more serious; it's a lot more nefarious than it was five or six years ago. And the fact that we have so many things connected and we have so many people connected, not just hundreds of millions of PCs, but growing on billions of phones, and rolling out more and more things all the time, this challenge is going to get tougher."

Mundie elaborated on the mantle he inherited. The current approach to Internet security, he said, was based on a fortress mentality. Defense systems protecting key parts of the Internet were akin to moated castles from which valuable assets could evaporate into the air or seep out through tunnels under the walls. And now to make matters worse, these castles had come under siege by an enemy with superior weaponry.

"It's sort of like we've been in the medieval age of computer networking and access. And we say, you know, we just have to build more and more fortresslike protections," says Mundie. "So we build thicker walls, higher turrets, put moats out in front, bigger drawbridges. And what we didn't really see coming yet is essentially the airplane and the air-to-surface missile."

CHAPTER 18

What Must Be Done

Try conducting this microsurvey. Make a list of a handful of people you interact with on a regular basis. Strive for a diverse mix of respondents. Consider including your relatives, your coworkers, your coffee barista, your church pastor, the refreshments mom from your kid's soccer team, your car pool seatmate, your hairstylist, your dog groomer. Ask them if they've ever experienced any form of identity theft or personally know anyone who has.

Many, if not all, of them are likely to answer yes. An amalgam of surveys and statistical summaries support this hypothesis. And the interwoven stories you've just read hopefully illustrate why your risk of having your personal data stolen, and worse, of having criminals use your data to perpetrate identity theft, seems certain to rise for the foreseeable future.

Even so, it is all too easy for the average person meandering along in our credit-driven, consumption-oriented culture to overlook this important matter. One might argue that ignorance is bliss, even preferable when contemplating the daunting digital world. Yet it could be that some part of the general apathy—perhaps a large part—can be attributed to conflicting messages about the scope and proximity of the threat.

On the one hand, report after report underscores that more people than ever are losing their personal data to crooks, and that more stolen data than ever is being widely put to use in financial fraud scams. On the other hand, marketing campaigns promoting Internet-enabled financial transactions convey a false sense of trustworthiness in current security systems. And lobbyists and researchers backed by the financial services industry have begun evangelizing the notion that Internet-related security and privacy threats actually are receding.

Chief among those who would argue that the perils described in *Zero Day Threat* are overblown is James Van Dyke, founder and president of Pleasanton, California–based Javelin Strategy & Research. At a March 2007 banking security conference in Washington, D.C., Van Dyke sat on a panel of experts convened to discuss ways to address rising consumer concern about the security of their personal and financial data. Van Dyke acknowledged that consumers perceive identity theft to be increasing, but he called this a "paradox," since Javelin's extensive research showed "identity fraud is declining."

He asserted that 81 percent of fraud is "nonelectronic," with criminals mostly stealing statements from mailboxes or burglarizing checkbooks and wallets. According to Van Dyke, just 16 percent of identity theft takes place via the Internet and just 3 percent of identity theft can be tied to data breaches. Van Dyke counseled the conference attendees to stop viewing technology as a negative that increases risk; he called on the audience to help educate consumers and institutions about the vital role technology plays in detecting and preventing fraud. Van Dyke failed to disclose to the audience that Javelin's research sponsors included CheckFree, Visa, and Wells Fargo.

Van Dyke's stance perfectly encapsulates the financial services industry's public posture about cybercrime: it exists, but at no greater level than financial fraud has always existed. Financial industry executives insist they have been mindful to minimize consumer risk. They acknowledge the security holes but say that consumer fraud in aggregate continues to represent less than 1 percent of all transactions, as it has for decades.

"Online banking is safe and getting safer," insists Doug Johnson, senior policy analyst at the American Bankers Association. In fact, Johnson argues that online banking services can help drive fraud even lower. Consumers can monitor online accounts any time of the day or night for discrepancies, instead of being restricted to making a phone call during business hours, or having to wait for a printed monthly statement, he says.

The financial services industry's self-serving position flies in the face of research dating back to October 2003, when the Federal Trade Commission, in a first-of-its-kind analysis, pegged the number of Americans victimized by identity thieves at 9.9 million. The FTC conducted phone surveys of 4,057 citizens. Its report estimated that businesses lost $48 billion to identity thieves in 2003, while individuals lost $5 billion in out-of-pocket expenses.

"These numbers are the real thing," Howard Beales, director of the FTC's Bureau of Consumer Protection, told CNN at the time.

The FTC repeated the identity theft phone survey in the spring of 2006 and took until November 27, 2007, to report the results, which showed that the number of identity theft victims in 2005 had decreased to 8.3 million. With scores of other analyses pointing to data breaches and Internet-enabled financial fraud locked into steadily rising curves, the FTC's results drew skepticism. "The numbers are unreliable," says Litan, the Gartner banking analyst. "The methodology is flawed. I think that's why they delayed the report."

Despite Van Dyke's assertions to the contrary, the occurrence and ongoing threat of identity theft have, in fact, remained palpable. Metrics recorded in late 2006 and early 2007 by leading tech-security firms provide tangible evidence showing this to be true. By the end of 2006, Cupertino, California–based Symantec found itself updating antivirus coding, called signatures, to block a record 70,000 virus variants, a legacy of Sven Jaschan, the idealistic virus crusader. Jaschan's technique of creating dozens of variants of his avenging antivirus virus, Netsky, in rapid succession became a model, and then an ingrained practice for virus writers. Internet viruses today mutate as prolifically as the common cold. Yet another measure of the ongoing virus surge comes from Boston-based security firm Sophos. In early 2007, Sophos recorded a record 23,864 distinctive malicious programs circulating in e-mail and lurking on tainted Web pages, as compared to 9,450 such threats in early 2006.

Meanwhile, e-mail spam continues to spiral out of control, despite the best efforts of determined antispam and antiphishing organizations. In February 2007, San Bruno, California–based IronPort Systems reported that the tidal wave of spam clogging the Internet had risen 109 percent over the previous twelve months, most of it originating from proxy servers implanted on home PCs. The deluge included record levels of unsolicited e-mail ads from purveyors of subprime loans, herbal remedies, and get-rich-quick schemes. It also included rising levels of "pharm spam" pitching fake drugs, and "stock spam" aimed at duping recipients into helping to drive up the prices of moribund stocks.

"This is the modern face of the e-mail threat," says Adam O'Donnell, director of emerging technology at message security firm Cloudmark. "Spam makes money."

In May 2007, London-based MessageLabs reported yet another criminal advance: for the first time the messaging systems security firm began intercepting scam spam laced with an enticement to click to a tainted Web page. Crooks were killing two birds with one stone.

"Why use two e-mails when just one will do?" says Mark Sunner, MessageLabs' chief security analyst. "Now we are seeing the bad guys layer on the threats—as if it's not enough to just scam someone and fill their in-box with junk e-mail, why not also infect and take control of their computer at the same time?"

By way of explaining why massive spam surges are sure to continue, Patrick Peterson, IronPort's vice president of technology, points to something he refers to as "the Poland problem." One day in 2006, Poland for no apparent reason zoomed to the top of the list of nations blasting out spam. It turned out that a Polish telecom company had recently embarked on a marketing push to persuade dial-up Internet account users to upgrade to high-speed connections.

"The people that were coming online with broadband connections didn't have home routers or antivirus or personal firewalls," says Peterson. "They were fresh meat, and they got infected and turned into new zombies at a remarkable rate."

In parts of Eastern Europe, Africa, and Asia, a vast supply of similar PC hookups can be expected in years to come, says Peterson. "There may not be an infinite supply of fresh zombies," he says, "but at the point we are now, it's close enough."

And let's not forget phishing spam. Research firm Gartner found in November 2006 that the number of consumers receiving phishing attack e-mails had doubled since 2004. Gartner banking security analyst Avivah Litan estimated that 109 million U.S. adults received e-mail that looked like, or definitely was, a phishing attack in 2006, up from 57 million in 2004.

Capitalizing on the fact that wealthier folks shop online more often than less-well-off consumers, phishers have begun to increasingly target adults earning more than $100,000 a year. Litan estimates that cumulative phishing-related losses in 2006 hit a record $2.8 billion. "The high-income earners clicked on links in phishing e-mails slightly less often, but when they did lose money, they lost almost four times as much as other victims," Litan says. "Women lost twice as much as men."

Infectious threats only begin with e-mail. Ever since the iframer gang tainted hundreds of Web pages with the zero day Windows Metafile infection in December 2005, tainted Web pages rapidly came into vogue. Video game fanatics, like the hackers who tainted the Dolphin Stadium Web site on the eve of the 2007 Super Bowl, hoping to snare World of Warcraft and Lineage game log-ons, jumped into the fray behind more serious-minded crime gangs. By the first quarter of 2007, 5,000 freshly infected Web pages were turning up on a daily basis, according to Sophos.

"It's shocking that such a high percentage of Web sites are vulnerable to hackers," says Ron O'Brien, senior security analyst at Sophos. "This is definitely a big concern."

Whether an infection spreads via e-mail, tainted Web pages, or some other means; whether it turns your computer into an obedient bot or plants a keylogger, or does both; all malicious software, in one way or another, contributes to the flow of stolen personal data into the cybercrime underground. That flow has become a torrent, fed also by insider data thieves, and by hackers of all skill levels incessantly probing for weaknesses in company databases.

Socrates was in a methamphetamine haze when he cracked the home page of the Michigan uniform company and downloaded 3,000 customer profiles. By contrast, the hackers who pointed a WiFi receiver at the Marshall's outlet in Minneapolis probably were clear-headed pros. They had to be in order to methodically crack deep into TJX's databases and extract the records of 94 million sales transactions over an eighteen-month period.

Fed by virus writers, insider thieves, and database hackers, the pool of stolen identity data—names, addresses, Social Security numbers, credit and debit card numbers, online account log-ins, medical records, driving records, tax forms, military records—has swollen into a rich sea brimming with enough nutrients to fuel cybercrime for years to come.

A conservative estimate as to the proportions of this sea of stolen data comes from the online document "Chronology of Data Breaches," launched by Privacy Rights Clearinghouse in February 2005, after ChoicePoint notified 166,000 individuals that their personal records had fallen into the hands of Nigerian scammers. Ever since that initial entry, new entries have been added to the chronology at the rate of several each month. By September 2007 the list included more than 770 disclosures from companies, institutions, universities, and public agencies reporting more than 240 million records holding personal information turning up lost or stolen.

As widely cited as the "Chronology of Data Breaches" has become, it represents a very conservative accounting of the outflow of stolen data. Only a fraction of data breaches are reflected on the list. An early 2007 survey of 1,400 tech-security administrators by Santa Clara, California–based security firm

McAfee found that 60 percent had dealt with a data breach in the preceding twelve months. One in three respondents agreed that a major data loss—whether malicious or accidental—could put their company out of business.

Thomas Harkins is familiar with such discussions. Harkins grew up in a middle-class Long Island family and never made it to an Ivy League school. But the Fordham University graduate's common sense and straightforward problem-solving approach served him well in a two-decade-long career as operations director for MasterCard International's fraud division. In helping MasterCard member banks stay a step ahead of criminals, Harkins gained an insider's view of the advancement of financial fraud, including the breakneck rise of cybercrime. Now chief operating officer of Bethlehem, Pennsylvania–based security firm Edentify, Harkins believes identity theft is spring-loaded to soar by a factor of twenty over the next two years.

"There's so many stolen identities in criminals' hands that [identity theft] could easily rise twenty times," Harkins says. "The criminals are still trying to figure out what to do with all the data."

*   *   *

The Internet began in the late 1960s as an experiment in open data exchanges by academics and military researchers collaborating as part of the Defense Advanced Research Projects Agency, or DARPA. It's doubtful any of the original members of DARPA ever envisioned the Internet evolving into the ubiquitous and empowering global phenomenon it has become today. The Internet enabled a great leap forward in human communication, matching, if not far exceeding, the disruptive impact of the Gutenberg press. Since 1995, it has come to enable grassroots communications and the open sharing of music, art, academics, science, engineering, and new ways of thinking on a global scale.

Yet the Internet's greatest strengths—its openness and anonymity; its robustness and global reach—instantly flip into its greatest weaknesses when the task at hand is not communication, but commerce. None of the Internet's intrinsic underpinnings were ever designed to support secure financial transactions. It's safe to say that no one at DARPA envisioned the day when the Internet would be intensively used to extend capitalistic consumption on a global scale.

Yet banks, credit bureaus, and data brokers rushed headlong into transporting the built-for-speed credit-issuing and card-based payments system—a system designed for the analog world of the 1980s and 1990s—to the digital Internet. The attraction was both obvious and irresistible. The Internet offered a way to reach new customers without buying real estate, erecting brick-and-mortar edifices, and staffing them with tellers and clerks. Since 2000, the Internet has rapidly won consumer acceptance as a convenient and trustworthy enabler of electronic commerce, especially in North America and Western Europe. U.S. online commerce topped $132 billion in the twelve months ending July 2006, climbing 58 percent over the previous two-year period, according to comScore Networks.

That kind of prodigious double-digit annual growth has executives at big tech, telecom, media, and entertainment companies salivating, and their strategists busily plotting out Internet-centric expansion plans. Yet, every day evidence mounts that security is falling behind to the point where that most crucial element—trustworthiness—is teetering on the brink. A telling example of this disconnection: Microsoft, Google, Yahoo, MySpace, and others have moved, herdlike, to find more and more uses for AJAX, hailing it as the enabling technology of ultracool Web pages. Then along comes a popularity-starved Los Angeles teenager nicknamed Samy, who figures out in his idle time how to corrupt AJAX to infect 1 million MySpace users—and thus opens the door to a vast new attack surface for profit-minded criminals to explore.

"The Internet is not going to die tomorrow," says Gadi Evron, head researcher for Israeli-based Beyond Security. "But, yes, all this pollution is becoming more and more visible, more and more disturbing."

Evron, a tireless contributor at security conferences and workshops, states the obvious in saying that Internet commerce, for the moment, remains viable. But on any given day, he says, it's all too easy to envision a scenario where the bottom drops out of consumer trust.

"We're doing good, but it's definitely not enough," says Evron. "E-commerce is still usable. We keep advancing more and more in our fight. But unless something more serious is done, whether it's two years from now or five years from now, eventually the Web channel will become unusable. We're still working on everything; we're still doing a lot to make this not happen. But it's a risk. It's something that we need to understand will happen one day if nothing significant changes."

An important first step would be for the financial services industry to progress beyond Pollyanna public assertions that data harvesters and cyberscammers pose little more than a negligible threat. Only then can serious discussions get under way to bring our credit-issuing and payment systems into the twenty-first century. Curtailing the practice of credit bureaus and data brokers routinely issuing credit reports and data dossiers rife with errors is a must, which is another way of saying consumers ought to be permitted, even encouraged, to assume more control over their own financial data. Jettisoning magnetic stripe payment cards and online authentication systems that rely solely on user names and passwords, and replacing them with technologies that actually hinder online counterfeiting and impersonation—not make it mere child's play—is also a must.

In short, the credit-issuing and card-based payment systems are due for a massive overhaul that will take us beyond the current solutions now on the table. Wider use of multiple-factor authentication won't be enough. Restructuring of the magnetic-striped-based payment system and reforming the business practices of credit bureaus and data brokers are in order. Such a metamorphosis would rock the status quo and cost billions. Thus, it will likely require sustained public outrage, enough to prompt a legislative mandate, to stir the financial services industry out of its lucrative comfort zone. As credit bureau lobbyist Eric Ellman well knows, consumer unrest has begun to percolate at the state level, where data-loss notification and credit-freeze laws are being adopted locally. But federal intervention will probably need to come into play. One can only hope that political leaders will emerge to champion the greater public good, and not be bulldozed by probusiness interests, as was the case with Senator Proxmire in the 1970s.

Meanwhile, the Internet itself is in need of a major overhaul, as well, if it is to endure as a grassroots communication channel and a commercial transactions channel. Technologists are hard at work on this problem, but competitive secretiveness and self-serving agendas complicate the challenge. What's clear is that the Internet's blanket openness and anonymity need to be refined so that crime groups are not able to so easily pervert those elements to carry out their scams. The trick will be to tighten down the

Internet without gutting its wonderful ability to empower the underclass and stir grassroots creativity and activism. Finally, consumers, particularly in the United States, need to be prepared to give up some conveniences, such as lickety-split access to online accounts.

On January 29, 2007, Microsoft CEO Steve Ballmer held court in a private suite on the thirty-second floor of the Grand Hyatt New York, high above Manhattan's Forty-second Street. Ballmer dutifully plowed through a string of one-on-one interviews with news reporters as part of the launch festivities for Windows Vista, Microsoft's oft-delayed new desktop operating system. By far the biggest delays stemmed from striving to ensure that Vista would be the most secure operating system the software giant has ever produced. With Vista, Microsoft, in essence, took the taunt issued by MSBlast's author in the summer of 2003 to heart:

```
billy gates why do you make this possible? Stop making
money and fix your software!!
```

Hardening Vista against cyberattacks turned out to be an agonizing process costing Microsoft and its partners, including chip maker Intel and PC makers Dell, Hewlett-Packard, and Toshiba, billions in sales opportunities lost because of the delays. But Ballmer was fully committed. He had experienced an epiphany about security, according to a tale Microsoft evangelists had been quietly circulating among tech-industry influencers, known as "the technorati," in the months leading up to the Vista launch. As a member in good standing of the technorati, Joel Shore, editor in chief of ITworld.com, heard the story of Ballmer's revelation at a workshop at Microsoft's Redmond, Washington, campus. Shore wrote about it in his blog:

```
Once upon a time not that very long ago, Microsoft CEO
and chief cheerleader Steve Ballmer was attending a
friend's child's wedding. One of the parents (I'm not
sure if was the groom's or bride's) complained that
his PC had slowed to a crawl and was performing miser-
ably. Would Steve mind having a look?
```

Ballmer spent the better part of the next two days trying to rid this PC of worms, viruses, spyware, malware, severe fragmentation, and well, you name it. Picture it: the world's 24th wealthiest person, a man worth $13.6 billion according to *Forbes* magazine, sitting at a table for two days, playing tech support. It was . . . a humbling experience.

Ballmer eventually gave up and instead lugged the machine back to Microsoft's Redmond, Washington, campus. There, several engineers spent several days, burrowing deep into the system to figure out the problem. Imagine, CSI: Redmond.

It turns out there were more than a hundred pieces of malware of various types. Things that these engineers using Microsoft's own private tools could not ferret out and fix. Some of these threats hooked themselves deeply into the core operating system and essentially lied about their existence. Other malware scoured the hard drive for anything containing the string "virus," and . . . would shoot them dead. The result was disabling any installed antivirus software.

It took a team of engineers to restore this system to health. And it was a real wake-up call.

The Vista launch event in New York was geared for mainstream media, not the technorati. So Ballmer came primed mainly to hype Vista's cool new features. He did so with characteristic zest. His last interview at the end of a long day happened to be with one of the authors. He recited perfunctory answers to the expected softball questions about what Vista meant to Microsoft's short- and long-term business prospects. But then the discussion turned to security. The reporter mentioned this book, and asked Ballmer what he thought about the notion that the very foundation of the Internet exposed consumers, tech suppliers, companies, and organizations—just about everyone—to the whims of data harvesters and scam artists.

The garrulous chief executive leaned forward and began to get physically animated. His pat answers about Vista yielded to a treatise on security, or lack thereof, when it came to routine online data exchanges. Ballmer spoke passionately.

Eyes wide open figuratively and literally, Ballmer advised the reporter that any attempt to secure the commercialized Internet was like trying to trying to reconfigure a superhighway without the ability to temporarily ban vehicles from the thoroughfare.

"On the Internet, we're replumbing while we're driving sixty miles per hour," he opined.

A complete overhaul, he said, was out of the question; piecemeal upgrades on the fly appeared to be the only alternative. But with cars continually roaring over the pavement, both the repairmen and the drivers necessarily assumed certain risks.

"In a fast-moving world," Ballmer observed. "People are willing to cope with reliability and security issues."

Microsoft had taken great pains to improve security, he said, but was only part of a much larger equation. Other folks had to step up and do their parts to help ensure the viability of Internet commerce. As yet, the matter was simply not urgent in the eyes of enough key constituents. After all, Ballmer observed, consumers appeared to be willing to put up with the current level of Internet security risks, in much the same way they tolerate erratic cell phone coverage. He did not bring up his friend from the wedding, who, presumably, got right back on the Internet.

The interview concluded. The reporter thanked Ballmer and stepped out into the hall to wait for the elevator. A few moments later, a burly bodyguard exited the interview room, scanned the hall, then whispered, "All clear," into an ear-piece communicator.

Flanked by a public relations handler and the bodyguard, Ballmer stepped lively into the elevator, alongside the reporter. With a sly grin, the executive turned the tables and assumed the role of interviewer. He wanted to know what the reporter had discovered while researching *Zero Day Threat*.

The reporter replied that it appeared as though the financial services industry may have moved too quickly into online services; someone failed to fully weigh how profoundly consumers would be exposed to data theft and identity scams.

"The Internet is sometimes about weighing financial opportunity with acceptable losses," Ballmer said. "It's something we all grapple with."

The elevator doors opened, and the chief executive of the world's largest software company—and the number one target of virus writers—hustled off into the frigid New York afternoon.

Epilogue

In April 2005, Vonkeman and Gauthier arrested Marilyn in possession of items to commit fraud. The detectives convinced Marilyn's mother to decline to pay her bail for a few days. After spending three days in lockup, Marilyn had an epiphany, of sorts. "Three days to me was a lifetime. It was horrible, just horrible," Marilyn said. From then on she stayed clean. She resolved the criminal charges against her and found steady employment. Raising her two children consumed her. She moved in with her mother, disassociated herself from the meth crowd, and began undergoing counseling. "I've cut all ties to the old lifestyle," said Marilyn. "I pretend I'm in a different city, a different country, a different universe. I'm in my own little bubble."

In May 2005, Frankie moved into a halfway house after spending eleven months in jail. He got a job as a laborer. "I'm just trying to get through each day," he said. At the time he had been clean and sober for seventeen months and was attending daily Narcotics Anonymous meetings. Every day was a struggle. "It was very hard to stop using. I think about using all the time," he said. On October 31, 2005, Frankie failed a urine test. That night he skipped out of the halfway house. He was arrested on November 13, 2005, in a car in the company of a known meth trafficker. In his possession Frankie had a laptop computer, a cell phone, and a magstripe reader/writer. He was returned to jail. Since his release in late 2006, Frankie has steered clear of the law. But Gauthier's sources indicate that Frankie may not always be steering clear of trouble. "I'm not hearing good things about him on the street," Gauthier said in the summer of 2007. "He's a guy I'm sure we're going to deal with again; that's only my gut feeling."

In early 2006, Yolanda entered herself in a four-week rehab program run by the Salvation Army. Once she was clean and sober, her innate intelligence and drive emerged. She became a leader among the patients. After completing the rehab program, Yolanda moved in with her mom and returned to work. She stayed straight, and in 2007 bought a house. "I attribute my sobriety and success to my mom," she said. "She has helped me a lot, giving me a place to stay and providing emotional support. And my boss has a lot to do with my sobriety, as well, just 'cause he gives me a lot of responsibility and trust. I love my job. Basically, that's all I'm about these days, family and work."

Biggie spent several months in jail following the Tower in the Park bust. He, too, appeared to turn a new leaf. In reality, Biggie had launched off on his own. In early 2006, he returned to the IRC chat rooms and tried to establish himself as an independent broker of stolen account data. He made the mistake, however, of selling U.S. bank log-ons and credit card numbers to an undercover agent of the U.S. Secret Service. At the request of U.S. authorities, Gauthier arrested Biggie on September 5, 2006. Biggie posted bail, got a job at a shopping mall, and avoided trouble. Jail was not to his liking. He was set to go to trial in December 2007 on charges of trafficking credit card data.

After his third arrest in July 2005, Socrates served ten months in jail, then moved into a halfway house. He was living in the halfway house and working as a busboy in June 2006 when he agreed to meet with one of the authors. About six feet tall, Socrates slouched and walked with a loping gait. He had put on about forty pounds since the frenzied days at Yolanda's Mill Woods walk-up. He chain-smoked cigarettes and often crossed his arms, as if hugging himself.

Socrates spent his Tuesday nights at a Narcotics Anonymous meeting and met on Thursday nights with a chemical dependency recovery group. He took prescription drugs to steady the constant trembling of his hands and to prevent the seizures that began once he stopped smoking massive amounts of crystal meth. Like Marilyn and Biggie, Socrates expressed an intense desire never to return to jail. "I want to be employed doing something with computers," he said. "It doesn't really matter what. That's something I'm good at. I'm not going to be doing fraud anymore. The frauds and the scams, that's over. I just want to work, stay out of trouble, go to church on Sunday with my parents. Be a normal person."

After successfully completing his time in the halfway house, Socrates got a job as a cook and began living with a girlfriend. In the fall of 2006, he appeared to be doing very well. But by the summer of 2007, Gauthier began hearing Socrates's name come up associated with a hustler named Contreras. Following his arrest at the Devonshire apartments in June 2007—his fourth at the hands of Gauthier—Socrates posted bail and moved back home with his parents. He was awaiting a trial date in Edmonton, probably in early 2008.

*   *   *

On May 12, 2007, detectives of the Newport Beach, California, Police Department wrapped up a lengthy investigation with the arrests of Christopher Aragon and his wife, Clara Aragon. The couple faced charges stemming from the fraudulent purchase of $13,000 worth of designer purses at a Newport Beach shopping mall using American Express gift cards whose magstripes had been re-encoded with stolen credit card account numbers. Clara Aragon quickly pled guilty to theft charges. Christopher Aragon faced more serious identity theft charges. While awaiting trial, Aragon began talking to the U.S. Secret Service about the supplier of the stolen account numbers: a thirty-five-year-old San Francisco man named Max Ray Butler, aka Iceman, aka Aphex, aka Digits, aka Darkest.

Aragon corroborated what several other informants had already told the Secret Service about Butler's activities—and filled in many blanks. In 2001 and 2002, Butler had served time in California's Taft Federal Correctional Institute after pleading guilty to hacking into systems at McChord Air Force Base, NASA's Marshall Space Flight Center, Argonne National Laboratory, Brookhaven National Laboratory, IDSoftware, and another unnamed Defense Department system. He was released in October 2002, but resurfaced in January 2004 when federal authorities brought him in for questioning regarding the hacking of Half-Life, a popular video game. (A version of Half-life was later modified to create Counter-Strike, Socrates's favorite game.)

By 2005, Butler and Aragon had struck up a partnership that would blossom in 2006, after Butler emerged as Iceman, the bold-thinking administrator of CardersMarket. According to Aragon, Butler maintained multiple online personas. As Iceman and, later, as Aphex, he was the self-righteous leader of CardersMarket, a self-proclaimed champion of free speech, meticulous caretaker of a top carding forum, and the online nemesis of one David Renshaw Thomas, aka El Mariachi. However, he would put Iceman's duties aside and spend long hours doing much the same thing as the hackers who swiped 45 million credit card records from TJX. According to a Secret Service affidavit, Aragon witnessed Butler "hack into numerous computers" at credit card data-processing centers and financial institutions using "two or more powerful desktop computers and a state-of-the-art antenna for his hacking activities." Upon harvesting a cache of account numbers, Butler would assume the online personas Digits and Darkest and proceed to sell the data to Aragon and to others worldwide via CardersMarket. From the affidavit: "When we asked how many credit card numbers he has received from Butler, Aragon stated that he has received 'tens of thousands' of illegally obtained credit card account numbers from Butler, and regularly received 1,000 such numbers or more per month from Butler."

An imposing figure at six feet five inches tall and 220 pounds, with long brown hair worn in a ponytail, Butler was a stickler for security who thrived on stealth. He continually maintained two safe houses, homes or apartment suites always rented by accomplices. He used bicycles, taxis, and rental cars to move between locations, and in the physical world used the aliases Sam and Daniel Chance. He made use of high-level encryption programs and even designed a "kill switch"—should he ever need to, Butler could destroy all evidence on his hard drives with two keystrokes. He was most active on his computers late at night.

Aragon functioned as the coordinator of various cells involved in money laundering. He was akin to El Flaco, the higher-up handler of Irving Escobar in Miami. Aragon's group re-encoded the magnetic stripes on the backs of American Express gift cards with account numbers supplied by Butler, in much the same fashion as Contreras had altered Mytreat Visa gift cards in Edmonton. Accomplices then used the doctored Amex gift cards in department stores to buy high-end goods, such as designer purses. Two named in the affidavit were Nancy Diaz Silva, aka Nancy 3, and Tsengeltsetseg Tsetsendelger, aka Alenka. Nancy 3 and Alenka served the same function in California as Hula Girl did in Edmonton and the Venezuelan did in Miami. Clara Aragon's job was to put the purses up for sale to the highest bidders on eBay under the account name Stylish_shelly. Christopher Aragon would divvy up the proceeds, routing some of the profits back to Butler, often in the form of prepaid Green Dot credit cards, easy to purchase online.

On September 5, 2007, U.S. Secret Service agents arrested Butler in San Francisco. A week later, a federal grand jury in Pittsburgh indicted Butler on three counts of wire fraud and two counts of transferring stolen identity information in connection with the sale of more than 100 credit card account numbers to a Pennsylvania resident cooperating with federal agents.

*   *   *

If immediate past history is a guide, the dismantling of the Edmonton cell and the arrests of Butler and Aragon will barely register as a deterrent. Cybercrime has evolved into a full-fledged, thriving economy operating on a global scale. Two distinct markets have emerged: one revolves around the harvesting of sensitive data, the other around supplying the goods and services needed to convert stolen data into tangible profit. The use of the Internet as a global communications and transactions channel for criminal pursuits has become ingrained. Meanwhile, law enforcement outside of North America remains negligible; banks, merchants, and media companies continue to enable more types of online transactions, and consumers continue to be seduced by the convenience of our card-based payments system and the Internet.

"There does not appear to be any saturation point," says Uriel Maimon, chief technology officer for RSA, the security division of EMC. "Both e-commerce and online banking adoption rates are increasing. The strategies that have been shown to reduce fraud are not in widespread adoption, meaning that the potential market for new victims is not shrinking. And there are more and more fraudsters joining the community all the time. They all seem to be making a comfortable living."

Appendix A
Personal Security and Advocacy

On November 21, 2005, one of the authors logged on to his Bank of America online banking account and discovered that an unknown party had somehow obtained his VISA platinum card account number and used it to purchase a MSN Plus Hotmail e-mail account. The amount charged was $19.95 for a one-year subscription, which bought two gigabytes of storage space at an e-mail address concocted by the thief.

The online purchase stood out because the Visa account had been set up to cover checking overdrafts. The actual Visa card was in a file folder and had never been used. At the time, the reporter had just returned from an investigative trip to Edmonton, where he learned how cyberthieves stored identity data in fraudulently set up e-mail accounts—for easy access and to avoid getting caught in possession of incriminating evidence.

A Visa phone representative advised the reporter that the fraudulent e-mail account upgrades were "not uncommon" and "seemed to be happening a lot" with AOL and MSN subscriptions. The reporter then called MSN, supplied his Visa number, and asked the rep to look up the subscription order. Heeding the MSN rep's request, the reporter recited his name and home address in Kingston, Washington. The rep immediately replied that the reporter's name and address did not match the information on the subscription order. He declined to disclose the subscriber's name, but after some cajoling revealed that the address associated with the subscription was in Greenville, Mississippi.

When asked how the account number on a never-used VISA card sitting in a file could have fallen into crooks' hands, the MSN rep said he had heard reports of crooks "throwing combinations of numbers" together until they worked. The rep said he had gotten seven to eight similar calls a day for the past couple of months. He also noted that the forty other reps in his department reported a similar level of complaints about fraudulently purchased MSN Plus Hotmail accounts.

It appeared that setting up e-mail accounts using stolen credit card numbers had become a widespread practice. Questions arose: Were cyber-crooks testing credit card numbers by making small online purchases at

MSN's and AOL's Web sites to see if they worked? Were they opening e-mail accounts with large storage capacities to stash stolen data? Those questions have gone unanswered.

Nonetheless, the reporter's firsthand experience as an identity theft victim underscored how participating in financial transactions—to any degree—can put your personal and financial data into active play among criminals.

So what can consumers do about it?

Unfortunately, there is no such thing as absolute, complete protection. That said, criminals generally target unprotected computers and easy-to-snatch data. And there is plenty a consumer can do to make himself or herself less of a target. It requires staying vigilant on several fronts and on a continual basis. Simply making it harder for data thieves and scammers to rip you off can be enough to discourage the crooks and send them looking for easier prey. Should you fall victim to an identity thief, catching the criminal activity early and alerting the merchants and banks involved is the best defense against getting deeply enmeshed in a frustrating and costly hassle.

Here are some basic guidelines for best consumer security practices in the digital age:

Financial Precautions

- Never use your debit card. If your debit card number and PIN ever flow into the stolen ID data pool, and thieves use it to make purchases or ATM cash withdrawals, the money taken is yours. It could take days or weeks to process the paperwork to recover your cash. Meanwhile, bills you were planning to pay may become a problem. And if you do not report debit card fraud within sixty days of the fraudulent transaction, everything gets much more complicated.

- If you're not using cash or a personal check, use a major credit card—Visa, MasterCard, Discover, or American Express—for all of your transactions, both online and offline, even the smallest purchases. Of course make sure you pay the balance down to zero each month and are never late with a payment. This takes discipline. But if you can master this habit, you get to use the bank's funds for free for thirty days. And you get great documentation of your spending, a key to sticking to a home budget. Should thieves ever steal the account number and commit fraud, you will not be held responsible. Since banks have great motivation to maintain public trust in the credit-issuing and card-based payments system, they've made dealing with instances of credit card fraud consumer friendly. Simply report the fraud via a phone call and promptly fill out any paperwork the bank sends you. The bank generally will not hold you responsible for the charges. It will discontinue the stolen card number and issue you a new card number. And all this will happen when you call to report the fraud.

- Keep very close track of all of your financial statements. If you bank or do other financial transactions online, check your account statements at least once a week, if not more often. Be vigilant for any suspicious activity, no matter how small, on your statements. Like a rapidly metastasizing disease, identity theft is more easily cured if diagnosed early.

- Consider subscribing to an identity theft detection or prevention service. There are about a dozen or so online companies that will keep close track of various aspects of your financial records for $8 to $10 per month. That's a small price to pay for peace of mind. LifeLock, TrustedID, and IDWatchdog are three that have gotten positive reviews from customers. LifeLock maintains and monitors ninety-day fraud alerts with credit bureaus on your behalf, and watches for crooks trying to open accounts using your data. It also removes your name from preapproved credit applications, which police refer to as "fraud starter kits." TrustedID implements and monitors credit freezes for users in states where credit freezes are allowed. If you become the victim of identity theft while a TrustedID subscriber, the company will guide you through recovery steps. IDWatchdog monitors the data dossiers compiled by data aggregators for suspicious activity linked to your information, and also goes to bat for you if you become an identity theft victim. Most of the services performed by these companies can be done on your own, if you're willing and persistent. If you choose to do it yourself, helpful guidance is available at the ID Theft Resource Center, www.idtheftcenter.org.

PC Precautions

- Keep current on all Microsoft security updates. Microsoft has done a commendable job of automating this chore for consumers. But figuring out how to access or enable certain functionalities for your particular PC can take a bit of work. Start by navigating to Microsoft's Security at Home Web page at www.microsoft.com/protect and work your way through the guidance you will find there that applies to you. Your goal should be to make sure you are automatically receiving and installing all security updates for Windows, Internet Explorer, and Office. You should also make certain you have a firewall activated and updated. To help with this, you can sign up for Microsoft Update, which can automatically install all security updates for you.

- Keep current on all Adobe, AIM (AOL's free instant messaging service), and Apple version upgrades, including upgrades for Apple iTunes. Virus writers have begun attacking vulnerabilities in software from these popular tech companies. Adobe, AIM, and Apple periodically send out version upgrades that include new features, but such upgrades can also carry important security patches, though they don't always make that clear. You may think your version of Adobe's Acrobat, AOL's AIM, or Apple's iTunes works just fine, and thus decline the upgrade. But in doing so, you may fall behind on important security patches.

- Keep current on antivirus, antispyware, and Web page scanner subscriptions. You should expect to pay $80 to $150 a year for some combination of all of these protections. If you've let your antivirus subscription lapse; if you rely on free antispyware software to clean up your hard drive; or if you don't bother to regularly use a Web page scanner to vouch for the safety of the Web page you're about to click to, then you increase your risk. In antivirus products, Symantec, Trend Micro, McAfee, Panda, and Kaspersky are the big names. In antispyware, Webroot's Spy Sweeper, Sunbelt Software's CounterSpy, and PC Tools' Spyware Doctor are the leaders. And in Web page scanners, LinkScanner Pro is a powerful tool that checks Web sites for signs of trouble in real time, while SiteAdviser Plus and CallingID check Web pages against a blacklist of known bad pages.

- Keep in mind that there are many worthwhile security products on the market with innovations and new approaches coming along every day. You may want to go with a suite of services from one company, or you may want to mix and match products from different suppliers, picking what you think is the best antivirus, antispyware, and Web page scanner for the money. Luckily, guidance is readily available from PC World, CNET, and eWeek; each publication regularly produces extensive reviews of tech-security products.

Web-Surfing Precautions

- Keep your Social Security number sacrosanct. Never type it anywhere online, as you may have a keylogger embedded on your computer waiting to capture and transmit it to the crooks.

- Use strong passwords. Make them at least eight characters with upper and lowercase letters as well as numbers. Frequently change your passwords.

- Download files judiciously. Download files only from Web sites you know and trust. Never agree to install free programs. Nothing is free. Clicking will often install spyware, or worse, a back door turning over control of your PC to an intruder.

- Never click on a banner ad or pop-up window, for the same reasons.

- Generally stay away from high-risk porno and gambling Web sites, for the same reasons.

- Lock down your wireless network. If not configured properly, your wireless network can be used to gain access to your local computer. Change the default user name and password set by the manufacturer on your wireless unit, which are widely known by crooks. Activate the encryption feature. This can be a little daunting, but persevere and figure out how to do it, or find someone who can do it for you. The wireless router manufacturer should have guidance available through the Internet or by phone.

E-mail Precautions

- Set your e-mail client to prevent attachments from being displayed or opened unless confirmed by you. Malicious software often arrives as attachments. Never open any attachments unless you're certain they're from someone you trust.

- Never click on a link unless you're sure it's from someone you trust. Think first; click later. Links can open tainted Web sites that load up malicious software.

- Use a spam blocker and be wary of scam spam that tries to get you to buy cheap drugs or penny stocks. Be highly suspicious of any e-mail that asks you to click to a link to a Web page where you are required to update account information, or fill in a form to qualify for lottery or sweepstakes winnings. This is a phishing attack, designed to lure you into giving up your account information and Social Security number.

*   *   *

With criminals staying far ahead of authorities—finding and exploiting new security holes faster than known vulnerabilities can be shored up—don't expect the above list of essential consumer security practices to diminish anytime soon. If anything, the burden on consumers to protect themselves will continue increasing. The surest way to reverse this trend is to compel the financial services industry to acknowledge the rising threat and overhaul the credit-issuing and payments system. This won't happen until consumers demand it, and so far consumers have been a sleeping giant.

"There is no consumer outcry yet from Joe Sixpack and Mary Tennis Shoes," says Paul Moriarty, director of product development for Internet content security at Trend Micro. "Unless there is a hue and cry from the man on the street, nothing will be done."

When you are ready to make your voice heard, there are consumer advocacy groups waiting to hear from you with systems in place to channel your outrage. Here are some of those groups and how they describe their missions:

Voicing Your Concerns

- U.S. PIRG, the federation of state Public Interest Research Groups. www.uspirg.org. "This group takes on powerful interests on behalf of the American public, working to win concrete results for our health and our well-being. . . . We stand up to powerful special interests on issues to promote clean air and water, protect open space, stop identity theft, fight political corruption, provide safe and affordable prescription drugs, and strengthen voting rights."

- CU, Consumers Union. www.consumersunion.org. "CU is an expert, independent, nonprofit organization, whose mission is to work for a fair, just, and safe marketplace for all consumers. CU publishes *Consumer Reports* and ConsumerReports.org in addition to two newsletters, *Consumer Reports on Health* and *Consumer Reports Money Adviser*, with combined subscriptions of more than 7 million. Consumers Union also has nearly 400,000 online activists who help work to change legislation and the marketplace in favor of the consumer interest and several public education websites."

- CDT, the Center for Democracy and Technology. www.cdt.org. CDT "works to promote democratic values and constitutional liberties in the digital age. With expertise in law, technology, and policy, CDT seeks practical solutions to enhance free expression and privacy in global communications technologies."

- EPIC, the Electronic Privacy Information Center. www.epic.org. "EPIC is a public interest research center in Washington, D.C. It was established in 1994 to focus public attention on emerging civil liberties issues and to protect privacy, the First Amendment, and constitutional values. . . . We have no clients, no customers, and no shareholders. We need your support."

- EFF, the Electronic Frontier Foundation. www.eff.org. EFF "has championed the public interest in every critical battle affecting digital rights. Blending the expertise of lawyers, policy analysts, activists, and technologists, EFF achieves significant victories on behalf of consumers and the general public. EFF fights for freedom primarily in the courts, bringing and defending lawsuits even when that means taking on the U.S. government or large corporations.

- PRC, the Privacy Rights Clearinghouse. www.privacyrights.org. "PRC is a nonprofit consumer organization with a two-part mission—consumer information and consumer advocacy. It was established in 1992 and is based in San Diego, California. It is primarily grant-supported and serves individuals nationwide."

- WPF, the World Privacy Forum. www.worldprivacyforum.org. "WPF is a nonprofit, non-partisan 501 (C) (3) public interest research group. The organization is focused on conducting in-depth research and consumer education in the intersecting areas of technology and privacy. The World Privacy Forum focuses its investigations on a broad range of emerging and maturing technologies."

- *Privacy Times*. www.privacytimes.com. Privacy Times "is the leading subscription-only newsletter covering privacy and Freedom of Information Law and policy. It is read largely by attorneys and professionals who must stay abreast of the legislation, litigation, and executive branch activities, as well as consumer news, technology trends and business developments. Since 1981, Privacy Times has provided its readers with accurate reporting, objective analysis and thoughtful insight into the events that shape the ongoing debate over privacy and Freedom of Information."

- Several federal lawmakers have weighed in with bills to protect consumers' sensitive data. Among them: Senator Dianne Feinstein (D-CA), Senator Mark Pryor (D-AR), Senator Daniel Inouye (D-HI), Senator Bill Nelson (D-FL), Senator Arlen Specter (R-PA), Senator Patrick Leahy (D-VT), and Senator Charles Schumer (D-NY). And as of late 2007, California state senator Joe Simitian, coauthor of California's data-breach notification law, the first of its kind in the nation, continued to push against a proposed federal bill he contended would water down more effective state laws modeled after California's bill.

Appendix B
Survey of Security Experts

To get the experts' consensus view of the cybercrime landscape, the authors conducted an online survey of 260 tech-security professionals. The survey was conducted in February and March 2007, and produced two major findings. The first was that there is a consensus expectation among security experts that computer intrusions, data theft, and identity fraud will continue on the upswing for the foreseeable future.

Criminals' use of the following attack vectors will track as follows through 2010:

	Decline	Stay the same	Rise
Viral e-mail attachments	25.2%	28.3%	46.5%
Botnets	5.7%	17.3%	77.0%
Phishing scams	7.1%	12.5%	80.3%
Keyloggers	7.6%	23.7%	68.7%
Rootkits	5.0%	27.5%	67.6%
Browser-based exploits	12.9%	17.9%	69.2%
Insider theft of personal data	2.7%	23.0%	74.4%
Database hacking of personal data	3.5%	18.6%	77.9%

Consumers' exposure to the following types of identity theft will track as follows through 2010:

	Decline	Stay the same	Rise
Personal data gets stolen	1%	7%	91%
Credit card gets used in fraud	3%	22%	75%
Debit card gets used in fraud	3%	24%	73%
Funds hijacked from an online account	4%	18%	77%
Data gets used in new account fraud	2%	13%	85%

The second finding, represented below, should remove any doubts about the intensity of data theft and identity fraud campaigns. A staggering eighty-two percent of *tech-security professionals* encountered malicious software on their computers and more than half had their credit cards accounts used fraudulently.

Have you or anyone in your family ever encountered the following:

	Security experts responding in the affirmative
Had computer infected by malware	81.5%
Had credit card used fraudulently	52.5%
Had personal data stolen or lost	33.2%
Had personal data used in new account fraud	12.7%
Had debit card used fraudulently	10.7%
Had funds hijacked from an online account	4.9%

Asked in an open-ended question for an opinion about where Internet-enabled security risks were heading in the next few years and what should be done about it, the survey respondents expressed a general consensus that things seem certain to get worse until consumers demand improvements—and companies and governments move to make major changes. Here's what the tech-security experts had to say.

Better Tech Tools

Some improvements can come from improving hardware and software, but technological advancements alone probably won't solve the problem:

- Better OS (operating system), browser, and antivirus software will offer better protection against virus, spyware, etc. However, phishing, man-in-the-middle, and other attacks will increase. As the value of personal data goes up (more things can be done with personal data), attacks to get personal data will increase—a combination of technology, social engineering and insider fraud.

  —Tech-security executive with more than six years of experience

- Security is like usability: You can't bolt it on after the fact. We need PC hardware that is designed with security in mind. We need operating systems that are designed with security in mind, and we need networks and credit systems that are designed with online security and fraud-prevention in mind.

  —Software researcher of less than two years

- Ultimately, risk increases with the complexity of systems. As fewer and fewer people actually understand how systems work, more of us become naive to the risks associated, making each of us more personally vulnerable. What makes this worse is that economic models dictate that security is bolted on after a new system (e.g., VOIP) has been proven economically viable, reducing our ability to effectively and efficiently secure such systems. Security must be considered as part of the design of any new system or technology.

  —Malware detection expert of more than six years

- Malware and exploits will become increasingly more sophisticated and hard to detect. The only way to combat this is to build security into the platform itself in a way that is transparent to computer users. This is something that won't happen in a big-bang fashion but should happen bit by bit. If this doesn't happen, I think that ultimately some sort of backlash will occur where users will abandon doing some tasks on their computers.

  —Tech-security researcher of more than six years

- Individuals with broadband access will be increasingly open to attack. Everything wireless on your person will open you up to attack whenever you are in a public place. Location-based services will be a stalker's playground. All services should be off and firewalled by default. Services should be enabled explicitly by the user. Firewalls should be application-aware, and only allow traffic for enabled services. Software should learn what the user does normally and warn when something unusual happens. Personal fraud detection.

  —Tech-security researcher of more than six years

- As the online channel and consumer-convenient channels like telephony and ATM become part and parcel of one's life, fraudsters are going to attack those channels in as many ways as possible. So, any institution that deals with consumers' personal and financial data needs to implement strong antifraud detection. At the same time, try to reduce the impact of such systems on the consumer. Risk- and layer-based fraud detection systems can play a major role in accomplishing it.

  —Engineer of more than two years

Consumer Awareness and Education

Individual computer users must take on more responsibility by educating themselves and embracing best security practices, but consumers cannot be counted on to make a big dent in the problem:

- The primary cause of identify theft is consumer negligence. The interconnected world that we live in has left consumers in an awkward place of not knowing who we are doing business with. Privacy policies are vague and full of legalese, which turns people away from reading those policies, leaving those consumers with no idea who has their data or how it will be used. People tend to forget that not every business is built on ethics. They follow the golden coin, not the golden rule.

  —Tech-security researcher with more than two years of experience

- Security is only as strong as its weakest link. In most cases, the weakest link is the individual. Individuals need to be aware of the risks and mitigate them via a system of knowledge sharing and education. In general, risk containment should be implemented through knowledge-sharing and education programs for businesses, security providers, and individuals. Quick reaction to new risks and associated development and/or patching of technology to reduce the risk is required. The most effective method to achieve this is through a knowledge-sharing process. Hiding the risk will only make the risk worse.

  —Tech-security researcher of more than ten years

- Social engineering continues to be the most effective technique and the greatest risk. Phishing attacks are some of the lowest tech and the hardest to protect against. Technology always advances faster than society's ability to cope with its consequences. It will take a while for the world's understanding of the threat to catch up with its ubiquity.

  —Tech-security researcher of more than ten years

- While I believe laws need to be created to address the criminality of online issues, I would hate to see the government create a bunch of regulatory legislation that does nothing more than stand in the way of progress. End-user education is the key. People need to be responsible for their actions, or lack thereof on the Net.

—Security expert with more than two years of experience

- Types of fraud reflect the sophistication of the thief. I only see increased activity here, since I see criminals getting more and more knowledgeable about the structure of Internet- and computer-based systems. And many of their "victims" will never know what happened.

—Tech manager with more than two years of experience

- Attackers will continue to break down the barriers between attack techniques, allowing them to rapidly roll out new and creative threats and monitor their effectiveness. Education may never be enough, since the threat landscape will be so dynamic.

—Software researcher with more than six years of expertise

- Already criminals use the Internet as a tool for money laundering, information theft, and safe communication. As the number of computers in the world increases, where third world countries become Westernized with no proper computer-security education plans, the amount of people vulnerable to computer-related crimes just increases. And there are enough criminals to take advantage of that. We need to educate the computer owners about security and the way they are able to defend themselves.

—Tech-security researcher with more than six years of experience

- The majority of risks are the ones that the average consumer is going to be blind to. It didn't take long for people to be educated about phishing and credit card scams, but I feel the new risks are going to be with worms, keyloggers, and identity theft through already available resources such as court clerk records, which are already online and anyone can access. Someone needs to be proactive in educating people, and I feel that all new PCs should come with malware/antivirus software trials installed as they do now.

—Tech-security expert with more than two years of experience

Stiffer Industry Standards and Government Regulation

The area that has the most promise for reversing the tide of cybercrime probably lies in some combination of the corporate world tightening up security standards and government accelerating that process via legislation.

- Risk is undoubtedly increasing, and disparate groups need to work together on a large scale to educate, develop better technologies, and create useful legislation to combat it.

  —Public policy expert with more than two years of expertise

- The current legislative emphasis on the consumer being held responsible is backwards. The consumer has no control of his data out of his possession. Instead, those granting credit or those accepting credit or credentials should be held responsible for the authenticity of the requestor and accuracy of the data they accept. If a third party is harmed by the action or inaction of credit-granting or accepting entity, the grantor or acceptor should be held responsible—not the innocent third party.

  —Network-security expert of more than six years

- Online crime and insider theft needs to be prosecuted. Companies need to be held liable for failure to do due diligence on security. The government needs to work internationally to crack down on criminal rings based in Russia, China, Eastern Europe, and elsewhere to slow the amount of online crime.

  —Tech-security researcher of less than two years

- Legislation doesn't do much without user awareness and action. Legislation should impose higher penalties to criminals. Whistle-blowers perhaps should get financial rewards where possible, as law enforcement can only do so much. Risk is going to continue on an upward trend as we begin to do more and more business, and put more and more personal information online.

  —Tech manager with more than ten years in the security field

- Job markets must improve so that the technical enablers of cybercrime have legitimate work available to them—if it means feeding his or her family, a PhD will start writing malware. Until law enforcement starts focusing on this phenomenon, criminals will have a distinct advantage. Please, do not encourage ignorant lawmakers to pass more ignorant laws about technology they do not understand.

  —Telecom-security researcher for more than ten years

- Internet threats will only diminish when prosecutions increase. The Internet is global in nature, but laws and law enforcement is not. Things will not get better until laws and enforcement improve dramatically and across the globe.

  —Fraud investigator of more than ten years

- What needs to be done is that local law enforcement needs to adapt to this type of fraud and actually take measures to prevent this by making arrests and seeking tougher penalties. Right now, if you are the victim of ID theft, all you can do is file the police report for the bank's insurance and hope that it doesn't happen again. The police do nothing to prevent ID theft nor make arrests.

  —Tech-security researcher of more than six years

A Mix of Solutions

Clearly a combination of better tech tools, higher consumer awareness, improved industry security standards, and heightened government regulation will be needed:

- There should be a multifaceted approach. Software vendors must do a better job in secure development. IT providers, including telecom, should move the battlefield off the desktop and away from consumers and do more to protect them. Consumers have to be better trained against technology intended to defraud them.

  —Security consultant of more than ten years

- Threats will continue to evolve as financially motivated cybercriminals seek to exploit the weakest links in the system, whether they be consumer ignorance, porous software, or lax corporate security policies. Consumers must be more vigilant and software makers more responsive to emerging threats. Corporations must also be much more proactive about protecting customer data. If not, they risk losing the trust of their customers and they could face massive lawsuits.

  —Journalist with more than two years of covering tech security

- The Internet, with its current infrastructure, must be viewed as bringing both risk and safety to consumers, industry, and law enforcement. ID fraud must engage the efforts of both provider and consumer of services, because by definition it attempts to impersonate one to victimize both. One-sided views only enable criminals, and educational efforts must present both sides of recommended actions. The individuals and companies we work with are often sorely lacking a factual model for creating and implementing risk-mitigation strategies. As a result, criminals' jobs are made easier.

  —Online banking analyst of more than ten years

- Systems, protocols, software, and services all need to be designed to meet the security challenges posed by the bottom 10 percent of Internet users in terms of experience and knowledge. Young children, first-time users, the illiterate, and the generally incompetent will continue to make up a large chunk of Internet users. The assumption must be made that these users will click on anything, will believe any phishing mail, will open any attachment that makes it through, and are not capable of configuring their firewalls or AV programs. If this bottom 10 percent of users continues to become infected regularly, the number of bots will consistently stay in the hundreds of millions. And with that many bots, the Internet as a whole will never be safe or stable.

  —Software researcher of more than two years

- The bottom line is that threats are becoming more serious in terms of how organized they are. The profit behind the threats is just beginning to come to light. Protecting data—the data itself as opposed to the perimeter—is an important step forward. The constant publicity and education regarding personal data breaches and security is the best defense moving forward.

—Security-software executive with more than two years of expertise

- Risk and fraud follow the money. The money is online. Consumers, merchants, and financial institutions all like convenience with transactions, and that's online, too. Issuer responsibility in accepting fraudulent applications and accepting change of address information is essential. As they pass the buck on all cards-not-present transactions to the merchant, there is no incentive to prevent or investigate the loss. Legislation will change that. Bill-payer authentication will become more intrusive. Alias/secure online accounts will become the standard. Strict controls will be placed on auction sites to meet the same FTC standards as merchants. As they are now, fraud trends will shift from consumer to commercial fraud, attacking independent credit departments' procedures. Companies that had trimmed back on head count will need to increase the manual review process, decreasing profitability. More service-oriented processing companies will expand their offerings to standardize the credit approval and collection process, possibly absorbing responsibility for losses. As this tightens the holes of opportunity for crooks, new trends will attack consumers.

—Tech-fraud investigator of more than ten years

- Risk is ever evolving. Twenty years ago, I would be worried about getting mugged. Now I don't carry cash at all. So my risk has evolved into my credit/debit cards getting stolen. It can be in my wallet or online. The thieves are a lot more active when the chances of getting caught are as small as they are online. I see risk changing and getting worse before it gets much better. It is important to realize it is a human problem, not a technology problem.

—Hacker of more than ten years

Glossary

admin—a person responsible for running technically advanced information systems.

adware—software that automatically plays, displays, or downloads advertising material to a computer after the software is installed on the PC or the software is in use.

aging fee—monthly fees charged to a bank-issued gift card, usually starting after six months.

AJAX (asynchronous JavaScript and XML)—technology that enables popular Web sites such as Google Maps and MySpace.com to come alive. Hackers and cybercrooks, however, have discovered that by corrupting one of the dozens of data exchanges AJAX handles while loading a Web page, a hacker can take control of the PC.

back door—a secret, unauthorized way for hackers to gain entry to an infected PC.

Bagle.A—the first strain of an e-mail computer worm that affected Microsoft Windows PCs starting in early 2004.

BASE I—a Bank of America processing system that was the catalyst for current-day card-based payment systems.

BASE II—based on BASE I, it computerized the settlement process.

the big three—credit-reporting agencies Equifax, Experian, and TransUnion. These data-handling giants track every loan, installment payment, and credit application for consumers. The information is distilled to individual credit reports, which form the basis for calculating interest rates and dictating repayment terms for all forms of consumer credit.

biometric authentication—the automatic identification of individuals by using their physiological and behavioral characteristics.

BIOS (basic input/output system)—a coded program embedded on a computer chip that recognizes and controls various devices that make up the PC.

black hat—a person who breaches the security of a computer system, usually with malicious intent, without permission from the authorized party.

bot—a compromised computer, remotely controlled by cybercrooks, to spread spam and carry out online scams. Also known as a zombie PC.

bot armies—thousands of compromised machines used in concert to extort protection money from Web sites, usually under the threat of flooding the site with bogus requests to slow its performance.

bot herder—a hacking specialist who assembles bot armies.

botnet—a network of hijacked computers.

carding chat channels—private online chat areas where stolen credit card information and ID theft are discussed and/or swapped.

carding forum—a Web site that mirrors the services of Amazon.com and the efficiencies of eBay. Criminal buyers and sellers convene at these virtual emporiums to wheel and deal in all things related to cyberattacks—and in the fruit of cyberintrusions: pilfered credit and debit card numbers, hijacked bank accounts, and stolen personal data.

CDV (consumer dispute verification)—documents containing complaints that are sent by credit bureaus to lenders.

challenge-response questions—one of several measures used by financial institutions to ensure that only an authorized user has access to his or her personal online account. Customers who try to log in from a computer away from home must answer a predetermined challenge question or questions to gain access to their accounts.

cob (change of billing)—an online banking account log-in, complete with PIN or other data needed to change the billing address.

Code Red—a computer worm targeting PCs using Internet-based services from Microsoft.

Consumer Data Industry Association—a lobbying group representing the big three credit-reporting agencies: Experian, Equifax, and TransUnion.

CVV—the card security code, sometimes called card verification value, is a security feature for credit or debit card transactions, to guard against fraud.

CVV2—the most cited CVV code, it is often requested by merchants to verify "card not present" transactions via the Internet, mail, fax, or phone. In Western Europe, it is mandatory to provide the CVV2 when the cardholder is not present.

DDoS (distributed-denial-of-service) attack—targeted attacks of Web sites with a deluge of data. Cybercrooks use the threat of a DDoS attack to extort protection money from businesses keen to keep their Web sites running.

drop accounts—banking accounts sometimes created by crooks, into which they transfer ill-gotten funds.

Fair Credit Reporting Act (FCRA)—law that regulates how the big three credit-reporting agencies (Equifax, Experian, and TransUnion) collect and disseminate consumer credit histories.

Financial Data Protection Act of 2006—legislation in Congress that would preempt laws in seventeen states that allow anyone to freeze their own credit. The bill would instead restrict that privilege to ID theft victims.

fraud starter kits—police slang for blank checks that banks mail to consumers to make it easy for them to tap into available lines of credit; popular with thieves skilled at money laundering.

fuzzers—hacker tools used to throw random data at popular software applications from Microsoft and Apple until they find a combination that crashes the program in a way that allows hackers to control the host PC.

Gozi—a program residing on tainted Web pages that, when viewed by a victim, infects his or her PC with a keylogger designed to steal typed-in data.

gray hat—a skilled hacker who acts with goodwill, but sometimes does not: gray hats are a hybrid between black hats and white hats.

honeypot PC—a PC set up to attract computer hackers so their actions can be observed.

iframers—Russian hacking groups who recruited porn, gambling, and other Web sites to taint their pages with malicious code.

Internet Safety Enforcement Team—a Microsoft group that helps law enforcement gather and distill cybercrime evidence, such as spam, computer viruses and worms, and phishing attacks.

IP address—the unique address of a computer; its digital fingerprint.

IRC (internet relay chat) channel—a form of instant messaging used in Internet forums for private discussions, often among cybercrooks.

ISP (Internet service provider)—also called Internet access provider, a business or organization that provides to consumers access to the Internet and related services.

key fob—a small device with a time-sensitive passcode used to log on to secure networks, often for financial transactions.

keystroke loggers, keyloggers—spyware designed to notice whenever the PC user types anything that looks like account information. It grabs the information and sends it to a bot for storage and risk-free access by crooks.

lead generators—middlemen in the credit industry who operate unfettered by the FCRA or any regulations. Lead generators make money by steering prospective borrowers to lenders for a finder's fee. They snap up mortgage triggers like candy, typically following up with telephone solicitations.

Linux—a computer operating system built on free software widely available on the Internet. Linux's source code can be modified, used, and redistributed by anyone for free.

LSASS (Local Security Authority Subsystem Service)—a Windows component designed to manage security and authentication.

malware—malicious software intended to infiltrate or damage a computer system without the owner's consent.

man-in-the-middle attack—a computer security breach in which a malicious user intercepts, and possibly alters, data traveling along a network.

mashup—an online scam in which attackers take the Internet address of a compromised PC and cross-correlate it with a detailed street location drawn from interactive maps supplied for free by Google.

Melissa e-mail virus—discovered in 1999, a virus that slowed Internet mail systems to a crawl with a barrage of infected e-mail. Its creator, David Smith, is believed to be among the first people ever prosecuted for creating a computer virus.

mortgage triggers—lists of recent mortgage applicants compiled by the big three and offered for sale to hotly competitive mortgage lenders and brokers.

MSBlast—a self-propagating computer worm that shuttered parts of the Internet in 2003. It bombarded the Web site Microsoft uses to dispense security patches with nonsense requests.

mule—a low-level collaborator for cybercrooks; mules often engage in reshipping, money laundering, and other cash-out schemes.

Mydoom—the fastest-spreading e-mail worm ever, it was spread quickly through spam in early 2004.

Mytob—a computer worm that became activated when the victim clicked on an attachment.

Netsky—software code that was the precursor to Sasser, one of the world's most malicious worms. The code was written by a German teen.

new-account fraud—criminal use of a false identity, made up or stolen, to open a new account, typically to obtain a credit card or loan. Consumers are typical victims.

open proxy—a proxy server that is accessible by any Internet user. See proxy server.

open relay—an e-mail computer server designed to let anyone on the Internet send e-mail through it.

open source programming—a worldwide movement whereby volunteer programmers collaborate on creating software applications free for anyone to use or improve.

Operation Firewall—an October 2004 dragnet in which federal agents in several states arrested members of an illegal card forum called Shadowcrew.

OS (operating system)—software that functions as the brains of a computer.

packet sniffer—software that monitors network traffic to steal passwords, credit card numbers, and other sensitive data.

patch—a fix for a software program.

Patch Tuesday—the second Tuesday of each month, when Microsoft releases the latest fixes for its Windows operating system and related software programs. Microsoft started the practice in 2003.

personally identifiable information (PII)—any piece of information that can be used to identify, contact, or locate a person.

pharm spam—spam (unwanted commercial e-mail) pitching fake pharmaceutical drugs.

phishing—a fraudulent attempt to "fish" sensitive information, such as passwords and credit card numbers, through fake e-mails that appear to come from established companies such as eBay and banks.

phishing kits—a dozen do-it-yourself kits containing bogus Web sites, programming code, and spam tailored toward customers of Citibank, eBay, and PayPal from which would-be cybercrooks can choose.

phone phreak—one of a group of a scattered, socially awkward, precocious teens and postteens who explored the phone system in the 1970s and 1980s.

point-of-sale terminals (POS terminals)—the electronic cash registers used as checkout stands by retailers, stores, hotels, and restaurants.

port—a connection that can be used by software programs to exchange data, rather than through a file or other temporary storage location.

proof of concept—often used as a synonym for a zero day exploit that does not take full advantage of a vulnerability.

proxy server—a computer system or application program that takes requests from individual PCs and forwards them to other servers.

remote procedure call (RPC)—a Microsoft Windows component that allows PCs to share files and use the same printer.

reshipping—criminal enterprise in which goods bought with stolen credit card numbers are shipped to a third party in the United States That party, in turn, reships the goods overseas, where the goods are sold. Often, reshippers are unwitting participants recruited by crooks under false pretenses.

ripper—an individual who rips off stolen personal information from carding forums, usually with bogus information or fake credit card numbers.

root kit—a set of programs designed to gain control of a computer operating system from its authorized operators. Root kits are widely available on the Internet.

Sasser—one of the world's most malevolent computer worms, it caused more than 1 million Windows-based PCs to crash and reboot.

script kiddies—inexperienced, unskilled hackers who attempt to infiltrate or disrupt computer systems by running prewritten scripts designed to crack those systems.

self-propagating worm—a computer worm that does not use e-mail to send itself. Rather, it independently searches the Internet for unprotected computers.

SDL (Security Development Lifecycle)—a 2006 Microsoft program that represented a major change in the company's approach to new products. Instead of placing emphasis on new features in a product, Microsoft now required engineers to first consider security.

Service Pack 2 (SP2)—a long-awaited security update for Microsoft Windows XP computers released in 2004 in response to a growing number of security shortcomings.

single-factor authentication—the use of only of a user name and password to gain access to an online account. Financial services are moving away, en masse, from such a vulnerable system.

skimmer—a small plastic device, about half the size of a pack of cigarettes, that can be used to capture and store magnetic stripe data found on the backs of credit and debit cards.

SoBig—a recurring e-mail virus that used infected computers to spread spam.

spam—unwanted commercial e-mail, often in the form of come-ons from Viagra and get-rich-quick schemes.

spyware—software installed surreptitiously on a computer to secretly intercept or take partial control of the user's interaction with the computer.

stock spam—spam (unwanted commercial e-mail) hawking "hot stocks." Some announce big news that will send shares rocketing. Others masquerade as private e-mails between a broker and a client, and due to your good fortune, are accidentally sent to you.

throttle down—the process between Thanksgiving and New Year's Day during which banks routinely "throttle down" and make fewer calls to consumers about suspicious activity.

thumb drives—also known as flash drives, they are typically small, lightweight, and removable devices that hold vast amounts of data. Commonly used by workers, they are also targets of data thieves.

Titan Rain—a program in which Chinese hackers launched a series of coordinated attacks on American computer systems at NASA and Sandia National Laboratories, dating to 2003. The attacks were traced to a team of researchers in Guangdong Province.

trigger lead—the name and contact information of recent mortgage applicants compiled by the big three and offered for sale to hotly competitive mortgage lenders and brokers.

Trustworthy Computing Edict—a high-profile initiative organized in 2002 by Bill Gates to shore up security on Microsoft products.

two-factor authentication—the use of something more than a user name and password to gain access to an online account.

Uniform Commercial Code (UCC)—a collection of rules setting legal limitations and defining liability for commercial businesses.

virtual private networks (VPNs)—a communications network funneled through another computer network, usually to secure communications over the Internet.

Web exploits—a digital attack in which the intruder embeds malicious code on a Web site, then sits back and waits. The victim activates the code simply by visiting a tainted Web page.

white hat—a hacker who, upon discovering a vulnerability in a computer system, alerts the system vendor to the problem.

WMF (Windows metafile)—a graphics file format on Microsoft Windows systems designed in the early 1990s, but not commonly used after the rise of the Web and popular graphics formats such as JPEG and GIF. The format has been exploited by hackers.

zero day attack—a cyberattack that exploits new security vulnerabilities on the same day such flaws become generally known, and weeks before patches are available.

zombie PCs—hijacked computers that cybercrooks herd into networks of a few hundred to more than half a million compromised PCs. The PCs are used for spamming and other illegal activities. They are also known as bots.

Zotob—a self-propagating worm that loaded adware onto PCs. What made it especially dangerous: It swept the Internet, infecting PCs with no user action required.

A Note on Sourcing

We had no way of knowing it at the time, but the foundation of this book really began to take root in a February 2004 memo written to Nancy Blair, *USA Today*'s senior technology editor, requesting her support for a rather open-ended project. The authors proposed teaming up to take a deeper look at the "convergence of viruses and spam." At the time, Microsoft had just been hit in rapid succession by SoBig, MSBlast, and Mydoom, phishing scams had begun to spread far and wide, and spammers were gravitating to the use of bot networks. There were plenty of news stories and industry white papers about such developments. But we could find no materials that satisfactorily explained how it all fit together.

The facts at hand seem to point to a growing correlation between the new strains of e-mail viruses and the resurgence of spam. It was clear that the motive of virus writers had begun to shift, and that well-funded criminal elements were getting increasingly involved. There was plenty of anecdotal evidence suggesting the existence of a thriving underground economy in support of rising criminal activities on the Internet. Yet no one in the tech industry, trade press, or mainstream news media had connected the dots in any meaningful way. So we asked Blair to let us give it a shot:

> The proposal would be for Byron and Jon to research all of the subsets associated with the major points outlined above. Each would build off past reporting, Byron on the virus side, Jon on the spam side. Byron would start by working with email tracking company Postini to see if we can document PCs infected by SoBig or MyDoom later spreading spam or phishing attacks. Jon will start examining the size and makeup of the pool of zombie PCs, and work his spammer contacts to piece together how the virus/spam economy is put together.

Thankfully, Blair went to bat for us and persuaded our senior editors to approve our proposal. The investigative reporting we did during the ensuing three-and-a-half years (and continue to do) has turned into the most intensive and exhaustive of our careers. We used the Internet extensively for research; conducted interviews by phone and e-mail; watched

Web casts and read blogs; attended security conferences and industry seminars (including one closed to the media); and created personas so we could communicate with denizens of the IRC chat channels and carding forums. In addition to interviewing technology, banking, and law enforcement sources in Seattle and San Francisco, our respective home-towns, we traveled to meet in person with sources in Edmonton; Vancouver, British Columbia; Atlanta; Las Vegas; Los Angeles; Sacramento; Grass Valley, California; Pittsburgh; Miami; Charlotte, North Carolina; and Jacksonville, Florida.

From the summer of 2003 to the fall of 2007, *USA Today* published more than 150 of our news stories and centerpiece features on Internet security and cybercrime, as well as thirteen investigative cover stories. By design, the shorter pieces served as important stepping-stones, allowing us to build our expertise, cultivate relationships with key sources, and refine the vague notions set forth in our original memo. Our shorter stories paved the way for us to break new ground in our investigative cover stories. We were the first in the mainstream media to comprehensively explain bots and bot networks, shed light on the role of banks and credit bureaus, and vividly illustrate cybercrime at the street level from the vantage point of the criminals.

Each story we produced was deeply researched and produced material far beyond what we could get into a daily newspaper. The idea to produce this book as a way to chronicle the antecedents of cybercrime in much greater detail began to take shape. The catalyst took hold in the summer of 2005. At the time we were keen to find a living, breathing cybercrook to write about. U.S. law enforcement and prosecutorial officials had proved reluctant to give us access to any charged suspects, and even if they did, we knew the defense attorney would likely throw up obstacles.

Then, while doing a search of news articles on the Internet, one of the authors ran across a front-page story in the *Edmonton Journal*. The story featured two detectives, Al Vonkeman and Bob Gauthier, expounding at length on what they believed to be a correlation between meth addiction and thievery. Contacted by phone, Vonkeman and Gauthier proved to be generously forthcoming about details of cases they were working. Gauthier told us they had just busted a twenty-one-year-old meth addict in posses-sion of 3,357 stolen credit card numbers hacked from the Web site of a Michigan clothing company. Later, we would piece together that the suspect, Hula Girl, had been given the stolen account numbers by Socrates, who was trying to woo her.

Vonkeman subsequently offered to help set up a phone interview with Frankie, who was then serving time in a halfway house. Eventually, Vonkeman and Gauthier helped us connect in person with four members of the Edmonton cell. Those interviews were conducted on two separate trips in November 2005 and May 2006, and included visits to many of the locations described herein, including the Beverly Motel, Hula Girl's west-end apartment, Yolanda's Mill Woods walk-up, and the Tower in the Park. Why were Vonkeman and Gauthier so generous in helping a couple of state-side reporters? They told us they thought our reporting would help increase public awareness of a growing problem. And they also hoped that inter-acting with reporters would somehow be helpful to the cell members as they struggled to make a clean break from drug addiction and thievery. Guiding drug addicts toward a productive life in society, they said, boiled down to saving the taxpayers money. But it went beyond that.

"We don't have a set of rules we're playing by, other than what's expected for ethics and behavior," Vonkeman told us. "We've been given a lot of lati-tude. Unfortunately, there's only so much we can do. We're way too busy, trying to investigate, educate, do intervention, and work out partnerships with banks and companies. So there's a lot on our plate. But it's also very satisfying intellectually, emotionally, and just on a human level, helping these guys. They're doing all right, turning it around and helping other addicts."

Yet, as veteran law enforcement officers, Vonkeman and Gauthier harbored few illusions about making anything more than a slight dent in what was obviously a rising global problem. Gauthier was pensive when one of the authors met him for coffee in Edmonton in the spring of 2006. "It's going to get a lot worse before it gets any better," he predicted. "How do you stop the Internet? It's like plugging your finger in the dike. For all the people we might catch up to now, there could be ten more networking, forming a criminal cell, expanding, and figuring out something new."

Chapter Notes

Chapter 1: Descriptions of the early activities of the Edmonton cell—here and in Chapter 2—are based on interviews with Marilyn and Frankie, corroborated by interviews with Vonkeman and Gauthier; we also reviewed police files and confiscated evidence. The description of VisaNet is based on a tour of Visa's facility and interviews with Visa executives and banking analysts. The chronicling of the evolution of malicious software—here and in Chapters 3, 4, 5, 8, 11, 12, 14, 15, and 16—derives from our ongoing newspaper coverage of Internet security, supplemented by interviews with tech-security experts done expressly for this book.

Chapter 2: The chronicling of how our credit-issuing and payments system evolved and currently operates—here and in Chapters 3, 4, 5, 6, 9, 10, 11, 12, 16, and 17—is based on news stories, surveys, research notes, and other literature generated by the financial services industry, along with interviews of industry analysts, consumer advocates, and identity-theft victims. The chronicling of the advancement of spam—here and in Chapter 3—derives from our ongoing newspaper coverage of Internet security, supplemented by interviews with tech-security experts done expressly for this book.

Chapter 3: Edentify's founder and CEO, Terrance DeFranco, and Gartner banking analyst Avivah Litan regularly supply expert commentary for our news stories on Internet security and cybercrime. At the request of the authors, Edentify graciously checked its databases to come up with the total number of Social Security numbers—5 million—that its systems have confirmed are being used fraudulently.

Chapter 4: Descriptions of the Edmonton cell's activities that revolve around Socrates—here and in Chapters 5, 7, and 10—are based on interviews with Socrates, Marilyn, Yolanda, and Biggie, and corroborated by interviews with Vonkeman and Gauthier. We also reviewed police files and confiscated evidence. The recounting of Sven Jaschan's activities draws from *Stern* magazine's June 2004 story "The Worm of the Wümme," by Sven Stillich. We also reported and wrote news stories about the Sasser worm, its aftermath, and Jaschan's arrest and prosecution. For those news stories we interviewed numerous experts. Insights about Jaschan from Microsoft's Tim Cranton and F-Secure's Mikko Hyppönen were particularly instructive.

Chapter 5: The descriptions on spyware, adware, and bots—here and in Chapters 6 and 8—derive from our ongoing newspaper coverage of Internet security, supplemented by interviews with tech-security experts done expressly for this book.

Chapter 6: Details of the activities of Olatunji Oluwatusin were obtained in interviews with Detective Duane Decker, Lieutenant Ronald Williams, and Detective Sergeant Joshua Mankini of the Los Angeles Sheriff's Department, and Special Agent Alice Tsujihara of the FBI. We also reviewed court records and confiscated evidence, including the applications Oluwatusin faxed to ChoicePoint to open the Gallo Financial and MBS Financial accounts. The description of the activities of bot herders Ancheta, Maxwell, and Essebar draw from police and prosecutorial records, supplemented by interviews with investigators and experts familiar with those cases.

Chapter 7: The chronicling of how credit bureaus and data brokers evolved and currently operate—here and in Chapters 8, 13, 14, 15, and 16—is based on news stories, surveys, research notes, and other literature generated by the financial services industry, along with interviews of industry analysts and consumer advocates. Evan Hendricks's seminal book, *Credit Scores & Credit Reports: How the System Really Works and What You Can Do,* was a pivotal resource, particularly in explaining the power politics behind the 2003 amendments to the Fair Credit Reporting Act.

Chapter 8: Descriptions of the Edmonton cell's activity that revolve around the meltdown at the Mill Woods apartment, and its aftermath—here and in Chapters 10, 11, 14, and 15—are based on interviews with Yolanda, Socrates, Marilyn, and Biggie, and corroborated by interviews with Vonkeman and Gauthier. We also reviewed police files and confiscated evidence.

Chapter 9: The recounting of David Joe Hernandez's trials is based on interviews with Hernandez and Rick Lunstrum, vice president of ID Watchdog; a review of the documentation assembled by Hernandez and Lunstrum; and interviews with the companies and agencies involved. The summary of milestone law enforcement cases from around the globe—here and in Chapter 10—draws from news stories in mainstream and tech-trade media, as well as discussions on blogs and forums. We also interviewed investigators, prosecutors, and tech-security experts familiar with these cases.

Chapter 10: Descriptions of criminal activities on the chat channels and carding forums—here and in Chapter 13—were compiled with guidance from tech-security experts, notably Yohai Einav, Idan Aharoni, and Uriel Maimon at RSA, the security division of EMC; Oliver Friedrichs and Jesse Gough at Symantec; and Dan Clements at CardCops.

Chapter 11: The recounting of Joe Lopez's trials is based on interviews in Miami with Lopez and his lawyers. We also interviewed law enforcement and banking officials familiar with his case.

Chapter 12: The recounting of Karl's experience—here and in Chapter 13—is based on interviews with Karl in Grass Valley, California; a review of the paper trail he kept; and interviews with law enforcement and banking officials. Similarly, George Rodriguez related his story and laid out the documentation for one of the authors, who visited him in Gastonia, North Carolina.

Chapter 13: Among the contacts we made with criminals, the engagement with Iceman was the most timely. One of the authors began exchanging private messages with Iceman in August 2006, at a time when Iceman was trying to hold together his hostile takeover of four rival forums. Screen shots saved of those communiqués, as well as screen shots of tutorials, marketing pitches, pricing lists, and miscellaneous discussions posted on Shadowcrew, CarderPlanet, CardersMarket, DarkMarket, TalkCash, ScandinavianCarding, TheVouched, and MexiCrew helped us document how carding forums operate.

Chapter 14: In chronicling the ongoing advancements being made to malicious software—here and in Chapters 15 and 16—we sought guidance from tech-security experts who could take us beyond the often disjointed daily news developments and help us grasp the wider context. We engaged scores of experts in phone interviews, e-mail threads, and instant messaging sessions. Among the consistently most insightful were Roger Thompson, of Exploit Prevention Labs; Jeremiah Grossman, of WhiteHat Security; Mikko Hyppönen, of F-Secure; Alan Paller, of the SANS Institute; Joe Stewart and Don Jackson, of SecureWorks; Dmitri Alperovitch and Paul Henry, of Secure Computing; Idan Aharoni and Uriel Maimon, of RSA, the security division of EMC; Graham Cluley and Ron O'Brien, of Sophos; Marc Maiffret, of eEye Digital Security; Jim Melnick and Ken Dunham, of VeriSign iDefense; Billy Hoffman and Caleb Sima, of SPI Dynamics; James Brooks, of Cyveillance; Dan Hubbard, of Websense; Alfred Huger, of Symantec; Martin Carmichael, of McAfee; Alex Shipp, of MessageLabs; Patrick Peterson, of IronPort Systems; Paul Moriarty, of Trend Micro; Gadi Evron, of Beyond Security; and Alex Eckelberry, of Sunbelt Software.

Chapter 15: The recounting of Daniel and Mary Braden's trials is based on interviews with the Bradens, privacy advocates, and Federal Trade Commission officials.

Chapter 16: Details of the activities of Irving Escobar and company derive from prosecutorial records combined with extensive guidance from Amy Osteryoung and John Wethington, assistant prosecutors for Florida attorney general Bill McCollum, as well as interviews with the Gainesville police.

Chapter 17: Details of the activities of Contreras are based on interviews with Detective Gauthier. The chronicling of Eric Ellman's lobbying activities is based on state hearing records and interviews with consumer and privacy advocates.

Sources of Documents

We reviewed public records from these agencies:

Edmonton Police Service; Federal Bureau of Investigation; Federal Deposit Insurance Corporation; Federal Financial Institutions Examination Council; Federal Trade Commission; Florida Department of Law Enforcement; Government Accountability Office; Securities and Exchange Commission; U.S. Department of Justice; U.S. Postal Service; U.S. Secret Service; U.S. Treasury; Washington State Attorney General.

We reviewed research notes, surveys, and white papers from these private entities:

America's Community Bankers; Anti-Phishing Working Group; Anti-Spyware Coalition; Application Security; Arbor Networks; AT&T; Authentify; Authentium; Bank of America; CardCops; Celent; Center for Democracy and Technology; Center for Responsible Lending; Cenzic; CERT; CheckPoint Software Technologies; Cloudmark; Computer Associates; Computer Economics Inc.; Computer Security Institute; Consumer Reports WebWatch; Consumers Union; CyberSource; Cyveillance; Debix; Deloitte Touche Tohmatsu; Edentify; eEye Digital Security; Electronic Frontier Foundation; Electronic Privacy Information Center; Endpoint

Technologies; Exploit Prevention Labs; ForeScout Technologies; Forrester Research; Fortify Software; F-Secure; Gartner; Getronics; Harbor Research; the Honeypot Project; IBM; ID Analytics; IDC; Identity Theft Assistance Center; Identity Theft Resource Center; IronPort Systems; Javelin Strategy & Research; Juniper Networks; Liberty Alliance; LURHQ; Markle Foundation; MasterCard; McAfee; MessageLabs; Messaging Anti-Abuse Working Group; mi2g; Mi5 Networks; Microsoft; Mindwave Research; MyNetWatchman; National Association of Consumer Advocates; National Association of Mortgage Brokers; Norman Data Defense Systems; Pew Internet & American Life Project; Postini; Privacy Rights Clearinghouse; *Privacy Times*; the Progress & Freedom Foundation; Qualsys; Rochester Institute of Technology; RSA, the security division of EMC; the SANS Institute; Secure Computing; SecureWorks; Security Innovation; Shadowserver Foundation; Simplicita; Sophos; SPI Dynamics; Stroz Friedberg; Sunbelt Software; Support Intelligence; Symantec; Tenebril; Tower Group; Trend Micro; Unisys; U.S. PIRG; VeriSign iDefense; Visa; Webroot Software; Websense; WhiteHat Security; the World Bank; World Privacy Forum.

Acknowledgments

Many hands helped make this book a reality. The assistance of Detectives Bob Gauthier and Al Vonkeman was, needless to say, invaluable. We're grateful that the members of the Edmonton cell, as well as the victims we wrote about, were willing to share their stories and help contribute to public awareness. The platform for this book would not have taken shape without the trust and support of Nancy Blair, Geri Tucker, Rodney Brooks, and Jim Henderson, our editors at USA Today. Our agent, Kathi J. Paton, persevered in finding someone in the publishing world who understood the larger story we sought to tell. Thankfully, she delivered Philip Turner, our editor at Union Square Press, an imprint of Sterling Publishing, whose enthusiasm and wise guidance on many fronts buoyed us at crucial junctures. We were the beneficiaries of insightful content editing from Phil and Keith Wallman, and scrupulous copyediting by Eileen Chetti; they helped strengthen and polish the draft manuscript considerably. And we could not have come this far without the unfailing encouragement and loving support of our spouses, Robin Acohido and Jackie Swartz.

Among the many tech-security, financial services, law enforcement, consumer advocacy and legal experts who patiently educated us, we'd like to thank Idan Aharoni, Nicholas Albright, Dmitri Alperovitch, Panos Anastassiadis, James Aquilina, Mitchell Ashley, Madison Ayer, Lawrence Baldwin, Ray Barber, Michael Baxter, Leonard Bennett, Pravin Bhagwat, David Bloys, Todd Bransford, Tom Brennan, James Brooks, Martin Carmichael, Scott Carpenter, Scott Charney, Michael Cherry, Steven Christey, Scott Christie, Richard Clarke, Graham Cluley, Mia Consalvo, Michael Cook, Russ Cooper, Greg Crabb, Tim Cranton, Raye Croghan, Todd Davis, Terrance DeFranco, Rohit Dhamankar, Harry Dinham, Steven Domenikos, Blair Drazic, Ken Dunham, Alex Eckelberry, Yohai Einav, Gadi Evron, Rick Farina, Richard Feferman, Paul Ferguson, Scott Finnie, Rob Fleischman, Craig Focardi, Mari Frank, Mike Freeworth, Patrick Frey, Oliver Friedrichs, Melodi Gates, Tom Gillis, Sarah Gordon, Jesse Gough, Tom Grasso, Jeremiah Grossman, Vinny Gullotto, Thomas Harkins, Mimi Hart, Evan Hendricks, Paul Henry, Gail Hillebrand, Billy Hoffman, Chris Jay Hoofnagle, Darold Hoops, Dan Hubbard, Alfred Huger, Mikko Hyppönen, Don Jackson, Benjamin Jun, Dave Kirby, Mary Landesman, Dan Larkin,

Chris Larsen, Avivah Litan, Guillaume Lovet, Rick Lunstrum, Marc Maiffret, Uriel Maimon, Steve Martinez, Danny McPherson, Barry Mew, Ed Mierzinski, Dale Miskell, Scott Mitic, H. D. Moore, Paul Moriarty, Bill Morrow, Brian Nagel, Jose Nazario, Ron O'Brien, Betty Ostergen, Amy Osteryoung, Martin Overton, Alan Paller, Sarah Patrick, David Perry, John Pescatore, Patrick Peterson, Scott Petrie, John Pironti, Stuart Pratt, Vivek Ramachandran, Mark Rasch, Randy Roberts, Stu Sjouwerman, Ed Skoudis, Lance Spitzner, Manoj Srivastava, George Stathakopoulos, Richard Steinnon, Joe Stewart, David Taylor, Roger Thompson, Stephen Toulouse, Brian Triplett, George Tubin, Johannes Ullrich, John Ulzheimer, Dan Verton, Adam Waters, Vincent Weafer, Ted Werth, Greg Wesley, Rick Wesson, John Wethington, Kimberly Zenz, and John Zurawski.

To connect with sources on the fly, we often had to rely on the help of public relations specialists. For continually hustling on our behalf, we'd like to thank Laura Ackerman, Art Adkins, Rachael Adler, Kristin Alexander, Juliana Allen, Claire Barton, Mike Bradshaw, Paul Bresson, Kim Bruce, Amanda Carlock, Marie Clark, Russ DeVeau, Paula Dunne, Kate Ennis, Lisa Eskey, Lise Feng, Bryan Ferarro, Jodi Florence, Lynn Fox, Tiffany Fox, Matt Furman, Marc Gendron, Don Girard, Matthew Grant, Kjersti Gunderson, Mike Haro, Heidi Harris, Sandra Heikkinen, Rosetta Jones, Keith Kameg, Steve Katz, Tony Keller, Richard Kolko, Kevin Kosh, Emily Langlie, Phil Lanides, Chris Leach, Steven Lee, Mike Lizun, Della Lowe, Jodi Lynn, Norm Magnuson, Suzanne Matick, Cameron McCrady, Dave McKee, Andy Murphy, Jay Nichols, David Oro, Stacy Pena, Erica Pereira, Paul Petrogeorge, Andrew Pontti, Joanne Rasch, David Rubinger, Nico Sell, Tom Shisler, Courtney Smith, Jessica Sutera, Elvira Swanson, John Tagle, Steve Thompson, Patricia Tobin, Juliet Travis, Sheri Walkenhorst, Kevin Whalen, Mindy Whittington, Hadley Wilkins, and Jessica Williams.

Finally, since basic research almost always starts with reading what others have written about the topic at hand, we're grateful that we were able to continually turn to the amazingly prolific work of a cadre of dedicated journalists covering Internet security including Brenno de Winter, Joris Evers, Sharon Gaudin, Dan Goodin, Matt Hines, Dawn Kawamoto, Brian Krebs, Eric Lai, Robert Lemos, Paul McDougall, Joseph Menn, Ryan Naraine, Bob Sullivan, Lisa Vaas, Jai Vijayan, and Kim Zetter.

Index

Acxiom, 161
Advanced Authorization, 13, 51, 197, 199
Advantage Financial, 72
Adware
affiliates, role of, 77, 81–82
antiadware movement, 67
defined, 65
distribution companies for, 66, 77
installing with bots, 78–85
installing with worms, 195
Affinity cards, 50, 64
Aharoni, Idan, 176
AJAX
criminal use of, 194–196, 237
functions of, 195
Alberti, Julio, 200
Allor, Peter, 84
Alperovitch, Dimitri, 107–108
Alvarez, Nair Zuleima, 200
Alvarez, Reinier, 200
American Express, origin of, 25
Ancheta, Jeanson James, 77–80, 104
Anna Kournikova virus, 18
Anti-Phishing Working Group (APWG), 68, 139–140
Anti-Spyware Coalition, 66–67
Aphex, 170, 245–247
Appleyard, David, 119–120
Arabo, Jason Salah, 69
Aragon, Christopher and Clara, 245–247
ATM withdrawals, 118, 124
February 2006 hit, 150–153
Authentication, two-factor, 139–140
Authentify, 213
Ayer, Madison, 187–188

Background checks, data suppliers, 174–176
Bagle viruses, 53–55, 57
Bahloul, Achraf, 85
Ballmer, Steve, 239
Bank(s)
monoline banks, 37
UCC and fraud cases, 142
Bank account fraud
ATM withdrawals, 118, 124, 150–153
bank responsibility, lack of, 141–144, 206
and debit cards, 114, 118, 150–153
drop accounts, use of, 33, 47–48, 96, 124–125, 172
Dumpster diving for information, 7–10, 22
eGold accounts, 132
e-mail transfers, 47–49
phishing for identity profiles, 123–124, 139–140
process of, 22–23, 47–48, 60, 73, 96, 123–125, 137, 149
Vonage phone numbers, use of, 48–49
Bank account fraud deterrence
challenge-response programs, 140
limitations of, 51–52, 113
two-factor authentication, 139–140
BankAmericard
first ads, 34–35, 138
origin/development of, 25–26
Bank Authorization System Experiment I and II (BASE I and II), 26–27, 50
Baxter, Mike, 93
Beals, Howard, 232
BearShare, 55
Benson, Bibiana, 72–73
Bereano, Bruce, 221
Beyond Security, 237

Black hats
    bot herding, 19
    hacking, motivations for, 17–18,
        21
    WMF (zero day flaw), 179–180
    working to beat patches, 83
Blackwell, Derrick, 172–173, 184
BoaFactory, 118
Borba, Steve, 62–63
Bots/botnets
    bot herding, 19
    botnet extortionists, 69–70
    defined, 19–20, 105
    high-end activities, 105–109
    identity-profile gathering,
        105–107
    to install adware, 78–85
    and MSBlast, 43
    Mydoom virus, 54
    Rxbot, 77–78
    sale of bots, 77–78
    Storm-infected bots, 212
Bourassa, Eric, 206
Braden, Daniel and Mary, 186–188
Braverman, Matthew, 43
Brennan, James, 161–162
Broadband, security precautions,
    258
Broder, Betsy, 128
Brokerage account fraud
    escalation of, 155–157
    process of, 153–157
    pump-and-dump scam,
        156–157
Brooks, James, 211
Bruesewitz, Jean, 13
Bruguera, Miguel, 203–204
Bubble Boy virus, 18
Budd, Christopher, 228
Bullet proofing, carding forums,
    166–167
Butler, Max Ray, 245–247

California, ChoicePoint disclosures,
    160–164
CallingID, 251
Capitol One, 37
CardCops, 104, 129
CarderPlanet, 104, 117–118, 129
CardersMarket, 112, 129, 130, 245–246
    expanded with hostile takeover,
        165–170
Carding forums
    administration/supervision of,
        130–134, 166–167
    bullet proofing, 166–167
    defined, 104, 129–130
    escrow services of, 133–134
    hostile takeover case, 165–170
    law enforcement difficulties,
        129–131, 166–167
    names of, 104, 117–118, 129
    operation, example of, 130–134
Carney, Marsha, 198–199
Carte Blanche, 25
Caselli, Michael, 69
Cashless society, 27, 138
Cell phones, new phone scams, 8,
    86–87
Cells (organized cybercriminals)
    operation of, 201–204
    See also Edmonton cell
Center for Democracy and Technology
    (CDT), 254
CERT (Computer Emergency Readiness
    Team), 17–18
Challenge-response programs, 140
Charge-backs, 114–115, 206
Chat rooms. See IRC (Internet relay
    chat)
Cherry, Michael, 31, 226
Chewning, Brent, 197
Chinese cybercrime, 41–42, 191–192,
    211, 228–229, 229, 261
Chinese X Focus, 41

ChoicePoint, 71–72, 160–164, 207
"Chronology of Data Breaches,"
   235–236
CipherTrust, 106
Claria, 66
Clarke, Richard, 121
Clements, Dan, 104, 129
Cloudmark, 233
Cluley, Graham, 56, 84
Cockerham, Rob, 63–64
Code Red, 19–21
Code Red II, 28
Collections agency, bogus, and identity
   theft, 71–74
Command-and-control servers, 78, 80,
   104, 105
Consalvo, Mia, 14–15
Consumer Data Industry Association
   (CDIA), 206–208, 218–223
Consumer dispute verification (CDV), 90
Consumers Union (CU), 254
Contreras, 214–217, 244
Cook, Mike, 176
Coreflood, 142
Counterfeit
   credit cards, 197–205
   drivers' licenses, 182, 185
   money, 10, 47
Counterspy, 251
Crabb, Greg, 203
Credit bureaus
   consolidation of, 98–99
   consumer dispute verification
      (CDV), 90
   credit reports, importance of, 89
   error-correction, limitations of,
      89–91, 93–94, 100–102
   federal probusiness position on,
      99–100, 102, 189
   functions/operation of, 88–89
   identity theft, lack of action in,
      93–94, 127

identity theft from, 71–74, 100
mortgage triggers, sale of, 186–189
origin/development of, 98–99
Credit card(s)
   application pranks, 62–63
   borrowing/buying, escalation of,
      35–38, 62
   credit monitoring, uselessness of,
      206
   default penalty rate, 74–75
   disclosures, limitations of, 76
   double-cycle billing, 75
   fees, complexity of, 74–76
   major, consumer use of, 249–250
   Marquette Bank case, 36–37
   origin/development of, 25–27,
      35–37
   predatory marketing tactics, 37,
      62–63
   proponents of, 64
   transactions, growth in dollars, 36,
      62
   VisaNet processing system, 11–14
Credit card fraud
   bank rectification of, 114
   bogus cards, 50, 51
   charge-backs, 114–116
   counterfeit cards, 197–205
   development of, 49–50
   e-mail setup, 248–249
   gift cards scams, 197–204,
      215–218
   new-account fraud, 32–33,
      127–128
   reshipping rings, 145–146
   tumbling, 48
Credit card fraud deterrence
   Advanced Authorization, 13, 51
   BASE I and II, 26–27, 50
   CVV2 numbers, 115
   holograms as, 50
   limitations of, 51–52

Credit.com Educational Services, 89
Credit freeze
  effectiveness of, 206–208
  laws related to, 220–222
  opposition to, 219–223
Criminal files, identity mix-up, 110–112
Croghan, Raye, 176–177
Cumbajohnny, 119–120, 130, 168–169
Cybercrime
  black hats, 17–21
  botnet extortionists, 69–70
  and bots/botnets, 19–20, 78–85,
    105–109
  Chinese rings, 41–42, 191–192, 211,
    228–229, 229, 261
  criminal collaboration online. *See*
    Carding forums; IRC (Internet
    relay chat)
  DDoS attacks, 19, 40
  and drug use, 1–3, 9–11, 47
  as global industry, 138–139
  global losses from, 103
  and hackers, 14–20, 68–70
  initial expansion of, 103–106
  Internet, benefits to criminals,
    116–117, 130
  mules, use of, 145–150
  and murder, 109
  organized groups (cells), 201. *See*
    also Edmonton cell
  perpetuation among cybercriminals,
    103–109
  and phishing, 61, 67–68, 139–140
  prevention/deterrence. *See*
    Cybercrime crackdowns; Security
  Russian rings, 4, 57, 81, 108, 118,
    129, 146–150, 156, 159,
    178–179, 191, 209–211, 229
  and spyware, 65–67
  surpassing illegal drug crimes,
    102–103
  Web exploits, 178–181, 192–193

  See also Bank account fraud;
    Brokerage account fraud; Credit
    card fraud; Identity profiles, theft
    of; Identity theft; Online
    purchases, fraudulent; Viruses;
    worms; *individual topics*
Cybercrime crackdowns
  on carding forums, 129–131
  cells, busting. *See* Edmonton cell
  federal operations, 120–122, 128–
    129
  law enforcement difficulties, 117,
    129–130, 166–167
  See also Security
CyberSource, 116
Cyveillance, 211

DarkMarket, 118, 166, 169
DarkProfits, 104, 129
Data-aggregation companies
  for background checks, 174–176
  largest data brokers, 161
  See also Credit bureaus
Data-breach notification laws, 100
  ChoicePoint case, 160–164
DDoS (distributed-denial-of-service-
  attacks)
  on adware suppliers, 107
  against criminal competitors,
    69–70, 77, 85, 169
  defined, 19
  and MSBlast, 43
  proxy servers for, 40, 105
  against RIAA, 57
  against SCO group, 54
  against White House, 20
Debit cards
  bogus, 118
  consumer precautions, 249
  development of, 50
  fraudulent activities, 114, 118,
    150–153

magnetic card readers, 151, 204
PIN data, decoding, 151–152
Debix, 114
Debt, consumer, escalation of, 37–38, 91
Decker, Duane, 71–74, 162–164
DeFranco, Terrance, 32–34
Delaware, credit card operations, 37
Diabl0, 81–85
Dias, Alex, 197
Diners Club, 25
Dinham, Harry, 188
Directions on Microsoft, 31, 226
DirectRevenue, 66
Dolphin Stadium Web site, infection of, 191–192
Drazic, Blair, 90
Drivers' licenses, counterfeit, 182, 185
Drop accounts, 33, 47–48, 96, 124–125, 155, 172
Drug use. See Methamphetamine
Dumpster diving, 7–10, 22–23
Dunham, Ken, 43, 190

Eckelberry, Alex, 180
Edentify, 32–34, 236
Edmonton cell
    arrests, 1–3, 182–185, 243–244
    Contreras cell, 214–217, 244
    development/activities of, 7–11, 22–24, 46–49, 60–62, 86–88, 95–98, 123–125, 135–138, 182–185
    See also Socrates
eEye Digital Security, 20
eGold, 131–132
Ekici, Atilla, 84
Electronic Frontier Foundation (EFF), 254
Electronic Privacy Information Center (EPIC), 254

Ellman, Eric J., 218–223
El Mariachi, 168–170
Elwood, Lee, 117–118
E-mail
    security precautions, 252–253
    virus infection, process of, 14–17, 53–55
    See also Adware; Spam; Spyware; Viruses; Worms
E-mail accounts, set up with stolen cards, 248–249
E-mail transfers, 47–49
Equifax, 72, 88–90
    and ChoicePoint, 161
    identity theft, lack of action in, 93–94
    mortgage triggers, 187
    origin/development of, 98
Eschouafni, Saad, 69
Escobar, Irving Jose, 198–205
Escrow services, of carding forums, 133–134
Essebar, Farid, 81–85, 104
Evron, Gadi, 192, 237
Experian, 88–89, 161
    mortgage triggers, 187
    origin/development of, 98–99
Exploit Prevention Labs, 16, 177–178, 190, 211
Extortion, botnet extortionists, 69–70

Fair Credit Reporting Act (FCRA), 90, 93, 99, 187
Farquhar, David, 81
Fathi, Ben, 226–227
FBI Cyber Crime Task Force, 81
FBI Internet Crime Complaint Center, 128–129
Federal Credit Reporting Act (1970), 208
Federal Financial Institutions Examination Council (FFIEC), 140

Federal Trade Commission (FTC)
  on cybercrime losses, 232–233
  on mortgage triggers, 187–189
Feferman, Richard, 90, 91
Feinstein, Diane, 255
Fergerson, Julie, 114–115
Financial Data Protection Act (2006),
  208
Fleishman, Rob, 107
Fraud detection. *See* Security
F-Secure, 41, 179–180
Furman, Matt, 162

Gambling sites
  avoiding, 65–66, 178, 252
  DDoS attacks, 69
Gammacash Entertainment, 77, 79
Ganeshamoorthy, Pathmathas,
  152–153
Gartner Research, 33, 234
Gates, Bill
  on credit-issuing system, 225
  enemies of, 38
  illegal practices, 17
  Internet Safety Enforcement Team
    (ISET), 84
  Trustworthy Computing initiative,
    30–31, 84, 179, 223
  virus writers' capture, reward for,
    58–59
  See also Microsoft Windows
Gator, 66
Gattis, Shaillie, 177–178
Gauthier, Bob, 1–3, 9–11, 47, 61–62,
  86–88, 173, 182, 214–218, 243–244
Getronics, 51, 146, 216
Gift card scams, 197–204, 215–217
Gnanakanthan, Sivagnanam, 153
Gold, eGold accounts, 132
Golden Goose computer, 1–2,
  123–124, 137
Google Maps mashup, 193

Gordon, Sarah, 18–19
Government Accountability Office
  (GAO), 74–76
Gozi, 209–210
Gray hats, 17–18
Greenbaum, Ben, 212
Guzman, Onel del, 16–17, 44

Hackers
  for-profit criminality, 52, 65, 68–70
  high-end activities, 105–109
  1999 variety, 14–16
  psychological factors, 18–20, 42,
    43, 46–47, 76–77, 80, 171–172
  script kiddies, 68, 105
  of video games, 46
Harkins, Thomas, 236
Havard, Douglas Cade, 117–118
Hendricks, Evan, 99, 102, 189
Hernandez, David Joe, 110–112
Hernandez, Dianelly, 200
Hock, Dee, 25–27
Hoffman, Billy, 195, 228
Hoops, Darold D., 36, 49, 51
House of Dabus, 57–58
Howard, Michael, 225
Hubbard, Dan, 191
Hyppönen, Mikko, 41, 179–180

IBM Global Services, 105
IBM Internet Security Systems, 84, 105,
  109
Iceman, 165–170, 245–247
ID Analytics, 176
iDefense, 43, 190
Identity profiles, theft of
  background-checking services,
    174–176
  from bogus collections agencies,
    71–74
  from bogus Web pages, 67, 210–211,
    233–235

bots, use of, 105–107
from credit bureaus, 71–74, 101
cybercriminal collaboration. *See*
    Carding forums; IRC (Internet
    relay chat)
Dumpster diving, 7–10, 22–23
Gozi, 209–210
keyloggers for, 105, 139, 142
man-in-the-middle attacks, 139,
    140
and mortgage triggers, 188–189
mother ships, 211
for online bank profiles, 123–124,
    139–140
from online businesses, 61–62, 97,
    106–107
packet sniffers, 139
from postal employees, 73
TJX heist, 198–199
Identity theft
case examples, 92–93, 110–112,
    126–128
credit bureaus, lack of action in,
    93–94
data-breach notification, 160–164
defined, 113
drug-use connection, 1–3, 9–11, 47
financial services sector on,
    232–233
losses related to, 232
personal information, access to.
    See Identity-profile gathering
Social Security numbers, use of,
    32–33
See also Bank account fraud;
    Brokerage account fraud; Credit
    card fraud; Online purchases,
    fraudulent
Identity-theft deterrence
credit freeze, 206–208
Edentify, 32–34
police task force for, 71–74

state laws, 100
theft-monitoring services, 176–177,
    250
IDology, 176–177
ID Theft Resource Center, 250
IDWatchdog, 111–112, 250
iframeCASH.biz, 178–181, 189–190
ILOVEYOU virus, 16
Inouye, Daniel, 255
Instant messaging. *See* IRC (Internet
    relay chat)
Integrated Search Technologies, 66
Intelius, 173–174
Interbank Card Association, 36
International Association for the
    Advancement of Criminal Activity
    (IAACA), 129–130
Internet, origin/development of,
    236–237
Internet Safety Enforcement Team
    (ISET), 84
IRC (Internet relay chat)
bot herding on, 19
chatting, examples of, 78–79, 165
cybercriminals connecting on, 19,
    38, 46–47, 61, 70, 77–80, 96,
    104, 107, 123–125, 128–130,
    172–173, 176, 182–183, 201,
    213, 244
defined, 19, 70
IronPort Systems, 233–234

Jackson, Don, 209–210, 212–213
Jaschan, Sven, 56–59, 83
Jayroe, Shannon, 203–204
Johnson, Doug, 232
Juniper Networks, 194

Kamardin, Aleksey, 156–157
Kaspersky, 251
Katz, Steve, 100
Kazaa, 54, 55, 66

Keyloggers
  defined, 105, 139
  and mother ships, 211
  uses of, 142, 191, 193, 252
King Arthur, 117–120
Kirkpatrick, Matthew and Lisa, 92–94
Kushnir, Vardan, 108–109

Larkin, Dan, 128–129
Last Stage of Delirium, 41
LaTorette, Steven, 208
Leahy, Patrick, 255
Leprechaun Software, 177
Lexis-Nexis, 161
LifeLock, 250
LimeWire, 55, 66
LinkScanner, 190, 251
Linux, 29–30, 54
Litan, Avivah, 33, 68, 113, 234
Llorente, Zenia Mercedes, 200
Local Security Authorization Subsystem
  Service (LSASS), 57–58, 80, 83
Lopez, Joe, 141–144
LOUDCash, 66, 77, 79
Love Bug, 16
Lunstrum, Rick, 111–112

Mafiaboy, 19, 70
Magnetic card readers, 151, 204, 216–217
Maiffret, Marc, 20–21
Maimon, Uriel, 170, 247
Majoras, Deborah Platt, 189
Malito, Lynn, 160
Malware, 15
  See also Viruses; Worms
Man-in-the-middle attacks, 105, 140
Mankini, Josh, 73
Mantovanni, Anthony, 119–120
Manzuik, Steve, 193–194
MasterCard
  origin of, 25–26, 36
  transactions, growth in dollars, 36

Maxwell, Christopher, 80–81, 104
Mayer, Martin, 27
MazaFaka, 129
McAfee, 251
McAfee Anti-Virus Emergency Response
  Team Labs, 53
McDonald, Kurt, 155
McKenna, Rob, 207
McNamara, Frank, 25
McNiven, Valerie, 102–103
Melissa e-mail virus, 15
Merchants
  charge-back losses, 114–116, 206
  as victims, bank response to,
    141–144
MessageLabs, 68, 233
Messaging Anti-Abuse Working Group
  (MAAWG), 106
Metasloit Project, 83
Methamphetamine
  cooking from ephedrine, 125
  and cybercrime, 1–3, 7–11, 22–24,
    47, 96–98, 125
  mechanism of action, 23–24, 125
Microsoft Windows
  hackers, motivations of, 17–18
  LSASS patch, 57–58, 80, 83
  MSBlast threat, 43, 190, 223–224
  Office attacks, 227–230
  patches, 18, 20–21, 41–42,
    43, 57
  Patch Tuesday, 83, 181, 191
  SDL (Security Development
    Lifecycle), 30–31, 224–227
  security vulnerabilities, 17–20,
    30–31, 41, 43
  Service Pack 2 (SP2), 179, 223
  Vista safety, 223–227, 239–241
  VML exploits, 192
  vulnerability researchers, 20–21, 83
  Windows Auto Update, 179, 189,
    193, 251

WMF (zero day flaw), 179–181,
189–191
XP safety, 30
See also Gates, Bill
Mierzwinski, Ed, 100
Mimail, 67
MNBA, 37
Monchamp, Brandon, 119–120
Money laundering
mules, use of, 145–150
via Internet, 155
Monoline banks, 37
Moore, HD, 83
Moriarity, Paul, 253
Mortensen, Brian, 115–116
Mortgage triggers, 186–189
Mother ships, 211
MSBlast, 41–45, 57, 83, 190, 223–224
Mules, reshipping, 145–150, 159–160
Multithreading, 44
Mundie, Craig, 224–225, 229–230
Munroe, Kevin, 128
Mydoom, 53–55, 57
MySpace worm, 194–195, 237
Mytob, 82–84

National BankAmericard Inc., 25–26
Nelson, Bill, 255
Netsky, 55–57
New-account fraud, 32–33
Nimda virus, 18
Northwest Hospital and Medical
Center, 80

O'Brien, Ron, 235
Ochoa, Armando, 200
O'Donnell, Adam, 233
Oluwatusin, Olatunji, 71–73, 160,
162–164
180 Solutions, 66, 77
Online purchases, fraudulent, charge-
backs, 114–116, 206

Open relays, spam routed through, 29
Operation Cardkeeper, 121–122
Operation Firewall, 120–121, 128
Operation Rolling Stone, 122
Operations Center Central, VisaNet,
11–14
Overton, Martin, 105

Packet sniffers, 105
Paller, Alan, 229
Panda, 251
Parson, Jeffrey Lee, 43
Passwords, security precautions, 252
Patches
negative effects of, 20
See also Microsoft Windows
Patch Tuesday, 83, 181, 191
Payment Card Industry (PCI) Data
Security Standard, 151–152
PayPal
log-in data, theft of, 61–62, 88,
106–107
Mimail virus, 67
Pescatore, John, 226
Peterson, Ed, 175
Peterson, Patrick, 234
Phishing
defined, 61
escalation of, 68, 139–140, 234
fraudulent activities, 67–68
information-gathering methods, 67
for online bank profiles, 123–124,
139–140
phishing kits, 67
security precautions, 253
targets of, 67–68
PIN data, decoding, 151–152
Pironti, John, 51, 146, 216
Poland problem, 234
Pop-up ads. *See* Adware
Porn sites, avoiding, 28, 44, 65–66,
106, 178, 190–191, 252

Postal workers, identity theft by, 73
Power blackout (2003), and MSBlast, 42
Pratt, Stuart, 91–92
Privacy Rights Clearinghouse, 235, 254
Privacy Times, 99, 102, 189, 255
Private.Eye.com, 174
Proof-of-concept exploit, 83
Proxmire, William, 99, 189, 206
Proxy servers
    for DDoS attacks, 107
    spam routed through, 29, 105
    viruses routed through, 39–40
Pryor, Mark, 222, 255
Public Interest Research Groups
    (PIRG), 253
Pump-and-dump scam, 156–157

Ray, Anthony, 197
Reavy, Mike, 227–228
Remote procedure call (RPC), attacks
    through, 41–42, 57
Reshipping rings
    defined, 146
    mules, use of, 145–150, 159–160
    recruitment Internet ads, 158–160
    Web sites of, 159
Retail Credit Company, 98
Roberts, Randal, 197–199
Robison, Jane, 73
Rodriguez, Anthony, 90–91
Rodriguez, Erick Fernandez, 198–200
Rodriguez, George, 153–155
Rodriguez, Irene, 159–160
Rodríguez, René, 76
Root kits, 178, 190, 227
Rouland, Chris, 105, 109
RSA Security, 170, 176, 247
Russian cybercrime, 4, 57, 81, 108, 118,
    129, 146–150, 156, 159, 178–179,
    191, 209–211, 229
Rxbot, 77–78

Samy, 194–195
SANS Institute Internet Storm Center,
    58, 180, 229
Sasser, 58–59, 80, 83
Savings rates
    decline of, 38
    twentieth century, stability of, 35
ScandinavianCarding, 166, 169
Schmugar, Craig, 53
Schumer, Charles, 255
Schwartz, Ari, 66
Schweitzer, Brian, 220–221
SCO Group, 54
Scott, Melinda and Greg, 126–127
Script kiddies, 105, 139, 194
SDL (Security Development Lifecycle),
    30–31, 224–227
Secret Service, 142, 201, 203, 246
Secure Computing, 106, 107
SecureWorks, 29, 38–40, 209, 212
Security
    advocacy groups, 253–255
    antivirus/antispyware programs, 251
    challenge-response programs, 140
    and consumer awareness, 259–260
    corporate versus home computers,
        193–194
    credit freeze, 206–208
    data-breach notification laws,
        160–164
    exploit prevention, 190
    future needs, 237–242
    holistic approach to, 262–264
    patches. See Microsoft Windows
    precautions for consumers,
        249–253
    regulatory needs, 261–262
    spam filters, 178–179
    technological tools, needs for,
        257–258
    two-factor authentication, 139–140
    and Vista, 223–227, 239–241

See also Bank account fraud deterrence; Credit card fraud deterrence; Identity-theft deterrence; Virus hunters; Specific security firms
Security hole, and zero day threat, 5
Security Socket Layer, data-gathering from, 209–210
Selembo, George, 148
Service Pack 2 (SP2), 179, 223
Shadowcrew, 104, 118–121, 128, 129
Shell accounts, 165
Shenning, Dave, 1–2
Shore, Joel, 239
Silva, Nancy Diaz, 246
Simitian, Joe, 255
Simplicita, 107
Singh, Jasmine, 69
SirCam virus, 18
SiteAdviser Plus, 251
Skimmers, 204
Smith, David L., 15–16
SoBig viruses, 40–42, 44–45
Social Security numbers
   identity-theft process, 32–33, 127–128
   security precautions, 252
Socrates
   assault on, 97–98
   capture/arrests, 1–3, 87–88, 173, 185, 217–218, 244
   cybercriminal activities of, 34, 47–49, 61–62, 77, 96–97, 123–125
   Golden Goose computer, 1–2, 123–124, 137
   personality profile, 46–47, 76–77
   postarrest, 173, 183–185, 214, 217, 244
   workspaces of, 60–62, 96
Solomon, Alan, 56
Sophos, 56, 84, 233, 235

South Dakota, credit card operations, 37
Spaceflash worm, 195
Spam
   antispam groups, 28
   with bogus Web page, 233–235
   botnets for, 106
   development of, 28–30
   escalation of, 233
   junk ads, 28
   open relays as route, 29
   phishing, 61, 67–68
   proxy servers as route, 29, 105
   spam blockers, 253
   spam filters, 178–179
   -virus connection, 28–30, 38
Spamcops, 29
SpamHaus, 29
Specter, Arlen, 255
Speier, Jackie, 161
SPI Dynamics, 195, 228
Sporaw, Andrej, 178–180, 189
SpySheriff, 178
Spy Sweeper, 251
Spyware
   antispyware movement, 67
   antispyware programs, 251
   defined, 65
   installing, 66
Spyware Doctor, 251
StealthDivision, 104, 129
Steigmeyer, Robert, 80
Stewart, Joe, 29, 38–40, 42, 44–45
StopBadware.org, 67
Storm virus, 212
Sullivan, Bob, 62–63
Summins, Scott, 127
Sunner, Mark, 233
Symantic Security Response, 65, 212, 251

TalkCash, 129, 130, 131–134, 165, 168
Taylor, David, 82–85
TD Ameritrade, 153–157

Telus, 87
The Vouched, 129, 166
Thomas, David Renshaw, 168–170
Thompson, Roger, 16, 177–178,
    190–191, 211
ThreatSeeker, 191
Titan Rain, 229
TJX identity-data heist, 198–199,
    202–203, 235
TransUnion, 88–89, 102, 161
    mortgage triggers, 187
    origin/development of, 99
Trend Micro, 251, 253
Triplett, Brian, 14
TrustedID, 250
Trustworthy Computing initiative,
    30–31, 84, 179, 223
Tsujihara, Alice, 73
Tumbling, 48
Two-factor authentication, 139,
    139–140

Ullrich, Johannes, 58, 180
Ulzheimer, John, 89
Uniform Commercial Code, 142–143
UnixCrew, 129
Unknown Killer, 168
Upgrades, importance of, 251
USA-People-Search.com, 174

Van Dyke, James, 231–233
Vector Markup Language (VML)
    exploits, 192
Veerasingam, Srikanthan, 152–153
Vega, Roman, 117–118
Veracity Credit Consultants, 187–188
Virtual private networks (VPNs),
    116–117, 119–120
Viruses
    Anna Kournikova, 18
    antivirus programs, 251
    antivirus virus, 55–56

Bagle viruses, 53–55, 57
Bubble Boy, 18
Code Red, 19–21
Code Red II, 28
improvement in versions of,
    44–45
and keyloggers, 139
Love Bug, 16
Melissa e-mail virus, 15
Mimail, 67
multithreading, 44
Mydoom, 53–55, 57
Mytob, 82–84
Netsky, 55–57
Nimda, 18
proxy servers as route, 39–40
remote procedure call (RPC) as
    route, 41–42
root kit cloaking, 178, 190
SirCam, 18
SoBig viruses, 40–42, 44–45
    -spam connection, 28–30, 38
Storm, 212
Virus hunters
    Netsky antivirus virus, 55–56
    SecureWorks, 38–40, 42
    tech-security companies, 39
    Virus Wars of 2004, 57–59
    of Web exploits, 16, 177–178, 190
    white hats, 17–18, 41, 83, 108
Visa
    origin of, 26
    transactions, growth in dollars, 36
VisaNet
    Advanced Authorization, 13, 51,
        197, 199
    operation of, 11–14
    progenitor of, 27
Vista, 223–227, 239–241
Vonage, bank fraud, use in, 48–49
Vonkeman, Allan, 9–10, 61–62, 86–88,
    97, 155, 173, 182, 214, 243–244

Voompeople.com, 174
Vulnerability researchers, 20–21, 83

Wallhacks, 46
Weafer, Vincent, 65
Web exploits 178–181
    defined, 178
    expansion, reasons for, 178–179
    prevention tools, 190
    Super Bowl (2007), 191–192
    WMF (zero day flaw), 179–181
Websense, 180, 191
Web sites
    bogus pages, 67, 210–211
    identity profiles, gathering of, 97,
        106–107
    Web page scanners, 251
WhenU, 66
White hats, 17–18, 41, 83, 108
White House, Code Red threat, 20
Wilson, Debby Fry, 181
Windows Auto Update, 179, 189, 193,
    251
Wireless networks, security precautions,
    252, 258
WMF (zero day flaw), 179–181,
    189–191

Woolford, Cator and Guy, 98
World Privacy Forum, 254
Worms
    MSBlast, 41–45, 57, 83
    MySpace, 194–195
    Sasser, 58–59, 80, 83
    Spaceflash, 195
    Yamanner, 195
    Zotob, 83–84, 104

Y2K, 14
Yamanner worm, 195
Yastremskiy, Maksym, 202–203
Ybarra, Carol, 175

Zabasearch.com, 174
Zango, 77, 107
Zero day attack
    defined, 5, 179
    Office attacks, 227–230
    WMF (zero day flaw), 179–181,
        189–191
Zombie PCs, 65, 69–70, 105,
    120
Zotob, 83–84, 104
Zumende.com, 174
Zurawski, John, 213

About the Authors

Byron Acohido joined *USA Today* in 2001 to cover Microsoft. He has held reporting positions at the *Herald*, in Everett, Washington, the *Dallas Times Herald*, and the *Seattle Times*, where he won the 1997 Pulitzer Prize for Beat Reporting, for stories linking a defect in the rudder controls of Boeing 737s to a string of deadly crashes.

Jon Swartz is an award-winning reporter with more than two decades' experience covering technology topics at trade publications and daily newspapers, including *USA Today*, the *San Francisco Chronicle*, and the *London Independent*. His writing has also appeared in the *Chicago Tribune*, the *New Orleans Times-Picayune*, and the *Daily Telegraph* (of London), and he has worked for Forbes.com. The body of work he created covering cybercrime with *USA Today* reporter Byron Acohido in 2004 won the Society of American Business Editors and Writers Best in Business Projects Award and reached the finals for a Gerald Loeb Award for Distinguished Business and Financial Journalism, in both 2004 and 2005.